AT THE MERCY OF THE MOUNTAINS

TRUE STORIES OF SURVIVAL AND TRAGEDY IN NEW YORK'S ADIRONDACKS

PETER BRONSKI

The Lyons Press
Guilford, Connecticut
An imprint of Rowman & Littlefield

The Lyons Press is an imprint of Rowman & Littlefield.

Designed by Lisa Reneson, Two Sisters Design

Distributed by NATIONAL BOOK NETWORK

Library of Congress Cataloging-in-Publication Data

Bronski, Peter.
    At the mercy of the mountains : true stories of survival and tragedy in New York's Adirondacks / Peter Bronski.
        p. cm.
    Includes bibliographical references.
    ISBN 978-1-59921-304-0
    1. Mountaineering accidents—New York (State)—Adirondack Mountains. 2. Wilderness survival—New York (State)—Adirondack Mountains. I. Title.
    GV199.42.N652A3415 2008
    796.522097475—dc22   2007042871

Printed in the United States of America

In memory of all who have lost their lives in the Adirondack wilderness while in search of adventure and the joy of the mountains

CONTENTS

PREFACE

*This is the most beautiful place on earth. There are many such places.
Every man, every woman, carries in heart and mind the image of the ideal
place, the right place, the one true home . . . .*

—Edward Abbey, *Desert Solitaire: A Season in the Wilderness* (1968)

When Ed Abbey penned those opening lines to his classic, *Desert Solitaire,* he referred specifically to the slickrock desert canyon country surrounding Moab, Utah. It wasn't Abbey's "true home" in the most literal sense; that was a farm in Pennsylvania where he was born and raised. But it was his adopted "ideal place," a landscape that gripped his heart and mind from the moment he started as the solitary ranger of a remote outpost in Arches National Monument (which became a national park three years after *Desert Solitaire* was published).

For myself, I'll take the mountains, and in particular, the Adirondack Mountains of northern New York State. Their combination of deep wilderness, dense forest, high summits, and innumerable backwaters is the essence of my ideal place. But the Adirondacks are not my home by birthright. Like canyon country for Abbey, they are an adopted landscape that, upon first introduction and in the years since, epitomize my ideal, seize my heart, and provide an outlet for my passion for outdoor adventure.

I wasn't born with mountains in my blood. I grew up surfing and fishing in the Atlantic Ocean on the south shore of Long Island, an hour's drive east of New York City's midtown Manhattan. At its highest point, the island gently rises to a height of 401 feet above sea level, though the overwhelming majority of the land lies below 110 feet in elevation. In fact, the entire island is predominantly composed of rubble transported from distant mountain ranges to the north, the sum total of two terminal moraines that marked the southern boundary of glaciers that advanced over the whole of New England during the last ice age.

The closest I got to mountains was our family's annual weeklong summer camping trip to North-South Lake in the Catskill Mountains, some 125 miles north of New York City. In truth, I later learned, the Catskills aren't actually mountains at all, but rather a dissected plateau; an uplifted mass of earth carved into shapes and forms resembling mountains by the erosional forces of creeks and rivers. No matter. Geologic authenticity aside, the Catskills are where my passion for the mountains and outdoor adventure began.

By the time I left home for Cornell University in the Finger Lakes region of upstate New York, two things were firmly established: my entrenched passion for the outdoors, and my status as an expert armchair mountaineer. Lacking an accessible mountain venue to learn and practice the craft, I voraciously read all the literature I could get my hands on related to mountain adventure and misadventure, climbing technique, and routes on the world's major peaks, vicariously living through the adventure writers who shared their tales from high places and far-off lands.

As a college student I finally had the independence and the ability to learn mountaineering technique from experienced guides, and to travel to "real" mountains to practice my newfound passion. Many of those early adventures took place close to home in places like the Gunks—or, more accurately, the Shawangunk Mountains just west of New Paltz, New York, above the Hudson River Valley—where I cut my teeth as a rock climber, and in New Hampshire's White Mountains, where I honed my winter mountaineering skills.

Soon enough, I'd become a self-sufficient adventurer, journeying to far-off mountain ranges in search of the same adventures I'd only read about years earlier. In the years since, I've climbed mountains in more than a dozen of the world's major mountain ranges, and stood atop 20,000-foot peaks shrouded in glaciers and precipitous slopes. In part by design and in part through providence, mine has been a life in the mountains. And, thanks to the overriding and inexorable law of probability, it has also been a life with more than one rendezvous with misadventure.

I've evacuated sick and injured companions from remote locales; run for my life down the summit ridge of a high peak while the mountains around me exploded with lightning from a sudden storm; struggled with hypothermia and acute mountain sickness; had more than a few close calls with natural and human-triggered rockfalls; had snow slopes disconcertingly *whomp* and settle beneath me; and I've had to ration food and water and spend unplanned days and nights in the backcountry.

Surely, in some cases I faced real and legitimate dangers; in others, my situation was more a matter of managing an unexpected change in plans or conditions. I don't know that any one experience would qualify as an epic, though such determinations are more often a matter of personal opinion than not. But I do know that those experiences collectively inform my decision-making, both consciously and subconsciously, making me a safer mountaineer today.

As I continued to travel and climb mountains, I realized that along the way I'd somehow managed to overlook a world-class mountain range virtually in my own backyard—the Adirondacks. That was until I somewhat unexpectedly settled north of Albany, New York, near the gateway to the Adirondack Mountains. Suddenly, a new world was at my doorstep. I would finally explore a region that had beckoned for so long, and it was a land full of opportunity for an outdoor adventure seeker like me.

I honed my ice climbing skills on the multi-pitch flows of places like Pitchoff North, put up a handful of new single-pitch rock climbing routes on the cliffs of the relatively unexplored southern Adirondacks, challenged myself with solo single-day enchainments of multiple High Peaks, skied the barren upper slopes of the highest mountains, mountain-biked singletrack in the Wild Forests of the eastern Adirondacks, and paddled the placid waters of the western Adirondacks' lakes and rivers.

There was one important additional element to my Adirondack adventures that was lacking in my travels to other ranges: For the first time, I became part of the community. Rather than being a transient visitor who comes for a few days or weeks, or even months, and then leaves, I invested myself in the region and its people.

My primary initiation to the Adirondack community came through Lower Adirondack Search and Rescue (LASAR) around the turn of the millennium. By then I had firmly adopted the 'Dacks as my home range, and felt an ever-increasing need to give back to the mountains from which I derived so much pleasure. That call to service was answered through the forty or so men and women who volunteered their time for LASAR. We met monthly in the music room at Warrensburg High School, north of Lake George, and there I met and befriended true North Country men and women. I earned my New York State Department of Environmental Conservation (DEC) Basic Wildlands Search certification, and every now and then my phone would ring late at night, and I'd be asked if I could rendezvous somewhere in the Adirondacks early the next morning to search for a lost or missing hiker. It added a new sense of purpose to my outdoor adventures—it was no longer just about me. I could now use my experience and relative youth to help others who found themselves at the mercy of the mountains.

That's not to suggest that I was suddenly exempt from my own misadventures. While my Adirondack years passed largely without incident, one experience still stands out in my mind:

Mid-January one year, I decided to attempt a solo ski mountaineering ascent and descent of Mount Marcy, New York's highest peak. Early Friday evening I drove to the trailhead at Adirondak Loj near Heart Lake (south of Lake Placid), and slept in the back of my Jeep. I awoke sometime around 3:30 in the morning and set off for Marcy, some 7-plus miles distant, in the predawn darkness, my entire world the illuminated glow from my headlamp. I've always enjoyed "alpine" starts, waking early, climbing by night, and being high on a mountain as the first light of day breaks on the upper slopes, and as I passed treeline on Marcy, the sun had just crested the horizon, bathing the summit in a gleaming white.

As I climbed higher, snow conditions changed. Deep drifts alternated with broad sheets of ice. Deciding that it would be safest to bootpack it from there to the summit, I strapped my skis to my backpack and continued on. Growing increasingly uncomfortable with the prospect of skiing back down over the terrain, I opted to turn around—having not quite made it to the summit—retreating several hundred yards to where I would don my skis and begin the cruise back to the trailhead. No sooner had I made that decision than I suddenly punched through the ice. I plunged in up to my armpits, the ice tight around my chest. Beneath me and the ice, loose, unconsolidated sugar snow wouldn't support my weight, and my legs were swimming around uselessly like I was treading water. Behind me, each ski had also punctured the ice in its own tight hole, restricting my movement.

The wind was blowing crosswise over the ridgeline, spraying my face with snow. I looked around at the endless mountains around me, wondering if anyone was coming up the trail somewhere behind, and if so, how far away they might still be at this early hour. At the very least, I'd followed my standard practice of leaving an itinerary with a friend, who would call the forest rangers to report me overdue if I didn't check in later that day. Nonetheless, I was fully aware of the irony of me, a search and rescue team member, possibly requiring his own search and rescue.

For ten or fifteen minutes I struggled, working to break the ice away from around my chest and ultimately belly-flopping onto the ice nearby, keeping my weight distributed so as to avoid repeating my previous predicament. I stepped into my skis and descended the mountain, enjoying the schuss through the trees every step of the way. I later saw a group of backcountry skiers several miles down the mountain; they would have found me, eventually.

I've since moved away from the Adirondacks, now making my home in Boulder, Colorado, where the Rockies serve as my new adopted home range. And I continue to travel the world in search of higher and more remote mountains to climb by ever more challenging routes. But I haven't lost my love or nostalgia for the Adirondacks. They are familiar mountains; my knowledge of them, intimate. I know I will return to them often, and one day will perhaps even make my permanent home among their valleys and communities.

Until then, I continue to want to give back to those mountains that have given so much to me; to share my love for those peaks with others; to tell the stories that unfold among the trees and rocks and rivers. This book is that giving back. The stories contained within its chapters are not my own. They are a collective human history of adventure and misadventure among one of America's most revered landscapes. And my hope is that this book will play several roles in contributing to that continuing legacy:

Honor the memory of those who have lost their lives in the Adirondacks;

Recognize and applaud the forest rangers, search and rescue teams, and individual volunteers who selflessly dedicate themselves to responding in times of need, "so that others may live";

Tell a cautionary tale, so that you might learn from the experiences of the people contained within the pages of this book and avoid finding yourself in similar trouble, whether in the Adirondacks or wherever your adventures take you;

Foster a respect and admiration for the Adirondack Mountains;

And finally, simply tell a good story, that you might be enlightened and entertained by these true tales from the mountains I have come to know and love.

I sincerely hope that you enjoy these stories from the comfort of your own armchair, that you experience joy in the mountains, and that your own adventures in the backcountry are conspicuously absent of misfortune.

INTRODUCTION

LAY OF THE LAND: THE PREHISTORY, PEOPLE, PLACES, AND POLICIES THAT DEFINE THE ADIRONDACKS

This region has always been and will always be under the dominion of Nature. Its altitude renders its climate cold and forbidding, while its rugged surface and light soil render it in a great measure unfit for cultivation. While the tide of emigration has rushed around it for almost a century, and filled the West with people for thousands of miles beyond it, this region, although lying along the borders of some of the oldest settlements in the New World, may still be said to be "a waste land where no one comes, or has come since the making of the world."

—Nathaniel Bartlett Sylvester, *Historical Sketches of Northern New York and the Adirondack Wilderness* (1877)

At more than 6 million acres (9,375 square miles), the Adirondack Park is a wilderness on the grandest scale. It is fully one-fifth the size of New York State, approximately equal to the size of the entire state of Vermont, and slightly larger than Yellowstone, Yosemite, Grand Canyon, Great Smoky Mountains, and Glacier national parks—combined. It is a patchwork of public and private lands that together make up the largest publicly protected natural area in the contiguous United States, and the largest designated wilderness east of the Mississippi River.

1

Of the 6.1 million total acres that make up the Park, 2.6 million (42 percent) is state-owned (1 million acres of which is classified as wilderness and is off-limits to motorized recreation). The balance is composed of sparsely populated private lands dedicated to open space recreation, forestry, agriculture, and tourism.

Yet the Park's overwhelming size fails to fully capture the Adirondack region. Restricting one's definition of "Adirondack" to the park boundary line as drawn on a map overlooks the rich and inextricably linked human and natural histories of the region. The Adirondacks' true extent reaches well beyond political divisions like park boundaries and county lines, and into the topography of the landscape—its mountains and rivers—and into the unique economic, cultural, social, and environmental idiosyncrasies that separate the Adirondacks from their neighbors to the north, south, east, and west.

Casting the widest net, the Adirondack region extends east to Lake Champlain and Lake George, which separate it from Vermont's Green Mountains farther east; is bordered on the south by the Mohawk River Valley; extends west to the Black River, beyond which lies the Tug Hill Plateau; and tapers off to the north in the St. Lawrence River Valley.

True to the region's wilderness reputation, that immense area is dotted with a little over one hundred towns and villages that are home to just 130,000 year-round residents and another 200,000 seasonal residents. But residents are only part of the population story: An estimated 7 million tourists visit the Adirondacks each year, and 60 million people are said to live within a day's drive.

BY THE NUMBERS: A TOPOGRAPHIC TALLY

Looking beyond the macro lens of sheer size and scale, the Adirondacks, upon closer inspection, reveal an impressive catalog of topographic, environmental, and recreational features that provide a seemingly tailor-made natural backdrop ripe for adventure—and misadventure.

Perhaps the premier attraction of the Adirondacks is the High Peaks—the forty-six mountains exceeding 4,000 feet in elevation, culminating in 5,344-foot Mount Marcy, the Empire State's tallest peak. The original list of forty-six was based on an early-twentieth-century survey, and in actuality contained some minor errors. More recent and accurate measurements revealed that four peaks—Blake, Cliff, Nye, and Couchsachraga—are just under 4,000 feet, and one mountain not included in the original list—MacNaughton—is just over 4,000 feet, but the original list of forty-six remains the standard definition of the Adirondack High Peaks.

Those High Peaks form a great drainage divide that separates the Hudson River to the south and the St. Lawrence River and Great Lakes watershed to the north and west. More than 30,000 miles of brooks and streams tumble out of the mountains, feeding another 1,200 miles of major rivers—including the Hudson, and also the Black, Oswegatchie, Grass, Raquette, Saranac, and Ausable. Of those, nearly 1,000 miles have been New York State–designated as Wild, Scenic, or Recreational.

In among the rivers and streams are roughly 2,800 lakes and ponds, totaling more shoreline than Vermont and New Hampshire combined. "A singular characteristic seems to mark all the rivers that flow in and around Northern New York. All of them . . . flow from and through great chains or systems of lakes," noted Nathaniel Bartlett Sylvester in his 1877

Historical Sketches of Northern New York and the Adirondack Wilderness.

Those lakes include tiny alpine tarns like Lake Tear of the Clouds, the headwaters of the Hudson River high on the upper ramparts of Mount Marcy, as well as major lakes like Upper and Lower Saranac, Big and Little Tupper, Schroon, Placid, Long, Raquette, and Blue Mountain.

Every now and then, as water flows from stream to river to lake, it dives into deep chasms and gorges. One such gorge is the Hudson River Gorge, a stretch of technical, and at times, violent white water where the river passes between steep rock walls as it flows south and then east between Newcomb and North River. Another such gorge is the Ausable Chasm, described by Seneca Ray Stoddard in his classic, *Old Times in the Adirondacks*, which tells the story of his adventures in 1873:

The river flowing quietly along the valley from the south and west, passes Keeseville, plunges over Alice Falls, square against a solid wall of rock, turns at right angles and, wheeling around in confused swirls, now right, now left, falls in a mass of foam over the rocks at Birmingham, then hurrying downward between towering cliffs and over rocks where the sun never shines, emerges from the gloom out into the glorious sunlight, and onward to mingle with the muddy waters of Lake Champlain.

This freak of nature is not alone of its kind, but one of a system of rents in the earth's surface that probably extend all over the northern portion of the State . . . .

With the exception of the highest peaks whose summits extend up above treeline and are home to the entirety of New York State's 85 acres of alpine tundra, the entire landscape is blanketed in dense forest. From the summit of Mount Marcy during an 1846 climb of the peak, J. T. Headley, one of the early adventure writers from the mid-nineteenth century, remarked on the sea of greens, grays, browns, and blacks—an endless wave of forest broken only by narrow gaps where he knew streams or lakes must exist out of sight below the treetops.

The region lies along a great north-south transition zone, and the forest changes character from a deciduous forest of beech and maple in the southern foothills to a coniferous boreal forest of firs, hemlocks, pine, and spruce in the north. And despite having been nearly logged over, the Adirondacks today look much as they did when Headley stood atop Marcy 160 years ago, once again blanketed in a thick and at times impenetrable forest. In fact, by one estimate there are still 500,000 acres of old-growth forest throughout the Adirondacks, 200,000 of which have never been logged in its history.

Wildlife, on the other hand, isn't as abundant as it once was, and mammals like wolves and panthers have been wholly extirpated from the region. Many species, though, are making encouraging recoveries. Moose began a return to the region from Vermont and New Hampshire during the 1980s, after an absence of more than a century, and today their population is nearly one hundred strong and growing. More than four thousand black bears make their home in the park, and beaver, nearly wiped out from the region at the turn of the twentieth century, are abundant once again.

Providing access to it all is an impressive network of entrance points, routes, and trails. More than forty roads enter the park (though there are no entrance gates or admission fees). More than 2,000 miles of hiking trails lace the region, constituting one of the largest hiking trail systems in the nation. Several notable long-distance trails are part of the network, including the 120-mile Northville-Placid Trail, which bisects the eastern and western portions of the High Peaks. A more recent addition to the network is the European-inspired Jackrabbit Trail, which is pieced together so that one may travel a day's distance in the backcountry and emerge from the woods at a town, permitting a hot meal and a warm bed before resuming the journey the next morning.

Hundreds of miles of mountain bike trails exist in the Wild Forest portions of the Park, and there are hundreds more miles of canoe routes that trace the great Adirondack waterways. They include the historic 90-mile Adirondack Canoe Route, from Old Forge to Saranac Lake, as well as classic destinations like the St. Regis Wilderness Canoe Area, the Fulton Chain of Lakes around Old Forge, the Saranac Chain of Lakes, and many more.

WEATHER

Despite its reputation for predictably unpredictable weather, the Adirondack climate can be succinctly summed up in its seasonal variation. Summer days are pleasant and sunny, warm but rarely too hot for outdoor activity. The landscape is lush and green, and outdoor adventure seekers are everywhere—rock climbers, hikers, backpackers, anglers, canoeists. As fall creeps in, the days and nights turn cool and crisp, and the trees explode in the vibrant colors of an iconic New England autumn. By October the first snows begin to fall, and soon the Adirondacks transform into a wonderland of snow and ice. Annual snowfall through the heart of the winter months ranges from 100 inches in some parts, to 400 inches or more at the higher elevations and in the western regions of the Park, offering an ideal playground for snowshoers and cross-country and backcountry skiers. Waterfalls and seeps in the rock cliffs freeze into enticing ribbons of ice, drawing ice climbers out of the woodwork. During spring the mountains rejuvenate, shedding their snow and coming back to life. The bugs come back to life, too, and for the first months of spring and into the earliest days of summer, blackflies reign supreme. At this time, a can of bug spray and a head net may be one's most indispensable pieces of outdoor equipment. Rivers flow full with snowmelt, challenging white-water canoeists, kayakers, and rafters.

NEW MOUNTAINS, OLD ROCKS: GEOLOGY AND ADIRONDACK PREHISTORY

The wilderness of Northern New York may properly be divided into three natural grand divisions, or belts . . . the Mountain Belt, the Lake Belt, and the Level Belt . . . each strongly marked by the distinguishing characteristics which suggest its name.

—Nathaniel Bartlett Sylvester, *Historical Sketches of Northern New York and the Adirondack Wilderness* (1877)

It looked as if the Almighty had once set this vast earth rolling like the sea; and then, in the midst of its maddest flow, bid all the gigantic billows stop and congeal in their places.

—J. T. Headley, *The Adirondack: Or, Life in the Woods* (1849)

With their rounded masses and relatively modest elevations, the Adirondacks are often assumed to be old mountains, worn down and blunted by the erosional forces of time. But, in fact, they are a young mountain range made of some of the oldest rocks on earth.

Contrary to popular belief, the Adirondacks share no geologic kinship with the Appalachian Mountains. They are more closely related to the Laurentian Mountains of Quebec than they are to any other range. And unlike the linear, elongated ranges of the Appalachians and the Rockies, the Adirondacks form a circular dome 160 miles in diameter and 1 mile high. Early explorers unknowingly recognized this distinction, often describing the Adirondacks as having five separate mountain ranges too convoluted and intertwined to tell apart.

The dome that constitutes the Adirondack Mountains is an extremely recent formation, at least geologically, having formed about 5 million years ago. The rock itself that comprises the dome, on the other hand, is more than 1 billion years old. Much of it is igneous anorthosite, the dominant component of the Canadian Shield, an enormous plate of billion-year-old rock that covers most of eastern and southern Canada and all of Greenland. The Adirondacks represent its southernmost extent.

The Shield, requiring intense pressure and heat to form, was born beneath an incredible 15 miles of overlaying rock. An ancient sea that covered the present-day eastern seaboard deposited layer upon layer of sediment, ultimately covering the nascent Shield to the required depth. Then, many millions of years later, repeated uplifts slowly raised the Shield while the forces of erosion stripped away the layers of sedimentary rock above, until the billion-year-old anorthosite reached the surface, exposed for us to see.

One can easily see that process continuing today in the form of the distinctive Adirondack slides, which are swaths of exposed bedrock that streak the flanks of the highest summits, laid bare of their soil and vegetation. In fact, the mountains are growing as much today as they ever have. During the 1980s, geologists remeasured old surveyors' benchmarks and, to their surprise, found that the Adirondacks are actively growing at the rate of 1.5 to 3 millimeters per year (an incredibly fast rate geologically that matches or exceeds the rate of growth of South America's Andes Mountains).

Although scientists aren't entirely sure of the cause, they theorize that a "hot spot" under the entire Adirondack region near the base of the earth's crust accounts for this rapid growth. Regardless of the cause, two things appear certain: The mountains are growing thirty times faster than they are eroding away, and at current rates of uplift, the Adirondacks will be the highest peaks in eastern North America within about 1 million years, reaching heights of 7,000 to 9,000 feet.

One can look elsewhere in the Adirondacks for clear signs of its geologic history and very active present. Great northeast-southwest fault lines—breaks and weakenings in the bedrock as a result of geologic uplift—allowed for differential erosion, ultimately becoming Long Lake and Indian Lake, as well as Indian Pass, Avalanche Pass, and the Johns Brook and Ausable valleys. Today, earthquakes remind residents that the Adirondacks are still very much alive. Smaller quakes are felt or recorded every year, and larger earthquakes—those measuring 5.0 or greater on the Richter scale—occur about once every five to ten years, including in 2002, 1993, and 1983.

But geologic uplift doesn't tell the whole story. The most recent ice age also left an indelible mark on the Adirondacks. While a massive continental ice sheet formed to the north, the high summits of the Adirondacks formed their own alpine glaciers. Those glaciers scarred the mountains, carving great *cirques*—bowl-shaped amphitheaters—into the sides of the mountain. One of the best examples is Whiteface Mountain, northern sentinel of the High Peaks. Glaciers formed on Whiteface's north, east, and west sides. As the glaciers grew and carved ever-larger cirques into the sides of the mountain, they slowly met and formed *arêtes* (sharp ridgelines that today give Whiteface its distinctive shape). Had that process continued, Whiteface might one day have come to look like Switzerland's Matterhorn.

The advance of the continental ice sheet trumped the alpine glaciers, however, eventually covering the whole of the Adirondacks. Its mark can be seen on the mountains as well. As the ice sheet eventually receded about ten thousand years ago, it left behind *erratics*—large boulders carried down by the glacier and deposited in the most unlikely places—which can be seen today everywhere from low-lying fields and meadows to the summit of Mount Marcy.

A PEOPLED WILDERNESS

God appears to have wrought in these old mountains with His highest power, and designed to leave a symbol of His omnipotence. Man is nothing here . . . .

—J. T. Headley, *The Adirondack: Or, Life in the Woods* (1849)

Almost from the moment the ice receded, humans began to leave their mark on the Adirondacks, and the region's history since then has reflected an intimate relationship between people and wilderness.

The first people to live near the Adirondack region moved to the shores of Lake Champlain shortly after the Wisconsin glacial ice melted back around ten thousand years ago. Native Americans—namely

Algonquin and Iroquois peoples from the Mohawk and St. Lawrence river valleys—hunted, fished, and collected plant foods from the wetlands, lakeshores, and river valleys throughout the region, though neither group seems to have had any permanent habitation among the mountains.

The Iroquois and Algonquin were hostile neighbors, occasionally fighting against one another, and the name *Adirondack* actually derives from the Iroquois "ha-de-ron-dah," meaning "bark-eater," a derogatory term that referred to their rivals, the Algonquin tribe. The Native American legacy can also be seen in other place names, such as Indian Carry on the Raquette River–Saranac Lake canoe route, and on the Oswegatchie River.

French explorers and missionaries were the next to arrive, when Samuel de Champlain and Father Isaac Jogues showed up within years of one another during the early seventeenth century. By the eighteenth century, a number of settlements and military posts were scattered along lakes George and Champlain (which would become a pivotal corridor during the French and Indian War, and later, the American Revolution).

In the late 1700s, the exploitation of the Adirondacks' natural resources began in earnest for the first time. The region's rich iron ore deposits had been discovered, and logging was by then abundant and would continue for the next century.

The first wholesale harvesting of the Adirondack forests had begun shortly after the English replaced the Dutch as the landlords of New Netherland and changed its name to New York. Then, after the Revolutionary War, Crown lands passed into the hands of New York State, and the original public acreage, totaling about 7 million acres, was sold for pennies an acre to repay the state's war debts. Lumbermen were welcomed to the interior of the Adirondacks with few restraints on their activities.

With the exception of the region's eastern fringe (the Lake George–Lake Champlain corridor), the interior of the Adirondacks remained relatively unknown, except to those hardy lumbermen, until the early nineteenth century.

Finally, in 1837, the Adirondacks became known by the name we call them today. Up until then, they had been known by any variety of generalities, including the Great North Woods, or simply, Deer Hunting Country, as indicated on a 1761 English map.

Rampant logging continued, such that in 1850, New York was the leading timber-producing state in the nation (thanks to the Adirondacks). But the "prestige" came to a quick close as rapid deforestation decimated the timber supply. Following 1850, the ongoing destruction of the Adirondacks became a growing concern as the deforestation of watershed woodlands reduced the soil's ability to hold water, accelerated erosion, and exacerbated flooding problems.

Then, in 1857, we saw the beginnings of what would ultimately become today's Adirondack Park, published in S. H. Hammond's *Wild Northern Scenes; or Sporting Adventures with the Rifle and the Rod*: "Had I my way, I would mark out a circle of a hundred miles in diameter, and throw around it the protecting aegis of the constitution. I would make it a forest forever. It would be a misdemeanor to chop down a tree and a felony to clear an acre within its boundaries."

In 1869, Rev. W. H. H. Murray published his pivotal book, *Adventures in the Wilderness*. His writing exposed the urban public to the wonders of adventure in the Adirondack wilds, spawning "Murray's rush." Sure enough, by 1880 the region had become a popular destination for the residents of crowded and polluted cities like New York, who vacationed in the northern wilderness for their health and well-being, and to cure tuberculosis in the crisp, clean mountain air. This was the beginning of the Adirondacks' Great Camps era.

Incidentally, by some accounts, this is also the time when the term *vacation* was coined. City residents "vacated" the cities, fleeing to the Adirondacks in search of fresh air to escape the stifling heat and deadly fevers of the city. Thus a distinction was born between American vacations and the British *holiday*.

Around the same time, Verplanck Colvin stepped onto the scene. Starting in 1872 he led the state survey of the Adirondack wilderness and would continue in that capacity for the next thirty years. The survey brought Colvin's profession into alignment with his passion for the mountains, and he used his annual reports to the state legislature to call for the creation of an Adirondack Forest Preserve. "Unless the region be preserved essentially in its present wilderness condition," he wrote in 1874, "the ruthless burning and destruction of the forest will slowly, year after year, creep onward . . . and vast areas of naked rocked, arid sand and gravel will alone remain to receive the bounty of the clouds, unable to retain it." His motives weren't entirely altruistic; the state needed to preserve the watershed as a water source for the fledgling Erie Canal.

In 1885, eleven years after that plea, Colvin got his wish. The New York State legislature established the Adirondack Forest Preserve, which "shall be forever kept as wild forest lands." That original Forest Preserve spanned 681,374 acres, which through targeted state purchases would eventually expand to its present-day 2.6 million. But Colvin dreamed of an even greater degree of protection for the region—a true Adirondack Park.

Seven years later, in 1892, a bill establishing the Park passed the legislature, indicating its boundary with a prominent blue line drawn on a map (which is why today, the Adirondack Park is often referred to locally as being "inside the Blue Line"). Ironically, however, the new Park actually weakened earlier protections placed on the landscape.

Then, two years later, at the 1894 Constitutional Convention, a new covenant meant to achieve meaningful protection for the Adirondacks was included in the new state constitution, and was enacted the next year—1895—through the popular vote of the people. To this day, the Adirondacks represent the only wild lands preserve in the nation whose fate lies in the hands of the voters of the entire state in which it is located. Any relaxation of the protection the Adirondacks enjoy requires the approval of a majority of the state's voters and two successive legislatures. Such relaxation is rarely given, and only twice have major measures been approved—the cutting of ski trails on Whiteface Mountain (1940), and the construction of the Northway (1958), the stretch of I-87 that runs northward from Albany to the Canadian border en route to Montreal.

The 1890s and the years that followed were precedent-setting. The language of the constitutional article establishing the Adirondack Park, and the decades of legal experience in its defense, are widely recognized as laying the foundation for the United States' National Wilderness Act of 1964. Also during this time, the Adirondack region was the birthplace of some of the country's first outdoor magazines, as well as hiking and paddling clubs; in addition, the rustic architecture synonymous with ranger stations and hunting lodges first started to take shape here.

The early twentieth century saw recreational use of the

Adirondacks increase dramatically, and Lake Placid's hosting of the 1932 Winter Olympics further put the region on the map.

But with the opening of the Northway in the mid-1960s (and the increased ease of access it offered), the Adirondack landscape once again came under threat, this time through new development pressures in private portions of the Park. New measures would be needed to protect the landscape from a new wave of destruction, and for a while, a hotly contested proposal to save the region by establishing an Adirondack Mountain National Park circulated among the people, though it never gained any serious traction.

A solution took shape in 1971 with the formation of the Adirondack Park Agency, whose task was to oversee and develop long-range land use plans for the public and private portions of the Park. They divided the Adirondacks into a series of land classifications: public lands were classified as wilderness, primitive, canoe, wild forest, or intensive use; private lands were designated as either hamlet, moderate density, rural use, or industrial use and resource management. The ultimate goal was to channel as much of the future growth as possible around existing communities in the Park, where roads, utilities, services, and supplies already existed, thus minimizing the impact on the overall Adirondack environment and wilderness.

It proved a double-edged sword, on the one hand providing much of the necessary protections required to sustain the landscape, but on the other hand placing intense restrictions on the private landowners in the Park. But, given the history of human exploitation of the Adirondack landscape, perhaps those tight restrictions were the only way to truly protect the Adirondacks. "No area in America has had a more miserable story of ruthless squandering of natural resources," wrote William

Chapman White in his 1954 *Adirondack Country*, "based on the supposition that the stock of fish and game, as well as trees, was infinite."

Indeed, the earliest adventure writers of the mid-nineteenth century extolled what they saw as limitless bounties of trout and deer and timber, and that attitude prevailed for nearly a century. But times have changed, and I suspect that if White were to evaluate the state of the Adirondacks today, his opinion might not be so pessimistic. Timber and mining are still major economic forces in the region, but now so is tourism, with a heavy emphasis on outdoor recreation. And while some scars of the region's exploitive history remain, the Adirondacks today are a wonderful success story—a testament to the power of good policy, and to nature's capacity to rehabilitate a compromised landscape, if given the opportunity to do so.

A MARRIAGE MADE IN WILDERNESS: THE GROWTH OF ADVENTURE AND MISADVENTURE

Visitors from the city who are ignorant of the dangers and difficulties attending an excursion into the forest frequently suffer for their lack of experience . . . . Many a pedestrian on reaching these woods is incredulous of the danger which he is told will menace him if he ventures out alone to indulge in his favorite pastime. But let him rest assured that there is no question as to the reality of this danger—the danger of losing himself in the forest . . . . And I very much doubt if there is any inexperienced person cool headed enough to face that calamity with absolute safety and calmness. Of course men have frequently been lost in the woods and have "come out alright" in the end. But more have been injured for life by the experience, and some have even died in the terrible labyrinth which their own fright and ignorance left them unable to penetrate.

—"Lost in the Adirondacks—Warning to Visitors to the North Woods; What Not to Do When You Lose Your Way and How Not to Lose It," *The New York Times* (March 16, 1890)

For as long as people have ventured into the Adirondack wilds, they've gotten lost, injured, or otherwise caught up in some type of calamity. Adventure was readily at their doorstep, and misadventure never more than a step away. It wasn't a matter of if something *would* go wrong, but rather *when*, for it inevitably would.

The Adirondacks have always been a rugged and remote wilderness that has challenged outdoor adventurers and defied straightforward exploration. For instance, New York's highest peak, Mount Marcy—which saw its first ascent in 1837—was the last of the New England state high points to see a person stand on its 5,344-foot summit, and the last to become familiar to outdoor adventure seekers. New Hampshire's Mount Washington was first climbed in 1642, and by the time Marcy was first climbed, Washington's summit already had summit buildings, hotels, and an auto road to the top. Mount Mansfield in Vermont was first climbed in 1772; Mount Frissel in Connecticut in 1781; Mount Greylock in Massachusetts in 1799; and even the remote and imposing Katahdin in Maine was first climbed in 1804.

Even more poignantly, by the time the last of the Adirondack High Peaks saw its first ascent (Couchsachraga on June 23, 1924), many of the West's prominent and lofty summits had already been climbed, some by technical routes. Colorado's 14,255-foot Long's Peak was first climbed in 1868 by Major John Wesley Powell, who also led the first expedition down the Grand Canyon of the Colorado River. Interestingly, Powell was originally scheduled to lead the Adirondack survey in New York State, but instead traveled west, leaving the task to Colvin, who began in 1872. The 14,441-foot glaciated Mount Rainier in Washington was first climbed in 1870; Oregon's Mount Hood in 1857 (and perhaps as early as 1845); and California's Mount Shasta in 1854, and Mount Whitney nineteen years later, in 1873.

Like her mountains, the Adirondacks' waterways have proven similarly elusive. Lake Tear of the Clouds, the source of the Hudson River high on the flanks of Mount Marcy, was discovered by Verplanck Colvin in 1872. But by then, several other notable finds had already occurred elsewhere. During the middle of the nineteenth century, prior to the discovery of the Hudson's source, John Hanning Speke located the source of Egypt's Nile River, Lake Victoria. Here in the United States, the famous Lewis and Clark expedition (1804–1806) had passed the headwaters of the Mississippi River seventy years before Colvin discovered Lake Tear, and Lewis and Clark went on to reach the mouth of the Columbia River at the Pacific Ocean. Twenty years later, and still fifty years before Lake Tear's discovery, David Thompson, a partner of the North West Company, discovered Columbia Lake high in the Canadian Rockies of present-day British Columbia; in so doing, he located the source of the Columbia River.

Could such examples be a case of the Adirondacks' being overlooked in favor of grander objectives in the West? Or, rather, did their rugged wilderness pose a barrier to early adventurers, a testament to the challenges inherent in penetrating and navigating the great Adirondack wilds? The answer is probably a little of both, but given the other successful and earlier explorations of other New England mountain ranges, one can be sure that the Adirondacks must have been on someone's radar screen.

Early writers of mountaineering in the Adirondacks criticized the mountains for their modest heights, with only fifteen summits higher than treeline. They noted that while the Adirondacks are home to some tall cliffs, for the most part the great rock walls lay elsewhere in the West and abroad. Most climbing in the 'Dacks was described as "simply mountain walking."

But those early writers largely missed the point. The defining elements that characterize the Adirondack experience are not those of the Alps or the Rockies or the Himalayas, or even the Whites in New Hampshire. The Adirondacks offer an experience all their own, and later writers recognized that some "limitations" are more than made up for with other qualities. "The Adirondack mountaineer is not likely to run out of opportunities in a lifetime," wrote one anonymous writer. The Adirondacks were valued, too, for the remoteness and solitude they offered the adventurer, and for the forest that stretches across their slopes to the horizon line.

Most of all, the Adirondacks were valued for their single most defining element—one that wraps all their other qualities into one succinct term—their wilderness. And that value is cherished by outdoor adventure seekers today as much as it ever was. Maintaining the Adirondacks' wilderness character and the frontier experience that goes along with it has been a top priority since the region was first protected as a Park, and that priority has been carried forward, generation by generation.

Percy Olton wrote in a 1938 issue of *Appalachia*, the Appalachian Mountain Club's semiannual journal of mountaineering, that many routes had been left "uncatalogued so that future climbers may share [to] some extent the pleasures of climbing an uncharted route." Don Mellor, in his authoritative *Climbing in the Adirondacks: A Guide to Rock and Ice Routes in the Adirondack Park* (1995), says that he intentionally left many wilderness climbs undocumented to allow others the opportunity for genuine exploration into the unknown. Even today, twenty of the forty-six High Peaks have been left without trails to their summits, to allow for greater opportunities for adventure.

EARLY ADVENTURERS AND THEIR MISADVENTURE

The earliest misadventures were a simple by-product of living life on a frontier. The Adirondacks represented an unforgiving landscape, rugged and virtually unknown. It was a time when the threat of predators—bears, wolves, panthers, bull moose—was very real, and stories of close calls and even hand-to-hand fights for survival were common.

One early account survives in the experiences and writings of Charles Dudley Warner. "The encounter was unpremeditated on both sides. I was not hunting for a bear, and I have no reason to suppose that a bear was looking for me," he wrote. It was a warm August day, "just the sort of day when adventure of any kind seemed possible." Warner ventured up to a series of clearings on the mountain behind his house to pick blackberries—even though bears had been seen there just the summer before.

"Not from any predatory instinct, but to save appearances, I took a gun. It adds to the manly aspect of a person with a pin tail if he also carries a gun," he continued. It would prove a crucial decision.

Arriving at the clearing, Warner set his rifle against a tree and started picking berries. As he filled his bucket, he glanced across the clearing and saw a bear standing on its hind legs, also lunching on blackberries. As Warner slowly backed away the bear saw him, dropped onto its forefeet, and started to approach. "Climbing a tree was of no use, with so good a climber in the rear," Warner later mused. "If I started to run, I had no doubt the bear would give chase and . . . get over this rough, brush-tangled ground faster than I could."

He placed his pail of berries on the ground as a lunch offering to the bear, distracting the predator long enough for Warner to flee. The tactic worked—initially. As soon as the bear's attention was focused on the pail of berries, Warner ran for his gun, reaching his rifle as the bear crashed through the brush behind him, "coming on with blood in his eye." Cocking the gun, Warner's life flashed before his eyes—he thought of his family; of the type of epitaph they would put on his gravestone; and of a newspaper subscription he had balked at paying years earlier. Then, his thoughts shifted to more practical matters: "I tried to think what is the best way to kill a bear with a gun when you are not near enough to club him with the stock." With little time to ponder, Warner raised his gun, covered the bear's breast with the sight, and fired. "Then I turned and ran like a deer," he said. The bear stopped, lying down in the brush. Remembering that "the best thing to do after having fired your gun is to reload it," Warner slipped in a new charge, but it would prove unnecessary. "Death had come to [the bear] with a merciful suddenness," he wrote.

Warner had survived his misadventure with Adirondack wildlife.

In contrast to these earliest stories, where disaster struck unwitting participants who were simply living their lives, adventure and misadventure as we think of them today—outdoor recreation with an element of risk—grew slowly, a series of gradual advances punctuated by major breakthroughs. The passage of time has made the names of a select few pioneers famous as their achievements have been recorded, but in truth, a long lineage of adventurers, both known and unknown today, contributed collectively to the growth of Adirondack adventure and misadventure.

The first 125 years of Adirondack adventure, beginning in 1800 and continuing until 1925, is divided into four distinct periods by Russell M. L. Carson in his 1927 classic, *Peaks and People of the Adirondacks*.

The first period, spanning the early to mid-nineteenth century, is known as the Emmons Period, named for Ebenezer Emmons, the state geologist who led the first ascent of Mount Marcy in 1837. It was a time when Americans were developing an increasing acceptance of wilderness, seeing the wilds as less of a threatening place that hid evil and the unknown, and more as an inviting landscape to be explored and appreciated for the spiritual enlightenment one's soul could find there. Much of this change of heart is due to the writings of Romantic philosophers like Ralph Waldo Emerson, who established the noted Philosophers Camp at Follensby Pond in the western Adirondacks, and Henry David Thoreau. The 1826 publication of James Fennimore Cooper's *The Last of the Mohicans: A Narrative of 1757*, which is partly set in the Adirondacks, helped as well.

Even so, the Adirondacks were still far from making the big time. *The Northern Traveler*, a popular guidebook to the northeastern U.S. that published various editions during the Emmons Period, omitted the Adirondacks from its pages. "The Adirondack region or mountains were not mentioned," notes Carson. "They were not slighted intentionally, but because at that time the northern mountain wilderness was practically unknown. The most important thing that the Emmons Period did for mountaineering was to give widespread public notice that in northern New York there were majestic mountains, beautiful lakes, picturesque streams, virgin forests, and an invigorating climate that made the region an ideal spot for recreation and the restoration of health. Previously, it had been thought of, if considered at all, as a cold, barren wilderness."

Several notable achievements on the part of Emmons contributed to this growing public exposure for the Adirondacks, including a partial ascent of Mount Colden's now-famous Trap Dike in 1837, and the first ascent of Mount Marcy in that same year. Yet, though they were slowly gaining attention, the 'Dacks were still largely "off the map." When noted Adirondack guide John Cheney guided adventure writer J. T. Headley to the top of Marcy in 1846, the mountain hadn't been climbed in six years. The High Peaks' relative inaccessibility and remoteness may have contributed to this "sluggish" era of Adirondack mountaineering. "A tramp of forty miles through a pathless forest to see one mountain is a high price to pay, but we have resolved to do it," wrote Headley of his 1846 trip up Mount Marcy. By comparison, aspiring Marcy summiteers today can arrive at the Adirondak Loj trailhead south of Lake Placid by car and follow a marked trail 7.4 miles to the summit.

Forget even making it up Marcy from a "base camp." Merely getting to the Adirondacks in the first place was an adventure in itself, a nineteenth-century version of *Planes, Trains and Automobiles*. Residents of cities like New York or Boston would leave around 8:00 a.m. on a Monday morning, and, assuming there were no unexpected delays, would arrive at Lower Saranac Lake to meet their guide around 5:00 p.m. on Tuesday. Along the way, they'd link up with a combination of trains, stagecoach lines, horseback riding, travel by canoe or larger boat, and possibly foot travel, traveling by one of three "established" routes that would lead them to Lower Saranac or wherever their prearranged rendezvous with their guide might be.

Regardless, by the period's close, only nine peaks had names, eight had been ascended, and the popularity of climbing peaks would die off for roughly a decade.

A new era of Adirondack adventure began in 1849—the Phelps Period—and would continue for the next twenty years. The period is named for Orson "Old Mountain" Phelps, one of the most famous of all Adirondack guides, perhaps best known for promoting the climbing of mountains simply for the sheer pleasure of it. During this time, the mountain climbing focus shifted away from the ironworks region near the present-day ghost town of Tahawus (named after the Native American title given to Mount Marcy, meaning "Cloudsplitter"), and toward Keene Valley, in the heart of the High Peaks region.

There were three new first ascents in the High Peaks, and both Marcy and Whiteface saw more regular ascents. Fourteen more peaks were named, and the process of trail cutting was started (though trails were still few and skilled guides were still needed by most people venturing into the wilds).

Also during this period, the earliest adventure writers, including J. T. Headley and Seneca Ray Stoddard, ventured into the wilderness with experienced guides and brought back harrowing tales of adventure and catastrophe for public consumption. In one such account, Headley describes getting hopelessly lost in the forests around Indian Lake. He was out with an Indian guide "driving trees"—the process of partially chopping the trunks of numerous trees, and then felling one tree so that it will "domino" into a succession of trees that topple with much less effort than if they had been individually cut down.

Headley was out hunting one afternoon when he shot a deer, wounding it, but not so badly that it couldn't flee. Headley followed the track of blood until darkness began to fall and planned to turn back to camp, only to realize that he had no idea which way to go. He wandered through the forest until total darkness fell, at which point he sat down, made a small fire, and resolved to wait until morning. Around 9:00 p.m. he climbed up onto a rocky knoll and built a new fire with the idea of escaping "the mosquitoes and blackflies that were devouring me at a rate that would soon leave nothing for the wolves to lunch on," he wrote.

As night wore on, the crackling of the fire and the sounds of unseen foxes and hedgehogs in the surrounding forest kept him awake. The soft glow of the fire receded past tree trunks and into the darkness beyond, and at one point he thought he saw a bear. Taking a "firebrand" in one hand and a rifle in the other, Headley investigated the sighting, only to discover it was a tree stump. Sometime later, a thunderstorm passed overhead, blotting out the stars. Suddenly, a bright flash of lightning revealed a figure standing in the trees, and then all was black again. Headley heard the strong sound of footsteps approaching, and when lightning flashed again, found himself standing face-to-face with his Indian guide.

The guide had seen Headley's fire, assumed he was lost, and had come to retrieve him from his predicament. As it turned out, Headley had wandered to within 2 miles of the settler's house from which he and his guide had originally started their adventure.

Aside from the adventures and misadventures of writers like Headley, this period also hosted a notable mountaineering achievement— the first successful ascent of Mount Colden's Trap Dike in July 1850 (and simultaneously, the first ascent of the mountain itself), one of the Adirondack's premier mountaineering and slide climbs today. For the climbers—Robert Clarke and Alexander Ralph—Colden's Trap Dike was merely a route to the summit, but soon, climbers would shift their focus to the climb itself, and not just on the achievement of standing on a summit.

As the Phelps Period came to a close in 1869, another writer burst onto the scene, setting the stage for the Colvin Period that would immediately follow. The writer was Rev. William H. H. Murray, and his book, *Adventures in the Wilderness; Or Camp-Life in the Adirondacks*, spawned "Murray's Rush"—a flood of tourists that flocked en masse to the Adirondacks, spurring the development of stagecoach lines and hotels throughout the region. *Adventures* was a veritable how-to guidebook for Adirondack adventure, with practical sections on why to go, what it costs, what gear to buy and where to buy it, how to get there, where to stay, when to visit, and what sections of the region to see—not to mention the actual stories of his adventures.

"Ladies, even invalids, can penetrate the wilderness for scores of miles without making any exertion which a healthy child of five years cannot safely and easily put forth," Murray declared.

It may have been a gross exaggeration, and other writers would soon come to strongly contradict Murray's declaration, but the message was out and the floodgates opened—the Adirondacks were the place to go for wilderness adventure. By 1875 there were almost two hundred hotels throughout the region, including the renowned Paul Smith's Hotel, and a railroad constructed from Saratoga Springs to North Creek.

So began the Colvin Period, lasting from 1870 until 1900. With the start of the Adirondack survey in 1872, and continuing through the survey's quarter-century-plus life span, Verplanck Colvin and his companions spurred a revival of mountaineering interest in the heart of the public. Twenty-three of the High Peaks saw first ascents, and fifteen more were named (leaving only eight without names). "They not only revealed to the outside world the glories and beauties of Adirondack lakes, woods and mountains," wrote Carlson, "but they pioneered the way toward an ever-increasing use of the Adirondacks for recreational purposes.

"Wolves and panthers were always more a threatening menace than a real danger to man in the Adirondacks," Carlson continued, "but the former became extinct, as far as this region was concerned, just as the Colvin period opened and the latter disappeared before it closed. The wildness was gone, but enough of hardship and difficulty remained to give a delightful, though mild, flavour of adventure to climbing the high peaks."

Menacing wildlife or not, the Adirondacks remained anything but mild, with their rugged wilderness and harsh winter climate, and plenty of people experienced a "flavour of adventure." Although by now many trails had been blazed, they were still unmarked, and shelters (such as today's ubiquitous Adirondack lean-to) were few and far between. As such, guides were in high demand, and the guiding profession at one of the heights of its glory. The 1881 edition of Edwin R. Wallace's *Guide to the Adirondacks*, for instance, lists the names and addresses of 546 guides. (I say the guiding profession was at *one* of the heights of its glory because four decades later, throughout the early and mid-1920s, guiding went through a renaissance, and there were more than 1,000 guiding licenses issued for the Adirondacks in any given year. That number would scale back to around 500 or so per year for the next fifty years thereafter.)

The Colvin Period also saw a number of notable pioneers show up throughout the Adirondacks. Colvin himself was perhaps the era's most important pioneer, with too many credits to list here, though it is worthwhile to note two special events: his discovery of the source of the Hudson River, Lake Tear of the Clouds, in 1872, and one of the first known accounts of primitive roped climbing on August 25, 1877, on the steep northwest side of Gore Mountain between Warrensburg and North River.

Another such pioneer was rock scrambler Newell Martin. The 1875 graduate of Yale honed his climbing skills, which he brought to the Adirondacks as a summer resident of St. Huberts, through the "art of steeple climbing," whereby he would scale the ivy-covered steeples and towers of the university's New Haven campus. In the Adirondacks, he cataloged several significant ascents, including the first ascent up Sawteeth, as well as the first climb of Gothics from the Ausable side, which involved a descent of the steep Rainbow slide. Newell and his guide, Charles Beede, left a large white handkerchief spread on the slab, plainly visible from the valley below, offered as proof positive of their climb.

While mountaineers like Colvin and Martin were exploring the High Peaks, other adventurers were busy plying the innumerable waterways of the western Adirondacks. George Washington Sears, a journalist and woodsman who went under the pen name of Nessmuk, was one of the most accomplished. Beginning in 1880, and continuing for a period of years, he filed an extensive series of reports for the New York City–based *Forest and Stream* magazine. His canoe explorations are legendary, the most revered of which is his 1883 "Cruise of the Sairy Gamp," during which he paddled and portaged a 10.5-pound Rushton-built canoe 266 miles from Boonville to Paul Smith's Hotel and back. His route followed what is today considered to be one of the classic and historic Adirondack waterways.

The fourth and final of Carson's eras of Adirondack adventure, the Conservation Commission Period, encapsulates the first quarter of the twentieth century, from 1900 to 1925. "Under the Conservation Commission's regime," he writes, "more has been done to open and preserve the Adirondack Mountains for recreational purposes than in any other period in their history."

During the early 1900s, raging forest fires, some of whose scars can still be seen on the landscape today, destroyed much of the Adirondacks. But prior to 1911, the woods and waters of the Adirondacks were under the overlapping jurisdictions of the Forest, Fish and Game Commission, Forest Purchasing Board, and State Water Supply Commission. Interested in inaugurating a streamlined forest fire protection system, Governor Dix in 1911 consolidated the various departments into the unifying Conservation Commission (which in 1927 became the Conservation Department, and later, in 1970, the Department of Environmental Conservation).

It was this agency that gave birth to the revered forest rangers, who were charged with the responsibility of forest fire protection, and have today become just as synonymous, if not more so, with Adirondack search and rescue. During this period we also saw the advent of both the automobile and good roads, which for the first time opened the Adirondack region to weekend visitors. The state began a major movement to preserve the high mountain region for recreational use through the purchase of large land tracts that otherwise would have been logged. Permanent log lean-tos were built along lengthy sections of trail and located near reliable supplies of water. And a trail marker system was instituted for the first time: Circular metal disks were attached to each side of selected trees along a trail (red markers on east-west trails, blue on north-south trails, and yellow on diagonal trails), and trailheads featured signs with names of, and distances to, destinations.

Adirondack adventure focused around several established hubs: Adirondack Lodge at Heart Lake, St. Hubert's in Keene Valley, and, after its construction in 1925, Johns Brook Lodge in the Johns Brook Valley.

Winter adventure also came into its own during this period. Previously, more often than not, the frigid Adirondack winters were considered something to be endured rather than enjoyed. But beginning in the last decades of the nineteenth century, a few hardy souls were venturing into the High Peaks on snowshoes, logging first winter ascents of Marcy, Whiteface, and other lesser mountains. Then, beginning in the mid-1900s and steadily growing through the 1920s, backcountry skiing made its entrance onto the Adirondack scene. Groups like the Sno Birds at the Lake Placid Club helped to boost its popularity, their winter forays growing from just six people in 1904 to several hundred by 1920. And with the sudden influx of winter adventurers came the inevitable stories of winter misadventure, adding a new component to the history of Adirondack exploration.

As the Conservation Commission Period—the final of Carson's four—came to a close, a new era called the Marshall Period began, named for Robert Marshall, who in 1924 made the last first ascent of an Adirondack High Peak, finishing out the forty-six. Although the Adirondack region was already home to a number of outdoor organizations, including the St. Hubert's–based Adirondack Trail Improvement Society, Marshall's 1924 climb roughly coincided with the founding of two outdoor clubs that would forever change the face of Adirondack adventure.

The first—the Adirondack Mountain Club (ADK)—was born in 1922. The club started small, but by the 1927 publishing of Carson's *Peaks and People*, its importance was already evident. "Perhaps it is too soon to say that the founding of the Adirondack Mountain Club was an event of major importance . . . for its 'long-run' programme is not much more than begun," Carson wrote. "But under . . . wise and devoted leadership . . . it has built the Northville-Placid trail; it has constructed the Johns Brook Lodge, besides a number of open lean-tos; it is conducting a campaign of education along the lines of good camping manners and proper care and use of the forests, mountain tops, and camp sites; and it is stimulating interest in mountain climbing."

Today, the ADK's (the Appalachian Mountain Club had already branded the initials "AMC" decades earlier) enormous contribution to Adirondack adventure is evident: The club is 35,000 members strong, and is probably the single most influential outdoor organization promoting conservation, education, and responsible recreation in the Adirondack Park.

The second group to take shape was the Adirondack 46ers. When Robert Marshall and his partners, George Marshall and Herbert Clark, climbed Couchsachraga on June 24, 1924, they became the first three Adirondack Forty-Sixers; those individuals who have climbed all forty-six of the Adirondack High Peaks. The movement would be slow to gain momentum, but the trio started a trend that over time has exploded by leaps and bounds. In the ten years following their 1924 accomplishment, only two additional people became 46ers, and by the beginning of World War II, a total of only thirty had reached the mark.

But in 1937, the 46ers of Troy formed to promote climbing in the Adirondacks, and in 1947 they disbanded to allow the formation of the present-day Adirondack 46ers, which officially incorporated in 1949. Under the group's direction, membership in the "club" exploded exponentially—by the end of 1971, there were 750 46ers; and by June 24, 2004—eighty years to the day after Marshall and company became the first 46ers—there were more than 5,300, and nearly 300 Winter 46ers (those hardy souls looking for the added challenge of climbing all forty-six High Peaks during the winter season, officially defined as falling between December 21 and March 21).

Two prominent personalities also left their mark on Adirondack adventure during the Marshall Period. John Case, a former president of the American Alpine Club and soon-to-be full-time resident of the Adirondacks, brought alpine skills and some of the first belayed climbing techniques to upstate New York, establishing the first official route up the imposing Wallface Cliff in 1933 (known today as the Case Route). In the years prior, he also completed first climbs on Indian Head and the cliffs of Chapel Pond Pass, as well as a ski descent of Whiteface Mountain.

At the same time, one of Case's climbing partners, Jim Goodwin, was busy pioneering new routes of his own. Described as a complete mountaineer—skiing, bushwhacking, rock and ice climbing—Goodwin combined skills he had learned in the Canadian Rockies with equipment he imported from the French and Swiss Alps. Along the way, he added several significant notches to his belt, including the first winter ascent of Colden's Trap Dike in December 1935 (completed with a long ice ax and ten-point crampons), and the first ice ascent of Chapel Pond Slab in 1936, which he completed with Bob Notman by cutting steps in the ice and belaying from chopped platform stances.

In the decades since, the Adirondacks have seen a steady evolution of adventure. Local legends like the Ski-to-Die Club and climber Don Mellor have pushed the boundaries of possibility. World-renowned adventurers have come to the 'Dacks, too, and equally left their mark; people like German climber Fritz Wiessner (who put up numerous new rock climbing routes and advocated the writing of a climbing guide to document historic routes before they are lost from memory), and ice climber Yvon Chouinard (founder of Patagonia and Black Diamond), not to mention the host of international names that show up at events like Mountainfest and the Backcountry Skifest.

Along the way, these modern-day pioneers have introduced new equipment (such as front-point crampons and technical ice tools), new techniques, and a higher technical standard. As a result, visionary new routes are opened, whether they be rock routes at a familiar crag, or a first ski descent on a remote backcountry slide. Now, the old classic routes (climbing, canoeing, skiing) are valued, revered, and cherished alongside the newest "projects."

Finally, as we move into the twenty-first century, a new era of Adirondack adventure may very well be unfolding. While old "traditions" continue, the Adirondacks are seeing an influx of three things: people, competitive adventure, and technology.

People are coming to the Adirondacks in ever-increasing numbers to experience their share of adventure. Some of those people will be well prepared; others, less so. But by sheer probability, it seems that the raw number of misadventures will rise, whether or not that increase is proportional to the growth in numbers of adventure seekers.

Adventure races—mountain biking, trail running, canoeing, multidiscipline—are bringing a competitive spirit to the mountains, along the way asking participants to at times test the limits of their physical and psychological endurance. Such testing of limits seems to invite a new series of misadventures, though hopefully the training and preparation of race participants, and the controlled environments of the races themselves, will minimize any consequences.

Technology and its application in the 'Dacks, on the other hand, is part of an ongoing debate that has no clear influence on the balance of adventure and misadventure. Cell phones, GPS units, and Personal Locator Beacons all have the potential to increase the margin of safety for adventurers, but if misused, have just as much potential to endanger the lives of both the outdoor enthusiasts who venture out with a false sense of security, and the rescuers who come to save them when they get into trouble.

THE ADVENT OF SEARCH AND RESCUE

Today, a well-established and skilled search and rescue system stands ready to respond when adventure turns to misadventure—a hiker reported missing or overdue, or a climber injured in a fall. But it wasn't always so. Like adventure and misadventure, search and rescue has evolved over time to meet the increasing needs of the backcountry public.

In the earliest days, search and rescue was very much an ad hoc affair. When help was needed for someone in the backcountry, local residents, outdoorsmen, police and fire personnel, doctors, and maybe a local rescue squad would come together, calling upon the local experts and their individual skills to pull off as best a rescue effort as they could.

Over time, the forest rangers, whose primary role since their founding was fire protection, played an increasingly important role in leading search and rescue missions. But even as recently as the 1940s and '50s, there was little or no support network of search and rescue resources—helicopters, other rangers—to aid the local ranger.

Many times, when an evacuation was needed, the call for help would come in after dark. This was before cable television made it to the Adirondacks, and on any given night a good-sized crowd could be found at the local bar, such as the Ausable Inn in Keene Valley. The ranger would literally go into the bar and recruit a team of young men (often in various states of sobriety) and head up the trail. Sometimes, for good measure, the motley crew would even bring along a few extra bottles and make a party of it. "Some of the people [rescuees] had every right to jump off the stretcher when a group like this arrived," jokes Tony Goodwin, editor of the semiannual accident reports for *Adirondac* magazine.

Throughout the '60s and '70s, as hiking use in the Adirondacks increased, the number of rescues increased as well. And for a time, a debate raged over whether or not the state should start charging for rescues. "I always said you should take a picture of these guys [drunk pub-crawlers-turned-rescuers] and post it at every trailhead," jokes Goodwin. If people thought such a motley crew would be coming to save them, it would serve as a significant enough deterrent to minimize unnecessary calls for help, he figured.

Similar debates still surface in the Adirondacks every now and then, often brought on by new developments—a proposal to put up telecommunications towers and improve cell phone coverage; the passage of search and rescue legislation in other states like New Hampshire, Colorado, or California; or the introduction and application of new technologies like Personal Locator Beacons. But search and rescue continues to be a service provided gratis by the forest rangers and the many people who contribute to any individual search and rescue effort.

Today, the forest rangers serve as the lead on any search and rescue in the Park, and behind their command lies a highly efficient and structured network of resources—trained rangers, state police, air force and National Guard personnel, helicopters, technical rescuers and climbers, and volunteer search and rescue teams.

That network is put into action today more so than ever.

Throughout the '80s and '90s, search and rescue missions in the Department of Environmental Conservation's Region 5, which covers all but the westernmost sliver of the Adirondack Park, averaged a fairly consistent 125 per year. More recently, however, rangers in the same district are averaging 250 search and rescues per year.

Thanks in part to the efficient and well-structured SAR network, the vast majority of those incidents are resolved within the first twelve hours, and the outcomes, when at all possible, are overwhelmingly positive. But every now and then, simple misadventure becomes an epic fight for survival, with the outcome in the hands of the direct participants more so than that of any rescuer.

MODERN-DAY MISADVENTURE: SEARCH AND RESCUE IN THE TWENTY-FIRST CENTURY

As debates over technology like cell phones and telecommunications towers continues, and as the Adirondacks are used by ever more people participating in inherently risky outdoor activities, we can be sure of one thing: True to their roots, the Adirondacks will retain their wilderness character, requiring independence and self-sufficiency on the part of outdoor adventure seekers. Should everyday adventure turn into epic misadventure, outdoor enthusiasts will bear the burden of responsibility for determining the outcome, whether the safety net of search and rescue is there to catch them or not.

Through the years, the nature of adventure has changed, but the surety of misadventure has not. Misadventure has always been a known part of the equation in the Adirondack wilds, and that isn't likely to change anytime soon.

A GUIDE'S STORY: MAGNET FOR MISADVENTURE

In passing through this region, one should never wander from his guide, for it does not require more than a mile's aberration sometimes to lose one effectually.

—J. T. Headley, *The Adirondack: Or, Life in the Woods* (1849)

Many stories are told indicating his coolness in times of danger, and his skill and daring as a hunter. An account of his perilous adventures would fill a large volume.

—Seneca Ray Stoddard, *Old Times in the Adirondacks: The Narrative of a Trip into the Wilderness in 1873* (1971). Courtesy of North Country Books Inc., Utica, NY

In the long, distinguished, and often colorful, history of Adirondack guides, a select few men and their exploits have withstood the test of time and become legends of Adirondack lore. Some, like Orson "Old Mountain" Phelps, are remembered for their passion for climbing mountains. All were highly regarded for their prowess in the wilds; for their expertise as guides and hunters, and in all things outdoor-related; and for the character of their personalities.

And then there was John Cheney. Perhaps no Adirondack guide attracted a more disproportionate share of misadventure, and certainly no other guide handled such situations with more grace under pressure than he. Historian Alfred Donaldson wrote that Cheney was of "the type that could face daily the primitive hardships and dangers of the woods, and yet survive. Surprise, agitation, fear were virtually unknown [to him]. [He] looked upon dangers and emergencies not as detached possibilities but as the woof and web of every hour . . . . For [him] the unseen was never the unexpected, and [he] reacted to it as normally as other men do to the commonplace."

His reputation made Cheney one of the most sought-after guides in the Adirondacks, and at one point or another, he guided many of the most prominent adventurers and writers of the period, including Ebenezer Emmons, J. T. Headley, and Seneca Ray Stoddard, to name a select few. Whether it was guiding high-profile clientele, heading out solo through the backcountry, or hunting for subsistence or for the market, the Adirondack wilderness was where Cheney felt most at home. "To him a good time meant a tramp through the woods," one unidentified friend remarked. Cheney himself admitted: "Even from childhood, I was so in love with the woods that I not only neglected school, but was constantly borrowing a gun, or stealing the one belonging to my father . . . ."

Cheney was born in New Hampshire on June 26, 1800, and spent the first thirty years of life dividing his time between there and Ticonderoga, New York, between northern Lake George and southern Lake Champlain. Then, wrote Cheney's wife, "finding that game was growing scarce, he shouldered his rifle, and calling his faithful dog, set out for the then almost unknown wilderness." The move took Cheney and his family to the vicinity of Adirondac, a mining village directly southeast of the High Peaks region. There, he became an instant part of Adirondack history when he guided the Emmons-Redfield party to the top of Mount Marcy during the first ascent of the mountain in 1837. In the years that followed, misadventure would be Cheney's most loyal companion.

"I've always had a great love for the woods and a hunter's life ever since I could carry a gun," he wrote to Seneca Ray Stoddard in 1873. "And have had a great many narrow escapes from being torn to pieces by bears, panthers, wolves and moose, and many a time have had to put a tree between myself and an enraged bull moose." Cheney wasn't kidding.

On one memorable occasion, a pair of bull moose attacked Cheney, the "saplings snapping under their charge." As they advanced, Cheney stepped behind a large tree to take cover and, waiting for them to roar past, fired a shot that went clear through one moose and lodged in the other, felling both with a single shot. In another instance, Cheney was out in the woods when he was caught in a gale, with large trees crashing down all around him. Another near-miss occurred while camped out with John McIntyre, son of the McIntyre Iron Works owner, Archibald McIntyre. The duo heard the sound of animals during the night, and waking, Cheney got up to investigate. McIntyre carelessly opened fire, just missing Cheney.

Such bite-sized anecdotes are just the tip of the iceberg in the life of John Cheney. His most harrowing tales and closest calls have become the stuff of legend, extensively retold in his letters to friends, in nineteenth-century magazine articles, and in the writings of the people he guided.

WOLVES

During one winter, Cheney unexpectedly came upon a wolf. She was floundering in deep snow and ravenous with hunger. Eyeing Cheney, the wolf became aggressive. Fearing for his safety, he raised a rifle that he carried on this occasion and fired. But almost simultaneously, the wolf sprang at Cheney and the bullet missed its mark. It struck the wolf, injuring it, but not seriously, which only angered it more.

Left with little more than an empty rifle, Cheney engaged the wolf in hand-to-hand combat. He clubbed the wolf's head repeatedly with the butt of the rifle's stock, shattering it into pieces, yet amazingly, the wolf seemed entirely unfazed by the blows. Cheney switched tactics and grasped the metal barrel of the rifle like a baseball bat, taking great swings at his attacker. It had an improved effect until the wolf seized the iron with her teeth, nearly tearing the rifle from Cheney's grip.

In the course of fighting at such close range, the wolf stepped on Cheney's snowshoes and he fell over, losing any advantage or equal footing he had maintained up until that point. Realizing that the momentum had shifted to the wolf's advantage, Cheney called out for his dogs, which were somewhere in the forest nearby. After what must have seemed like an eternity, the first dog—a young hound—came into view, and just as quickly retreated into the forest with his tail between his legs.

Fortunately, his second (and clearly, braver) dog arrived a moment later and came to its master's aid. The dog attacked the wolf, sinking its teeth into the wolf's jawbone and tearing it away from Cheney. Taking advantage of this momentary reprieve, Cheney regained his feet, and with a well-directed blow of the rifle, crushed the wolf's skull and ended the ordeal.

GUNS

As Cheney became a more seasoned outdoorsman, and thanks in part to his wolf encounter, he lost his taste for a rifle, finding the weapon "unhandy," and instead opted for a custom-built pistol. The simple gun was unadorned but highly accurate and reliable, with a birch root stock and an 11-inch-long barrel. It weighed nearly 3 pounds, and fired a half-ounce ball (or roughly, forty bullets to the pound).

In 1849, a writer for the *Spirit of the Times* asked Cheney how far he could shoot with the pistol. "Twelve rods [1 rod = 16.5 feet], with a sure chance of bringing my game to the ground; but I have killed deer much farther," he replied. "And, a pistol is a very bad thing to shoot with on the jump, and when I do bring down game with it on the jump, I feel as if I had done something." It was one of Cheney's most prized possessions, and the only weapon he used for many years, always carrying it on his person in a leather holster.

Looking at the gun with a glance of affection during that interview, Cheney mused: "That pistol has killed 22 moose, and how many deer I certainly could not tell you." Ironically, it was while hunting for deer with that pistol that Cheney survived one of his most notable misadventures.

He was in a canoe, paddling after a large buck swimming across a lake (later named Cheney Lake in honor of this very misadventure). "I was pressing hard upon the animal," he wrote, when "my pistol slipped under me in some queer way and went off." The ball struck Cheney halfway between his knee and his ankle, and came out just below the knee. "But being 14 miles from any habitation and alone," he continued, "I only stopped long enough to see what harm it had done."

Having inspected his wound, Cheney grabbed the oars again and resumed rowing after the buck. "The thought struck me," he wrote, "that I may need that deer now more than ever." He succeeded in catching up with the deer, made "short work" of killing it, took it ashore, dressed the carcass, and hung it up. Cheney soon realized, however, that he didn't have time to wait in the backcountry. His boot had filled with blood and his ankle was in extreme pain.

Ever the resourceful woodsman, Cheney cut two "crotched sticks" and used them as crutches, taking eight hours to extricate himself from the wilderness. "I only stopped to sit down once, it was so hard to start again," Cheney wrote in the conclusion to an 1873 letter relating the story to S. R. Stoddard. "I succeeded in walking 14 miles to my house where I was confined to my bed from October until April. My leg got entirely well, and is now as good as ever."

A short time after Cheney's recovery, however, he was present at the tragic scene of another pistol-related mishap. It was September 1845, and Cheney was one of the guides leading a party of men from the McIntyre Iron Works. The Works' supply of water had become inadequate, especially during times of dry weather, and the party's goal was to investigate the feasibility of combining two branches of the Hudson River where they were only a few miles apart.

Daniel Taylor, the company's engineer, assembled a five-man party that, in addition to himself and Cheney, included David Henderson (an important Iron Works business partner and the man who named Cheney Lake in honor of the namesake's incredible tale of survival), Henderson's ten-year-old son, Archie, and Tony Snyder, another guide. The team set off into the wilderness prepared to spend the night, and soon came to a small unnamed pond a short distance southwest of Flowed Lands and Lake Colden, known simply as "the duck hole."

Exactly what happened next (and how) is not entirely clear, as a variety of accounts exist, but one thing is certain: As David Henderson set his backpack down upon a rock, a pistol contained within whose hammer had been left cocked struck the rock and fired, mortally wounding him. The other members of the party rushed to his aid. "What an accident, and in such a place!" Henderson proclaimed. "This is a horrible place for a man to die." Calling his son Archie to his side, Henderson added: "Be a good boy, and give my love to your mother." Fifteen minutes later, he was dead.

Snyder hurried to the nearest village to get help, and later returned with a crew of men that would carry Henderson's body out of the wilderness. Along the way, they cut back trees and shrubs to allow the passage of the corpse, which had to be carried 30 miles to the closest passable road. That widened path became the standard "tourist" route up Mount Marcy in the years immediately following. In fact, just one year later, in 1846, Cheney guided writer J. T. Headley up Marcy via that very route. As they approached the site of the accident, Cheney pointed to a log alongside the trail. "There," he said, "I sat all night and held Mr. Henderson's little son in my arms. It was a dreadful night."

Today, the "duck hole" bears the name Calamity Pond; the stream flowing into it, Calamity Brook; and the mountain looming over it, Calamity Mountain . . . all in memory of the tragic misadventure that played out there more than 160 years ago.

PANTHERS

No Adirondack beast ever struck fear in the hearts of men more than the panther. It was elusive, stealthy, and predatory. Cheney, likewise, was sufficiently startled when he stumbled upon a panther crouched in a tree, peering down at him. The feline, Cheney realized, was in a position to pounce, and well within range to do so. "I asked him how he felt when he saw the animal crouching so near," Headley recounted. " 'I felt,' Cheney said coolly, 'as if I should kill him.' "

But such superficial calm belied the nerves within. Cheney admitted to friend George Shaw that his hair stood on end and that he felt the perspiration start on his face. He pulled out his faithful pistol and fired at the panther, which fell from the tree. Not knowing whether the panther would attack or not, Cheney readied himself for a fight to the death. He stamped down the snow around him, fashioned a club from a cut piece of wood, and fired several additional shots from behind a tree.

It all proved unnecessary. The initial shot had killed the panther, which never stirred after falling from the limbs of the tree. Later that same day, thanks to colder-than-expected temperatures and less than sufficient clothing and supplies, Cheney supposedly had to shoot a moose and spend the night sleeping inside the gutted hide to keep warm.

The veracity of that assertion aside, Cheney was known for heading into the Adirondack wilds classically ill-equipped, at least by conventional standards. The only three things Cheney could be assured of bringing along were his dog at his side, his pistol in its holster, and an ax on his back. Anything more was considered sheer luxury. Fittingly, every Cheney-guided expedition started with the same simple questions: Have you the pork? Have you the sugar and tea? Have you the spyglass and matches? Then let us be off!

BEARS

On yet another occasion, Cheney was out hunting, wearing snowshoes, when he broke through the snow and his leg plunged into the cavity created beneath the roots of an overturned tree. Unluckily for Cheney, the feet of snow that had fallen over the cavity created a well-insulated hollow that had been chosen as the winter hibernation den of a bear.

The thrust of Cheney's leg woke the bear, which burst out through the snow with a growl that sent Cheney reeling backward. Unfortunately, earlier in the day Cheney had given his knife to a hunting companion who had gone ahead to the other side of the mountain where they planned to meet up later in the day. This left Cheney with only his pistol.

With the bear closing in fast, Cheney leveled the pistol, aimed between the bear's eyes, and pulled the trigger. The cap exploded but somehow failed to discharge the gun. With no time to reload, Cheney gripped the pistol by the muzzle and struck at the bear's head, but the bear swatted the pistol with its paw, sending the gun flying 10 yards away. The two tangled together and tumbled down into the snow.

Cheney was clearly in a perilous and losing situation until his faithful dog, Buck, again came to his aid. Buck bit at the bear from behind, causing the bear to turn and fight the dog, and in doing so, to let go of Cheney. Cheney scrambled to his feet, located his pistol sticking out of the snow, loaded a fresh cap, and tightened his snowshoes, which had loosened in the course of battle.

Meanwhile, Buck and the bear were locked together in a grueling fight, but the bear eventually overpowered the much smaller dog and shook him off. Buck was badly hurt, "torn all to pieces," in Cheney's words. Yet still, Buck had some fight left in him, and together with

Cheney, the two pursued the bear, Buck leaving tracks of blood in the snow as they went.

When they came within range, Cheney called Buck to a halt and took aim at the bear's head, hoping to kill the beast with a single shot through the brain. His first shot hit low, tearing off the bear's jaw but leaving him more than capable of fighting. Cheney reloaded and fired a second time, again striking the bear, but it still would not go down. Finally, after a third shot, the bear fell for good and Cheney and Buck were out of danger.

Cheney carried Buck out of the woods and nursed him back to health, but the dog was never the same. "That fight broke him down," Cheney said. Nevertheless, Cheney held Buck in the highest regard. "You may not believe it, but I have seen a good many men who were not half as sensible as that very dog. Buck is now four years old, and though he's helped me to kill several hundred deer, he never lost one for me yet . . . . Buck is of great use to me, when I am off hunting, in more ways than one," he wrote. "If I happen to be lost in a snowstorm, which is sometimes the case, I only have to tell him to go home, and if I follow his tracks I am sure to come out in safety; and when sleeping in the woods at night, I never have any other pillow than Buck's body."

THE LATER YEARS

As Cheney grew on in years, he lost none of his passion for the outdoors, or his propensity for stumbling into misadventure. In 1875, at the age of seventy-five, Cheney managed to tangle with yet another bear. This one managed to take a chunk out of Cheney's abdomen with a swipe of its paw, and bit him badly on the arm and leg, and yet Cheney came out on top, killing the bear and ending up none the worse for wear, save for a few wounds that were still healing when his wife wrote of the incident in a letter to *Forest and Stream* on July 16. She was rightfully proud of John in his later years, boasting in 1873 that he "can run in the woods now and beat most any of 'em [younger men] when he feels like it."

By the time Cheney passed away in Newcomb in 1887, he had amassed a staggering tally of animals hunted and killed during his lifetime in the Adirondacks (especially considering that he never hunted on Sundays): 600 deer, 400 marten, 30 otter, 27 bears, 22 moose, 7 lynx, 6 wolves, 1 panther, and 1 beaver.

Such incredible numbers may surprise, shock, or even horrify and anger readers in today's conservation-minded era. But Cheney, too, had developed his own hunting and conservation ethic over the years. He supported "ethical" hunting that gave game a sporting chance, and spoke out against methods that didn't offer game a reasonable chance of escape. He respected the animals he hunted, none more so than the deer. "There isn't a creature in this whole wilderness that I think so much of as a deer," he wrote. "They are so beautiful, with their bright eyes, graceful necks, and sinewy legs . . . . I wish I could get my living without killing this beautiful animal!" And finally, he had a deep appreciation for the Adirondack wilderness that he called home. The beauty of the natural landscape and his connection to it are things he valued until he left this world.

2

A CARNEGIE HERO'S RESCUE ON LAKE CHAMPLAIN

What lies behind us, and what lies before us, are tiny matters compared to what lies within us.

—Ralph Waldo Emerson

On Friday, February 11, 1927, twelve men walked out onto the ice of Lake Champlain destined for a series of ice-fishing shanties—small, movable wood-frame buildings 8 feet square—where they would spend the weekend angling for landlocked salmon, lake and brown trout, northern pike, yellow and white perch, crappie, and smelt—or at the very least, whatever would bite on the bait at the end of their lines. They hailed from Willsboro, a small rural town on New York's western shore of the lake across from Burlington, Vermont. First settled in 1765 on the Boquet River north of Essex, Willsboro was a tight-knit community intimately connected to the lake on its doorstep.

Cradled between New York's Adirondack Mountains and Vermont's Green Mountains, Lake Champlain is a freshwater jewel 120 miles long along its north-south axis, and up to 12 miles wide. Its 435 square miles of lake reach depths of up to 400 feet, hugged by 587 miles of shoreline. Sometime in early December, ice-fishing season opens in the northern reaches of the lake where the water freezes in the protected coves and bays. The fishermen follow the ice line, where the fishing is best, slowly marching farther and farther into the open waters of the lake. And by mid-February, on average, the lake has frozen over entirely at its widest point.

Fishermen have been lured out onto the waters of Champlain for centuries, but in winter the lake becomes a harsh and dangerous landscape of windswept snow and ice that threatens hardy ice fishermen. "It freezes late in winter, and even when it seems solid, the ice can be treacherous," wrote Martha Wardenburg in 1977, a part-time resident of Willsboro during the 1920s. "It is incredibly beautiful on a brilliant day in winter . . . but those who live along those shores are wary of her charms and treat Lake Champlain with great respect."

Champlain has more than once demonstrated her capacity to claim lives. In early March 1936, Abel Duso, from Keeseville, attempted to walk across the frozen lake from New York to Vermont to visit his brother in Burlington. Six miles from shore, and 2 miles beyond Four Brothers Island, Duso slipped on the ice, fell, and injured himself so that he could not move. He died of exposure two hours later. Searchers found his body lying half-buried in a snowdrift with his suitcase resting nearby.

One year later, in February 1937, a fifty-three-year-old father and his ten- and nine-year-old sons went ice fishing in a shanty on North Harbor in Westport Bay, several miles north of Westport village. Locals considered the area especially dangerous due to strong currents and deep water. Returning from a day of fishing, the three were walking back to shore when they broke through the ice and slipped beneath the icy waters several hundred yards out from the beach. All three perished, and only the father's body was later recovered.

But the twelve men walking out onto the frozen lake that Friday in 1927 had no such worries on their minds. The ice was thick—6 to 8 inches near shore, and at least 3 inches thick farther out. The temperature was 10 degrees above zero Fahrenheit. Their only concern was making it to their destination—the relative comfort and shelter of their shanties, which were located a mile offshore from Cedar Point, and about a mile and half north of the town of Essex.

Earlier that day, Martha Wardenburg arrived in Willsboro just before dawn. For much of the year she lived in Wilmington, Delaware, with her father and mother, but would occasionally come up north to visit her father's farm on the western shore of Lake Champlain. George and Maud Hathaway looked after the farm and lived permanently in the north wing of the large farmhouse, the only section heated in winter by the furnace. Their nineteen-year-old son, Winifred "Waiter," had quit school two years earlier in February 1925 to work, but days before Martha's arrival, he was laid off from the paper mill where he earned $80 per month. His father immediately put him to work on the farm, making full use of Winifred's 5-foot-5, 124-pound body.

After settling in to her room in the south wing of the farmhouse, Martha decided she would like to see her family's summer cottages in the snow. Together, she and Winifred walked to the cottages on a bluff above the lake. From their elevated vantage point, they could see that the ice was frozen straight across to Vermont. Scattered about on the ice were tiny shanties, and besides the shanties, little dots—people—on the snow.

On the way back to the farmhouse, Winifred and Martha stopped at a shed behind the cottages. Though it was locked, they peered in through the windows and admired Martha's canoe, which was stored inside, upside down on a pair of wooden sawhorses. It was a 16-by-3-foot Sponson with air pockets along the side, built of a light but sturdy wooden frame and covered with canvas.

Content, they returned to the farmhouse. That night, Martha, the Hathaways, and the entire town of Willsboro went to sleep, unaware that their family and friends out on the ice were about to enter a fight for their survival.

Early Saturday morning, February 12, the twelve men on the ice of Lake Champlain were fishing in two groups of six. In one group were Ernest Wade and his son, Clarence; Henry King and his son, Leroy; Donald Calkins; and Liston Dickerson. The second group of six included fifty-six-year-old Henry Mero, who could not swim; Henry's twenty-year-old son, Leslie; sixty-one-year-old Albert Reynolds; twenty-seven-year-old John Pedro; fifteen-year-old James Moore; and twelve-year-old Clarence Sayward.

A strong wind blew across the lake out of the west-southwest, estimated at 40 miles per hour. Without warning, the ice suddenly started to break up into multiple floes, each one 2 to 3 acres in size. Sitting in his shanty tending to the rig that descended down through a hole bored in the ice, Henry Mero noticed the unusual dragging of his fishing line. When he looked outside, he was speechless. A half a mile to the north there was a wide expanse of open water. To the west, another wide break in the ice cut him and his group off from the lake's western shore. To the southwest, Mero watched as Wade's group jumped across cakes of ice, eventually making it to the safety of the New York shoreline.

Mero and company started running south off their floe, jumping over cracks in the ice and hopscotching across pads and chunks of ice until they became stranded on a floe 400 feet across, surrounded by open water and crushed ice.

At home at the farmhouse on the west end of Cedar Point, Winifred was out with his father cutting wood when they saw tiny dots running from one shanty to the next. They had never seen the ice break up that fast.

In the south wing of the house, Martha was still asleep when she heard a knock on her bedroom window. It was a frantic Winifred. "The ice is breaking up! The wind's rising. They thought it was solid," he told her. "I know them all. They're going to drown. My father says so, too."

Meanwhile, the strong wind blew the six stranded men farther out into open water away from the New York shore and toward the still-distant shoreline of Vermont. The waters of Lake Champlain, by this point, were turbulent, with the ice floes heaving and crashing into one another, slowly grinding into smaller and smaller pieces.

Word of the accident quickly spread through tiny Willsboro. Friends and family rushed to the Essex shoreline in automobiles, feeling helpless to save their loved ones out on the lake. Albert Sanburg and Leon King, the son of Henry who had made it safely to shore when the ice first started to break up, pushed off in a small rowboat, intent on saving the fishermen. But they immediately turned around and returned to shore, fearing that their boat would be crushed between the massive floes.

Sometime around 11:15 a.m., acting out of pure instinct, Winifred and Martha broke into the shed behind her family's cottages and got her canoe. With his hunting knife, Winifred cut a length of rope into two equal pieces and tied one to the canoe's bow and the other to its stern. He grabbed an oar to use for a paddle. Then, together, he and Martha dragged the canoe down to the shoreline. Winifred got in and told her to stay behind.

He started paddling to the east. It was extremely difficult going, with the wind and waves and crashing ice. Two hundred feet out from shore, fearing that the canoe, like Leon King's rowboat, would be crushed, Winifred tried to turn around. But with the forceful wind blowing out of the west, he found it impossible. Left with no other option, he turned back to the east. One hundred feet farther on, Martha watched as Winifred and the canoe shoved up against a large floe of ice. Then, he disappeared into the distance, and she was left standing alone on the shores of the lake.

Back at the Wardenburg farmhouse, the Hathaways were just sitting down to eat when Martha walked in and told them that Winifred had gone off in her canoe to save the men. George and Maud responded with disbelief at first, but when they realized that Martha was telling the truth, their emotion shifted to deep concern.

"Off and on during the day, we all went down to the shore. Neighbors who lived a few miles away joined us," Martha later wrote. "News of the tragedy, increased now by [Winifred's] disappearance on the lake with my canoe, spread throughout Willsboro. Families were grieving . . . . [Winifred's] mother fed us all but we could not eat much.

"By afternoon," she continued, "all hope was lost." Then, darkness fell.

When Winifred and the canoe drifted out of Martha's sight, shoved against the floe and pinned by the wind and the current, he got out and dragged the canoe up onto the ice. Laboriously, he pulled the boat across the floe until he reached its other end. Then, carefully, he set off again into the open water.

It was exhausting work. Continually, he would come up against another impassable floe of ice and be forced to repeat the process—open water to ice floe back to open water. Forty-five minutes later, he reached the men. By then their 400-foot floe had decreased in size to 300 feet across, and the wind had shifted out of the northwest and pushed the floe southeast into thicker ice that halted their drift. The six men pulled Winifred and the canoe up onto the floe.

As a group they decided to travel southeast toward the east shore of the lake where ice conditions were better. Putting the plan into action, they dragged the canoe to the southeast edge of the floe. Twice, a fatigued Winifred fell into water up to his waist while traversing broken sections of ice, but he kept his tight grip on the canoe and thus avoided slipping into the frigid waters entirely.

Linking up patches of ice and narrow strips of thin ice and open water, they continued on. At times they used the canoe to span a divide too wide to jump across, walking across it like a bridge. In other places, they were forced to paddle across open stretches of water. With Winifred paddling, the canoe could only transport two of the men at a time, and he was forced to make multiple trips to ferry the men. At other times, Winifred would paddle while the men remained on a floe, holding tight to the canoe's stern line. Reaching the next floe, Winifred would get out onto the ice and take a firm grip of the boat's bowline. The men would pull the canoe back, climb aboard, and shuttle forward to the next floe where Winifred waited.

Having forged on for what seemed like an eternity, the seven exhausted men finally reached the Vermont side of the lake near the town of Charlotte, some 4 miles distant from the original site where the ice had first started to break. They were welcomed in to a local farmhouse where they warmed up and ate some food to regain part of their lost strength. Then, they set out again into the cold night and headed south for several miles along the lakeshore before crossing back to the west on firmer ice.

As night wore on, Martha and George and Maud Hathaway grew increasingly depressed, convinced that they would never see their friend and son again. Sometime close to midnight, a tired and upset George answered a knock at the door, expecting the worst. It was Winifred. Out on the road behind him, men in a car shouted cheery farewells.

Sitting at the kitchen table, Winifred explained the ordeal of the rescue, and outlined how they had taken a train back to Willsboro and been picked up in a car by George Mero. The men were bruised from all their scrambling over the broken ice, but otherwise none the worse for wear. Winifred was utterly exhausted.

Relieved to have her son safely back under her roof, Maud Hathaway looked at the group huddled in her kitchen, and through shining eyes, said, "Well, best get to bed."

In the days that followed the harrowing rescue, newspapers touted Winifred as a hero: BOY RESCUES LIVES OF 6 ADRIFT ON ICE, proclaimed the *Adirondack Record-Elizabethtown Post*. He told reporters that he didn't think about the risk to his own life at first, and was only concerned for the men on the floe. In hindsight, though, he realized how close he actually came to losing his own life in the frigid waters.

The six men he saved later gave Winifred a gold watch with their names engraved on it.

And, perhaps most nationally important of all, the Pittsburgh-based Carnegie Hero Fund Commission awarded Winifred a bronze medal and a $500 award—equivalent to half his father's yearly salary—to "be used for a worthy purpose." The Carnegie Hero Fund was founded in 1904 after a January 25 coal mine explosion in Harwick, Pennsylvania, outside of Pittsburgh that killed 179 miners and two rescuers. Forever a pacifist who abhorred war, Andrew Carnegie sought a way "to recognize persons who perform acts of heroism in civilian life." He called those persons "heroes of civilization," in stark contrast to the nation's typical military "heroes of barbarism."

"We live in a heroic age," he wrote. "Not seldom are we thrilled by deeds of heroism where men or women are injured or lose their lives in attempting to preserve or rescue their fellows." Carnegie probably first got the idea for the fund eighteen years before the Harwick mine tragedy when, in 1886, a seventeen-year-old boy drowned while rescuing a friend in a loch in Carnegie's native Dunfermline, Scotland. He donated a substantial sum of money to fund the building of a monument in the young rescuer's memory.

Carnegie called the Hero Fund his "ain bairn," or "own child." Of all the institutions he founded or endowed, the fund was the only one solely of his own creation and motivation. He established the Hero Fund with a $5 million trust and a twenty-one-member commission, and charged them with the task of recognizing worthy heroes with a medal and financial assistance. To date, nearly nine thousand medals have been awarded over the fund's hundred-plus-year history, and more than $28 million in awards have been given out. Winifred was number 2,403.

And though he valued the medal into his late years, Winifred earned his true reward that February day on the lake. "He was a hero in the village, his exploit published in the papers," Martha later wrote. "But I knew that his own fulfillment came that night when he led the ice fishermen safely across the lake, and they returned to the world of the living."

3

THE BOY SCOUTS VERSUS WALLFACE

The famous Indian Pass is probably the most remarkable gorge in this country, if not in the world . . . . Majestic, solemn and silent, with the daylight from above pouring all over its dread form, it stood the impersonation of strength and grandeur . . . . Persons not accustomed to scenes of this kind, would not at first get an adequate impression of the magnitude of the precipice. Everything is on such a gigantic scale—all the proportions so vast, and the mountains so high about it, that the real individual greatness is lost sight of. But that wall of a thousand feet perpendicular, with its seams and rents and stooping cliffs, is one of the few things in the world the beholder can never forget.

—J. T. Headley. *The Adirondack: Or, Life in the Woods* (1849)

Deep in the heart of the Adirondacks' High Peaks region lies Wallface Cliff, one of the tallest, and considered by many to be the greatest, of the wilderness rock faces in the eastern United States. The cliff and its companion, Mount McIntyre (today called Algonquin Peak), together form the dramatic Indian Pass. It is an otherworldly place—immense talus fields are home to boulders the size of buses; ribbons of ice persist in the dark corners of the pass deep into summer. The cliff itself towers, on average, more than 600 feet tall, standing guard over one of the most remote and wild places in all the North Country.

Wallface "is the place where climbers define themselves," notes Don Mellor in his classic climbing guide to the Adirondacks. "Some have seen it as the best of Adirondack adventures . . . others . . . have vowed never to return . . . routes here are especially committing . . . rescue is a day away in the best of circumstances, and impossible in the worst."

Early explorers to Wallface immediately sensed the cliff's grandeur, but grossly overestimated its height, proclaiming it to be anywhere from 1,000 to 2,000 feet tall. Yet accuracy aside, its intimidating face captured the hearts and minds of armchair adventurers, and captivated climbers who dreamed of scaling its heights. Still others, owing to its awesome and fearsome reputation, were compelled to spin tall tales of misadventure, having never actually faced the cliff themselves.

Henry Van Hoevenberg, a nineteenth-century Adirondack innkeeper, had one of the most colorful reputations for entertaining his guests with wild stories told 'round the fireplace. In one memorable yarn, he regales listeners with his epic tale of an ascent of Wallface's 1,000-foot cliff:

Old legend held that a secret Indian treasure was buried in a cave hundreds of feet up the side of the cliff. Learning of the treasure's location, a solitary woodsman made the ascent—barefoot and by moonlight, no less—making extensive use of shrubs and other vegetation for handholds, and making one desperate lunge across a blank slab of rock. He succeeded in reaching the cave and the treasure, but was driven out by the ghost of the first ascent party. He fell hundreds of feet, surviving only by crashing through the branches of a hemlock tree that was an indispensable hold for the ascent. With the tree thus smashed, a third ascent of Wallface became unjustifiable and impossible.

In truth, by the early 1930s, despite the attempts of several notable and accomplished climbers, the Wallface Cliff had never been scaled. But three naive Boy Scouts from Plattsburgh thought they would change all that.

Actually, there were seven of them . . . at least, at first: nineteen-year-old Tyler Gray, seventeen-year-old Bob Glenn, sixteen-year-old Bill Ladue, fourteen-year-old Robert Ladue (Bill's younger brother), nineteen-year-old Paul Allen, Paul's fifteen-year-old brother, Frank, and Harry Hitchcock, an Allen family neighbor. They were all part of Scout Troop 17, and met regularly in the basement of the YMCA in Plattsburgh.

On Tuesday, August 29, 1933, they piled into the Allen family seven-passenger Franklin car and drove to Heart Lake, south of Lake Placid, planning to spend two days in the Adirondacks. Around 7:30 that morning the seven boys started out from the trailhead at Adirondak Loj, destined for Indian Pass. More than 6 miles later, they had reached the famed locale. Paul, Harry, and Frank continued on to a lean-to farther down the trail. Tyler, Bob, Bill, and Robert stayed behind in the pass.

The four who stayed behind later disagreed about whether they had planned to climb Wallface from the beginning, or whether they got the idea to give it a try once they reached the cliff in the pass. Regardless, "we knew no one had ever climbed it and it looked so easy, so we decided to try it," Bill later said.

Bill, along with Tyler and Bob, started up the cliff. Young Robert waited below in the pass, watching his older brother and two friends climb higher and higher. According to an August 31 *New York Times* article, "after they had gone fifty feet, there was no turning back." By 11:00 a.m., the intrepid young climbers had ascended more than halfway up the rock face, and were nearly 400 feet above the ground. Then, one of the three dislodged a large boulder that fell, smashing several hand- and footholds that were crucial for the ascent up to that point, cutting off any chance of retreat. Robert watched from below, terrified as he saw their near-miss.

Undaunted, the boys continued upward, assuming they could simply climb to the top. But still more than 200 feet from the top of the cliff, they became stuck on a narrow ledge and couldn't move, unable to climb higher or descend lower. The precarious ledge was 12 feet long, only 2 feet deep, and worst of all, down-sloping. "We had a hard time staying on it," Bill later recalled.

Yelling at the top of their lungs, Tyler, Bob, and Bill attracted Robert's attention in the pass far below. Using semaphore codes (arm signals) they had learned in the Boy Scouts, they communicated with Robert and let him know that they needed help. Robert immediately ran for help, sprinting 9 miles back to the nearest civilization where help could be obtained, along the way cutting his arms and face as he tore down the trail through bushes and brambles.

Around 2:30 p.m., Clarence Graham, a doctor from Albany, New York, and his son, John, were relaxing in their tent near Adirondak Loj, enjoying a peaceful afternoon, when young Robert came tearing into camp, frantic. Through heaving breaths, he explained his fellow Scouts' predicament as the two Grahams, and Jed Rosman, a guide and caretaker at the Loj who was also present, listened intently.

The elder Graham immediately sent his son, John, on his way to the pass with provisions, accompanied by Robert. While they sped back to the pass, he hurriedly arranged what would become the first primary rescue party and set out for Wallface as well. At the Lake Placid Club, a second rescue team was assembled, composed of Robert Downs, the Club's camp and trail director, George Reynolds, a halfback for Colgate University's football team, and Paul Stevens, an undergrad from Harvard University. At the same time, state troopers formed a six-man rescue team that headed into the wilderness behind the other two teams.

Meanwhile, Fred McLane, a pilot from Lake Placid, received a telephone call from Harry Wade Hicks at Adirondak Loj. Hicks asked McLane to fly over the pass, locate the boys on the cliff, and report their condition and location. Around 4:30 p.m. that afternoon, roughly two hours after Clarence Graham had first received Robert's desperate plea for help, the three boys stranded on the cliff saw a plane come into view over the pass. It was McLane.

As he flew into the pass, he turned off the plane's engine and glided close enough to the cliff face to be able to yell to the boys. He told them that help was on the way, and that they should not move. "It was a long time before we saw the airplane," Bill later recalled. "From the moment we saw the plane come sailing down over the mountain . . . we knew we would be taken down and just waited." Bob added: "That first pilot was a great guy. We felt better after he had cheered us up."

A short time later, Clarence Graham and the first rescue party, as well as Stevens, Reynolds, and Downs in the second rescue party, reached the pass. It was nearly dark, and Graham's son, John, had built a fire. The boys waited impatiently up above as they watched Stevens, Reynolds, and Downs attempt to climb up with ropes from the bottom. The attempt was unsuccessful, and they aborted the climb after just 75 feet. "No one had been known to have before attempted to scale the cliff where the boys ascended and their position was viewed by the most venturesome as difficult and precarious," the *Lake Placid News* reported.

The older Graham stripped the bark off a birch tree and rolled it into a megaphone to call to the boys. It was too late and too dark to attempt to mount another rescue attempt, he explained. The boys would have to wait on the tiny ledge until morning.

Overnight temperatures in the pass, despite having been warm during the day, dropped below freezing, and the rocks grew a thick coating of frost. The boys had matches, but almost no wood to burn on their narrow ledge. The roaring fire of the rescuers, visible far below, taunted them throughout the night.

Dressed in little more than light day-hiking clothes, the boys huddled together, taking turns in the middle to keep warm. They were exhausted, and desperately wanted to sleep, but were afraid of rolling off the ledge while they napped. Bob and Tyler devised a plan where, using a combination of their belts and their shoelaces, Bob would secure himself to a sturdy bush at the rear of the ledge, and Tyler would secure himself to Bob. They slept for maybe an hour. Bill, meanwhile, sat awake all night.

Early Wednesday morning, August 30, McLane once again flew over the pass and confirmed for rescuers that the boys had safely spent the night on the ledge. Graham and the three rescuers who had unsuccessfully attempted to climb up to the boys the previous evening hiked two hours to the top of the cliff, where they met other waiting rescue teams. Throughout the morning, additional rescuers continued to appear on the top of the cliff, having ascended from the mountain's gradual north side.

George Reynolds was carefully lowered from a rope 100 feet down from the cliff top so that he could pinpoint the boy's location and help place the other ropes in proper position. Rescuers lowered a pack to the boys that contained oranges and sandwiches. It had contained water as well, but the jug smashed against the cliff face, spilling its contents onto the rock.

Late Wednesday morning, rescue teams lowered a small, narrow rope to the boys tied with a rock to weight it down. The three Scouts flipped a coin to see who would tie in first to be hoisted to the top. Bill won. Tyler would go second. Bob, the heaviest, would go last.

Bill tied a bowline knot in the rope and slipped it under his armpits. But as rescuers started to raise him up off the ledge, the rope proved too weak for the combination of his weight and sharp rock edges. The rope broke, dropping Bill back onto the tiny ledge. Rescuers immediately realized they would need a longer and stronger rope to safely rescue the three boys. Harold Muller, a member of one of the rescue teams, ran one hour and fifteen minutes back to Adirondak Loj in search of suitable rope.

Realizing that time was of the essence, and not wanting to potentially expose the boys to another night out on the ledge, Muller recruited Lyle Churchill, a pilot from Plattsburgh, to fly over the mountain and drop a pair of ropes to the waiting rescuers on top of the cliff. Sometime after 2:30 p.m., Churchill appeared overhead. He dropped the first coil of rope, which missed the mark and landed far down the mountain. But his second drop landed virtually in the arms of the rescuers. The rope was 260 feet long and 1 inch thick.

Rescuers tied one end of the rope to a stout tree set back from the cliff's edge, and lowered the other end to the boys. Each Scout tied himself in, one at a time, using a bowline. Then, a rescuer aimed his revolver pistol into the air over the cliff and fired several shots, letting the boys know that it was time to start hauling. Initially, five strong men pulled, hand over hand, hoisting each boy to the top. Eventually, twelve men in all joined the effort to bring the boys up one at a time.

"It was a thrilling experience when we saw the ropes hanging down with the package of food for us," Bill told the *Plattsburgh Daily Press*. "But that was nothing compared to the thrill when I was actually swung out into space at the end of [the rope]." *The New York Times* reported that Bill "was unafraid as he was hauled in as his body was dangling over the darkening gorge." "We were never frightened for a moment," he maintained, "during the two days we were prisoners on the narrow ledge."

Yet, though they later said they were not scared, the three boys were reportedly white-faced as they were pulled to the top, and "clung wildly" to the arms of their rescuers. Most important, though, they were finally safe. That night the boys—with abrasions from being hauled up the cliff—and about thirty rescuers hiked out to Adirondak Loj, arriving at around 7:30 p.m. to a waiting crowd of more than a hundred people. In total, the boys had spent more than thirty-one hours on that remote ledge.

Back at their homes in Plattsburgh, the boys' mothers fed them while their fathers, who had aided in the rescue effort, chastised them. "If you ever do that again, I am going to leave you there," Bill's father was reported to have said. Elsewhere in New York State, a seven-point buck deer was also making national news and sharing headlines with the Boy Scouts, having caught the country's attention while getting stranded on a cliff above Watkins Glen in the Finger Lakes region during the same time that the boys had spent their time on Wallface.

Later that same year, Wallface would finally see its first successful ascent. John Case, a former president of the American Alpine Club and soon-to-be full-time resident of the Adirondacks, had been exploring the cliff with Adirondack pioneer Jim Goodwin. The pair had picked out a potential route up the face, and had succeeded in climbing most of its height, but as of 1933, they were still unsuccessful in making it all the way to the top.

Case returned later that year with his son and Betty Woolsey, and the trio succeeded in wandering to the right of Case and Goodwin's original attempted route and discovered the natural line of what today is known as the Case Route. Case himself maintained that surely someone else must have climbed the route, it was so natural and "easy," but no previous climbs had ever been documented.

He climbed it in the purest style of the day, never placing any protection (it ruined the rhythm of the climb, he said) and climbing by the old mantra that the climber must never fall. Even today, climbers with modern equipment and refined technique often pause as they contemplate the route's final exposed moves 600 feet above the ground. Case would return to the cliff many times, re-climbing the route solo for years.

A few years later, in 1938, renowned German climber Fritz Wiessner arrived at Wallface and succeeded in finishing the climb that had denied Case and Goodwin the honors more than five years earlier. Wiessner used Case's route as a descent, and later praised it as "possibly an even nicer climb than ours . . . cleaner . . . interesting crack and face work." He fell in love with Wallface, and regarded it as the most beautiful cliff in the Northeast, noting its "feeling of altitude" and "charm of solitude."

In the years since those early climbs and misadventures, Wallface, and its immense and challenging cliff and routes, has been home to several other notable accidents. For a time it held the title as the deadliest cliff in the Adirondacks. And no season of misadventure is more remembered than the late 1970s and early 1980s.

On August 13, 1977, a group of nine climbers—six from Rochester, New York, and three from New York City—split into several rope teams and attempted different routes on Wallface. One group, led by twenty-nine-year-old William Mollet, started up Wiessner Direct, a more direct finish to Fritz Wiessner's original 1938 route. Although not especially difficult technically, it is still a serious and committing undertaking, with demanding route-finding. As Mollet approached the top of the cliff, he diverged off-route to the left where the rock steepened considerably. As he led the final pitch, he placed four pieces of successive protection—two nuts (tapered metal stoppers wedged into cracks) lower down, and two slung trees (short lengths of webbing tied around the base of the trunk) higher up.

As he was executing the final moves of the climb, a large loose block shifted and Mollet fell. Three pieces of gear ripped out during the fall, but the lowest nut held, stopping Mollet just below his belayer. He had taken a 60-foot fall. It was about 4:00 p.m.

Two other climbers ran out to Adirondak Loj for help, alerting the forest rangers around 7:30 p.m. By 11:30 p.m., the first rescue team had arrived, and a short time later, a second team as well. But by then fair weather had turned to rain, wind, and fog. Despite having all the equipment they would need to self-rescue, the climbers involved in the accident failed to do so. They left Mollet tied in to an anchor on a small ledge. He was unconscious, bleeding from the mouth, and had a weakening pulse. His climbing helmet was crushed on one side.

The next day thunderstorms prevented both rescuers and

helicopters from reaching Mollet. Finally, on the second day after the accident, August 15, a paramedic was able to rappel to Mollet. He was dead. An autopsy later revealed that he had a broken neck, a severed spinal column, broken ribs, a punctured lung, and other internal injuries, but no damage to his head or brain.

Less than six years later, on July 3, 1983, thirty-two-year-old Lee Fowler and twenty-two-year-old Andrew Metz were also climbing Wallface. The pair was more than 300 feet off the ground, with Fowler leading a pitch 6 to 8 meters above Metz, who was anchored to the cliff with only a single piece of gear. Fowler fell, having not placed any additional protective gear between himself and Metz. The woefully inadequate anchor ripped out of the rock, and, roped together, the two men fell to their deaths 300 feet below.

In a world where improvements in technology, skill, and resources have vastly improved the margin of safety for outdoor adventurers, Wallface cuts fiercely against the grain. The intimidating cliff remains as wild and imposing as it ever was, its capacity to claim, or at least attempt to claim, human lives undiminished.

4

THE CRASH OF AMERICAN AIRLINES FLIGHT 166

Of course we weren't lost. We were merely where we shouldn't have been, without knowing where that was.

—T. Morris Longstreth, *The Adirondacks* (1917)

On Friday evening, December 29, 1934, American Airlines Flight 166 took off from Syracuse airport in upstate New York, destined for Albany, the state capital, several hours to the east. It was the middle leg of a longer flight heading from Cleveland to Boston, landing in Syracuse, and then Albany, along the way.

There were only four men on board, three crew and one passenger—Ernest Dyer, the pilot; Ernest's brother, Dale, the copilot; J. H. Brown, another pilot "dead-heading" on the return to his home airport in Boston; and P. D. Hambrook, an official with the U.S. Department of Education in Washington, D.C.

It was a nascent time for American Airlines, and commercial air travel in general, in the United States. Eight years earlier, in 1926, Charles Lindbergh was credited with flying the first regularly scheduled flight of American when he flew a bag of mail from Chicago to St. Louis. One year later, in 1927, Colonial Air Transport, a forerunner of today's

American Airlines, operated the first passenger flight in the country, taking six passengers from Boston to New York City (and in so doing, also documenting the first scheduled passenger flight in New England).

On January 25, 1930, four companies, including Colonial Air Transport, consolidated into American Airways, the immediate predecessor of American Airlines. Then, ten months later, on October 15, they inaugurated the nation's first all-air transcontinental service from Atlanta to Los Angeles, with stops in Texas and Arizona. In 1933, the eighteen-passenger Curtiss Condor airplane came onto the scene, and along with the Condor, the first flight attendants (then called stewardesses). By 1934, American Airways had introduced the first in-flight meal (and one year later, the first hot meal service). On April 11, 1934, American Airways officially became American Airlines, and on May 5 they unveiled a new sleeper version of the Curtiss Condor.

Seven months later, on December 29, the four men on board Flight 166 took off from Syracuse and disappeared into the night sky.

Around 9:30 p.m. that Friday night, Ernest Dyer radioed the airport in Albany to report his position. Flight 166 was north of Utica, New York, proceeding on schedule over the southwestern Adirondacks. But fierce snow squalls were sweeping down from the north throughout the entire region, and Albany never received another radio transmission. When the plane failed to arrive, aerial search parties were immediately sent out, but flying conditions were nearly impossible in the winter storm. The search for American Airlines Flight 166 was temporarily called off before midnight on Friday. Weather permitting, it would resume the next day.

Early Saturday morning, December 30, a hastily mustered air fleet set out to search for the missing plane. The initial search covered an immense area spanning from Utica to Albany, and north to Speculator, an area of more than 3,500 square miles. The growing public fear was that the airplane had crashed on a mountainside in the blinding snowstorm, and that all those on board were dead. But what would turn out to be a well-substantiated report began circulating that airplane flares had been seen and that at least some of the men on board were believed to have survived. The question then became: If the men were alive, where were they?

Somewhere in the Adirondack wilderness, J. H. Brown hooked up Flight 166's radio, which had also survived the crash, to a battery that was fading fast in the extreme cold. Around 9:15 a.m. that Saturday morning, he started making radio transmissions, repeating "One-sixty-six, calling Albany." He added that they were all safe, but were somewhere between Utica and Albany in deep snow, high on a mountainside 2,500 feet above sea level. Beyond that, the survivors had no idea where they were.

Seventy-five miles away, Albany heard their calls, and answered. But what Albany didn't know is that 166 couldn't hear them. Even still, Albany had enough information to now center the search in earnest over the lower Adirondacks. By late on Saturday, additional airplanes from American Airlines, TWA, United Airlines, the National Guard, and the Army Air Corps had all joined in the search. But as darkness fell, searchers still hadn't located the downed plane, and didn't know how long it would be before they found the survivors, who would be forced to endure a second night in subzero temperatures.

On Sunday, December 31, the air over the southern Adirondacks was swarming with search planes, looking for any sign of the survivors or their wrecked airplane. Finally, around 5:45 p.m., more than forty-five hours after Flight 166 had first taken off from Syracuse, rescue planes at last located the survivors. The first person on—or, more accurately, above—the scene was Dean Smith, a veteran pilot for American Airlines and former pilot for Rear Admiral Richard Byrd during his first Antarctic expedition. Also on board with Smith were Ralph Damon, from the Curtiss-Wright Corporation, builders of the downed Condor plane; Albert Leo-Wolf, a pilot with the State Conservation Department; and Philip Reynolds, Smith's copilot.

"It was about sundown, the sun low in the sky getting dark fast, when I saw the fire they had built," Smith told reporters. "I noticed that every now and then it would flare up as if they put gasoline on it and I knew it must be them." Flight 166 had gone down on the northwest side of a "round snow-covered hill." The plane had crashed in a stand of fir, pine, and other evergreens, and off to one side, there was a broad marshland.

"I dove low and switched on my landing lights," Smith continued. "Then they put on more gas and oil and it lit up so that I could see the plane clearly. I flashed the landing lights and they answered with a blinker, '166-166.' That was the plane's number and they kept repeating it."

Smith radioed the Albany airport with the encouraging news. The survivors were about 15 miles north of Little Falls. As planes overhead refined the survivors' location for ground search teams, they at first believed Flight 166 was on Bull Hill, about 5 miles from Gray in Herkimer County. Finally, they pinpointed the plane's location on Wilder Mountain, near Morehouseville.

For the next two hours, Smith circled overhead, routinely swinging back to a nearby highway where he hoped automobile traffic would deliver ground searchers that he could guide to the crash site. Rescuers, meanwhile, established a base on the nearby farm of Axel

Malmberg, where they set up a portable radio station. Six state troopers, led by veteran woodsman Douglas Johnson, prepared to attempt the 6-mile slog to the crash site, pulling a bobsled over the snow.

Simultaneously, a troop of National Guardsmen attempted to reach the survivors by way of Wilmurt. They encountered fresh snow, 2.5 feet deep on average, with higher drifts throughout the rolling and rugged country. The region's only road, a one-track lane, ended just outside Gray.

Eventually, Smith saw a team of rescuers step into the woods from the highway. Once he saw that they were headed on the right track, he circled higher to attract the attention of other planes in the area. From overhead, pilots could make out the four men standing alongside a fire. They could also see the outline of the plane, half-hidden under snow and tree branches. But the site was still extremely difficult to locate. One plane carrying food supplies never succeeded in finding the location. Another pilot said that the crashed plane would hardly be visible from 1,000 feet in clear weather.

Around 9:00 p.m. on Sunday night, Ray Jones, another American Airlines pilot, also spotted the wrecked plane. Over the radio, he reported that the crash site was "about a mile north of the vertical point of an L-shaped lake." Smith continued to circle overhead for a total of five hours, helping to guide other planes and ground searchers to the remote spot. At one point, Smith was forced to return to Albany briefly to refuel, and used the opportunity to guide a series of military planes back to the site where they could drop food and clothing from their bomb racks. An expert army pilot swooped low and dropped the supplies. Rescuers in the air knew the survivors had received the parcel when two flares were ignited.

In Hoffmeister, 5 miles south of the crash site, another ground rescue team made up of twelve men set off through waist-deep snow and temperatures that dropped below minus-15 degrees Fahrenheit. At 10:45 p.m., Smith was replaced by another pilot who would circle a plane overhead to guide the rescuers. Thinking that the survivors were about to be rescued, Smith returned to his home in Summit, exhausted, and went to bed. He was scheduled to fly the "night sleeper" the next evening to Chicago.

When the replacement pilot saw that rescuers were "almost there," he left and returned to the Albany airport, where he landed at 12:55 a.m. Monday morning. He had spent thirteen hours in the air aiding in the search and then guiding the ground rescue teams as Smith's relief, and flew back to Albany for gasoline under the false assumption that rescuers would make it to the four men before he even landed in Albany. He was wrong.

The pilot's premature departure left the ground searchers with no point of reference—no target toward which to aim. They fired their shotguns and lit flares while attempting to continue the search, but they received no response from the survivors and couldn't see through the dense forest of fir and pine. After an hour they were forced to abandon the search and return to Hoffmeister to regain contact with the air search teams, having gotten tantalizingly close to the survivors yet still out of reach.

Early Monday morning, January 1, New Year's Day, Lieutenant C. I. Emerson from the Massachusetts National Guard flew overhead with a crate of supplies—blankets, milk, sandwiches, whiskey, matches, gloves, and cigarettes. He dropped the crate to the four men waiting below, but to his dismay, he watched it lodge in the top of a high tree, well out of reach of the men. Determined, he raced back to nearby Utica, retrieved an ax, and dropped it to the men from a small parachute so that they could cut down the tree that held their lifesaving supplies.

A short time later, the first ground search party finally reached the downed airplane. The seven-man team was led by Lester Pertello, a forest ranger from Cold Brook. They traveled on snowshoes, bringing with them a toboggan, the only type of sled that could reasonably be dragged and pulled across the soft snow.

The crash site, it turns out, was about 3 miles from the Utica-Speculator Highway; not a terribly far distance by most standards, but in this case spanned by incredibly deep snow and a "thick and well-nigh impenetrable forest." When they arrived they saw the plane partly covered in snow, but much of it was still propped up on the trees. The two motors appeared to be undamaged; the propeller was whole but bent; one wing was torn and broken.

Their findings on the ground confirmed what pilot Ernest Dyer later said about the crash: He had lost his way in the snowstorm, and when he realized that they were going down, he pulled the Curtiss Condor into a slow stall position and waited for it to hit. It did, and in the process flattened the trees that cushioned its fall as it came down on the mountain.

It was a skilled bit of flying, but one that also included a fair amount of luck, or perhaps, divine providence. "It was the only place on the whole mountainside where the plane could have fallen and not killed everybody in it," rescuer Edward Hughes later said. "In fact, there isn't a place for miles around where it could have dropped and done so little damage."

Rescuers found the survivors huddled in a makeshift lean-to constructed from airplane debris and fabric torn from the plane's wing. They had gathered twigs and branches from beneath the snow to supplement their dwindling fuel supply, and had ripped the seat coverings from inside the plane to wrap their hands and feet and protect them from the cold.

With the searchers and the survivors finally united, rescuers could begin the evacuation. By Monday afternoon, all four men were saved and removed from the wilderness that had held them for so many days, and they could at last tell their story.

As Ernest Dyer had piloted the Curtiss Condor through the raging snowstorm Friday night, things suddenly took a turn for the worse. Sometime after he made his last transmission to Albany at 9:30 p.m., "snowstatic" made the radio unworkable. Then, about twenty minutes before the crash, the plane lost one of its engines when a carburetor froze. The remaining engine would have normally provided enough power to allow the plane to find a safe location to land, but ice buildup on the wings made the airplane too heavy.

Dyer rang the plane's bell and alerted Brown and Hambrook in the main cabin that the Condor was going down. Treetops suddenly appeared just below the airplane. Brown, who was standing at that moment, braced for the crash and was hurled down the plane's center aisle. Everything happened too fast for anyone to be afraid, the four men later said.

"For several minutes before the crash we knew we were in for it. Some minutes, or it might have been only seconds, before the actual crash, the plane struck something. One motor was dead, the other was racing. The wing was getting heavier every moment with ice and snow," Hambrook later recalled. "The two boys in the cockpit struggled to hold us aloft. Their efforts failed. We first snapped off two huge trees as we struck the forest. The wings sheared off the plane. The cabin, bereft of its wings, struck on its nose but flattened out immediately and bumped into the ground, the limbs of the surrounding trees breaking the fall . . . we crawled out. It was snowing hard. It was cold and dreary. But above all it was lonely and silent."

Just as they crashed, one of the Dyer brothers threw the ignition master switch to shut off the electricity. On the ground, all four men climbed out and got away from the plane for five minutes, being cautious about the threat of fire, and allowing the plane time to cool down.

The fuselage survived the crash largely intact, cradled by the tree branches, and for two nights the men called it home, taking shelter within its walls from the cold and wind. But on the third night, the temperature dropped below minus-25 degrees Fahrenheit, and they moved outside to be close to the fire they had built beside their makeshift lean-to, made from the plane's wreckage.

It was anything but a romantic stay in the woods. They had no ax with which to chop wood for a fire, and they had to fight hard to stay awake in the cold. "Sleeping meant freezing," Hambrook said. Saturday morning dawned crisp and cold, but the four survivors heard no sign of life. "We were too tired to care," Hambrook continued.

As time wore on, the men became half-starved, half-frozen, and began to lose hope that they would be rescued. Brown rigged the radio with one of the plane's dwindling batteries. They tried to contact someone—anyone—by radio, but it didn't seem to work. The men were left utterly demoralized. (Albany heard their calls and responded, but the men never received those transmissions.)

Sometime early Sunday morning—their second morning in the wilderness—they heard the droning of an airplane. It passed somewhere nearby, although the men never actually saw it. Then, as the sound receded into another deafening silence, they "gave up." By that afternoon, Hambrook said, "we were prepared to sleep our way out of life."

The sight and sound of Dean Smith's plane circling overhead gave them renewed hope as the Dyer brothers, Brown, and Hambrook realized that they'd been spotted. One of the pilots threw a pail of gasoline on the dimming fire, making certain that Smith could be sure it was them. Though not yet literally and figuratively out of the woods, it appeared that they were saved.

Around midnight the men found a supply of wood that had been dropped from one of the search planes and used the fuel to keep warm through the coldest night of their ordeal. At 7:00 a.m. on Monday morning, Emerson from the Massachusetts National Guard flew overhead and dropped his crate into a tree. Then, the ax came down. And not long after that, the weary survivors were greeted by the friendly faces of twelve rescuers who appeared out of the forest.

It was amazing they had all survived, and the men were in remarkably good condition, all things considered. Still, after three full days out in the harsh wilderness, they were in rough shape by most standards.

Ernest Dyer had frozen hands and feet, and was suffering from a bout of pneumonia. He had to be taken out of the wilderness on the toboggan to a waiting Civilian Conservation Corps ambulance.

His brother, Dale, walked part of the way but suddenly collapsed before reaching the edge of the forest. Rescuers strapped him to the toboggan with his brother. An examination at the hospital later revealed that he had a broken jaw and an injury to his eye, both sustained when the plane hit the mountainside.

Brown and Hambrook walked out under their own power, sinking up to their waists in snow along the way. Even so, rescuers had arrived none too soon. "We knew that if no one found us last night, we were done for," Hambrook told reporters. By the time they were rescued, the men's supply of wood was low, and none of them had enough strength to gather more.

J. H. Brown, who suffered from "exposure and dehydration," was hailed by rescuers and newspapers for his "fortitude and resourcefulness." "That man is a hardy guy," said one rescuer. Brown traveled 1.5 miles around the mountain and countryside, searching for a way out of the woods. He worked hard to gather fuel for their fire—at one point near the end of their plight, he crawled through the snow on his hands and knees and scraped at the frozen earth with his numb fingers to retrieve twigs and branches; on the way back to the crash site, he stumbled several times, dropping some of the precious wood he had gathered. And of course, he jury-rigged the plane's radio and batteries, which enabled Albany to learn that the men were alive and begin to pinpoint exactly where they might be.

Ernest and Dale Dyer and J. H. Brown spent New Year's night in St. Elizabeth's Hospital in Utica. Late that night, a heavy snowfall pushed through the region and nearly buried the downed airplane. Had the men not been rescued when they were, and had they still been in the

Adirondack wilderness, their story might very well have had an entirely different and tragic outcome.

P. D. Hambrook, for his part, was apparently none the worse for wear. With "his confidence in air travel unshaken," wrote *The New York Times*, he boarded a plane in Utica that same afternoon, destined for Washington, D.C. In a cruel twist of irony, Hambrook's plane was forced down in bad weather and landed in Newark, New Jersey, where he spent the night at the Hotel McAlpin. The next morning, he took the train to Washington.

5

STRANDED: THE RESCUE OF MARIA GERSEN

It is now early in summer and we hasten to admonish all,
especially ladies, about going into the Adirondack wilderness to do
mountain climbing without a guide. Better have someone along who
knows the way.

> —"Chicago Woman Physician Alone All Night on Mt. Whiteface,"
> *The Elizabethtown Post* (July 5, 1906)

Late in the afternoon on Wednesday, July 7, 1938, a chauffeur left from St. Huberts in Keene Valley destined for Westport, where he was scheduled to pick up his employer at the train station. It was a new car, and he drove slower than usual to gently break in the engine, and to enjoy the dramatic scenery of Chapel Pond Pass. As he leisurely motored past the shores of Chapel Pond, he heard a woman's voice calling for help. Craning his neck upward, he scanned the mountains and cliffs towering over the pass, looking for the source of the voice. Then he saw her—a small figure motioning for help and waving a white handkerchief. She was stuck on a tiny ledge high above the pass.

The anonymous driver honked his horn several times to let her know she'd been seen. "I'll go for help," he shouted up to her. "Don't fall off." And with those words, he headed back toward St. Huberts.

The young woman's name was Maria Gersen. She was an eighteen-year-old German immigrant who had only been in the United States for six months. Gersen worked as a nursemaid for Dr. Paul Wolfe, a Congregational minister from Evanston, Illinois, who spent the summer in Keene Valley with his family. Wolfe owned a cottage at the Ausable Club on the private Adirondack Mountain Reserve property near St. Huberts, and Gersen, along with several servants, attended to the family's needs, including looking after the Wolfes' three young daughters.

Earlier in the day, with Dr. and Mrs. Wolfe away in New York City, and with the three girls attended to by other servants, Gersen set off for Dix Mountain (4,857 feet), the Adirondacks' sixth-tallest peak. The trail was overgrown and difficult to follow, having been neglected for years while responsibility for maintaining the trail slowly shifted from the Appalachian Trail Improvement Society to the Department of Environmental Conservation.

Despite early challenges, Gersen succeeded in safely reaching Dix's high and remote summit several miles south of St. Huberts. On the return, she would need to follow an obscure turnoff through a thick growth of raspberry bushes. But there were many such thickets of berries, and Gersen missed the trail's change of direction entirely. She continued hiking down valley to the north, realizing her error much too late.

To the right in front of her, Gersen recognized the distinctive summit of Round Mountain, which along with Noonmark's contrasting pointed summit, are two of the most instantly recognizable and easily seen peaks in the Keene Valley region. Gersen knew that a road twisted through the tight valley—Chapel Pond Pass—on the other side of Round, between it and Giant of the Valley. If she could make it to the top of Round Mountain, Gersen reasoned, she could then head toward

Giant, and in so doing would be guaranteed of stumbling into the road, which she could then easily follow back to St. Huberts. Having decided on her change of plans, Gersen determinedly marched through the forest, set on making it to the top of Round.

Chapel Pond Pass is easily one of the most dramatic roadside settings in all of the Adirondacks. The steep walls of the mountains on either side of the valley constrict and close in on the road, then known as the Montreal–New York Highway—although in actuality, it was little more than a rough dirt track, and today is known more simply as Route 73. On the south side, the pass's namesake, Chapel Pond, sits calmly at the base of steep cliffs and soaring slabs of rock—the King Wall, Emperor Slab, Chapel Pond Slab, and a series of other cliffs—that in places rise up more than 700 feet from the pond and road below. To the north, Washbowl Cliff, the immediate area's tallest vertical rock face, stands guard over the pass, while the Giant's Washbowl, a beautiful hanging lake, sits just up above on the middle ramparts of Giant of the Valley.

In devising her plan, Gersen had failed to account for this abundance of rock that would greet her as she descended the north side of Round Mountain. Soon enough, she reached the summit of Round, and oblivious to what lay below, she started straight down for Chapel Pond Pass. Almost immediately, she ran into cliffs and ledges and steep rock, the mountain falling away beneath her, and she was forced to carefully pick her way down, weaving through gullies and along the tops of cliffs. Hundreds of feet below, she could see the shimmering waters of Chapel Pond, and along its northern shoreline, the dirt track that she hoped would lead her home.

At one point, she stood at the top of an angled slab of smooth rock with a wide ledge at its base. Cautiously, she slid down the slab and landed on the ledge, where a number of blueberry bushes provided a welcome snack. Her plan was to walk along the ledge to its other end, hoping to find a way down from there, but it became too narrow to traverse. Gersen attempted to climb back up the smooth angled slab of rock, but it denied her attempts. Unable to move either up or down, and fearing that she would fall to her death if she tried, Gersen realized that she was stranded.

From her perch above the pass, she could see and hear cars driving on the road below. She called for help at the top of her lungs, and ripped a white strip of cloth off her shirt to wave as a flag, but no one saw or heard her. Cars usually climbed the road to the pass in a loud gear, the noise compounded by the jarring of the rough road itself, and drivers and passengers alike had no chance of hearing Gersen's faint, high voice. And with the late-afternoon sun dropping below the mountains to the west, Gersen's position soon became shrouded in dark shadow.

She contemplated attempting to jump into Chapel Pond far below, but wisely reconsidered. Then, a short time later, the chauffeur from St. Huberts leisurely idled into the pass in his boss's shiny, new—and quiet—car, and heard a desperate woman's cry for help.

Maria Gersen wasn't the first hiker to stray off-trail onto technical terrain in the Adirondacks, scrambling over steep rocks and becoming stuck or falling to her injury or death. And she certainly wasn't the last.

On December 3, 1942, thirty-seven-year-old Charles Donnelly from Lake Placid was enjoying the view from the top of Whiteface Mountain with friends. During the descent from the summit, Donnelly stepped off-trail and tripped on an outcrop of jagged rocks, falling more than 20 feet over a short cliff. He broke both arms and both legs, as well as his nose, but survived.

On June 2, 1991, eighteen-year-old Robert Mahar and several friends scrambled up Rogers Rock on Lake George, which in recent years has seen the development of a number of technical rock climbing routes on its main face. Mahar marked their route with strips of cloth tied to trees and bushes, but like Gersen, lost his way during the descent. Mahar slipped and fell to his death, 100 to 200 feet off a ledge.

Less than a month later, on June 29, twenty-one-year-old Jason Chicoine from Champaign, Illinois, and two friends attempted to scramble to the top of Roaring Brook Falls, a picturesque cascade on the lower flanks of Giant. Fifty to 60 feet off the ground, one of Chicoine's handholds pulled out of the cliff, sending him tumbling to a ledge below. He was pronounced dead at the hospital. The trail-accessible view from the top of the Falls has proven equally perilous over the years; from this expansive vantage point, the water flows over a concave lip of rock. Careless hikers wanting a glimpse down the Falls inch forward, lured by the slowly developing view, until the friction of their sneakers or boots can no longer withstand the pull of gravity on the steepening rock.

Giant of the Valley and its many slides above Roaring Brook Falls have also been home to a number of mishaps where hikers have fallen over ledges or tumbled down a slide and been badly injured, requiring helicopter evacuations.

And most notorious of all, Mount Colden's Trap Dike—the Adirondacks' premier slide climb in summer and mountaineering route in winter—has such a fearsome reputation for luring hikers onto technical terrain that it has earned its own chapter in this book.

When Maria Gersen's call for help finally reached Keene Valley, nine men led by local constable William Isham responded. The rescue party also included James Brown, the brother of 1936 Olympic two-man bobsled champion, Ivan Brown. They set off for the cliffs above Chapel Pond armed with two long ropes.

Brown attempted to climb up to Gersen from the base of the cliff, but did not succeed. The rescuers changed tactics, opting to hike to the top of Round Mountain from a gentler aspect, and descend to where they could rescue Gersen. By the time they began their descent through the maze of cliffs, it was dark. At one point the men paused on an 8-inch-wide ledge to rest. When they pointed their flashlights over the edge, they were unable to see to the bottom of the cliffs.

Meanwhile, a crowd of onlookers had wandered up from St. Huberts to watch the rescue efforts from the shores of Chapel Pond. "Relax if you can and be comfortable," someone shouted up to Gersen, hoping to help her remain calm while waiting for her rescuers. "I'm comfortable," came her reply. "I'm sitting down."

At long last, the nine rescuers succeeded in locating Gersen on the ledge below them. By that point she had been trapped on her ledge for more than ten hours. One rescuer, Alan J. Slater from Keene Valley, tied into the ropes and the other men lowered him down to a point along Gersen's ledge. Carefully and slowly, he inched his way over to the young woman. According to one newspaper report, Slater had to traverse nearly 1,000 horizontal feet along a ledge that narrowed at times to just 18 inches.

When he reached Gersen, he removed the rope from his own body and retied it around hers, so that the eight men above could hoist her to safety. "She remained cool and calm while the rope was passed around her body and she was pulled to firm ground," *The New York Times* later reported. Slater, in his turn, was also hauled back up to safer ground. Gersen was tired and a bit scratched up, primarily from trying to climb the angled slab down which she had slid, and her clothing was badly torn, partly of her own doing in fashioning a flag to wave for help, but she was otherwise uninjured and none the worse for wear.

By the time Gersen and her rescuers had hiked back to the top of Round Mountain, it was late. They decided to build a fire and camp on top for the night, waiting until dawn before returning the rest of the way home. Around 5:30 a.m. on Thursday morning, Gersen was back in the Wolfes' cottage at the Ausable Club, ready to get some much needed rest, and the rescuers returned to their normal pace of life in nearby Keene Valley. Alan J. Slater was hailed as a local hero for his efforts in reaching Gersen on the ledge, and later that same year, in November, he received the Light for Life Foundation Award for Life Saving.

6

GRAND AMBITION: TWO MEN, FORTY-SIX HIGH PEAKS, FIVE DAYS, AND ONLY ONE SURVIVOR

For a true mountaineer, the summit is never off-route.

—Gerry Roach, *Colorado's Fourteeners: From Hikes to Climbs* (1999)

Getting to the top is optional, but getting down is mandatory. A lot of people get focused on the summit and forget that.

—Ed Viesturs, mountaineer

In the late spring of 1972, two men had a vision for a trip that would test them against the Adirondack Mountains, and against the calendar and the clock. Their names were Chris Beattie and Joe Lamb, and together they planned to climb all forty-six of the Adirondack High Peaks in five successive days. "We thought it'd be neat for some boys in Lake Placid to have the record, instead of someone from outside the area," Beattie says today. If successful, they would best the previous record, which had stood for more than ten years, by nine full days.

Both men were in fantastic physical shape. Earlier that year, Lamb had competed as a U.S. Olympian in the Nordic Combined—ski jumping and cross-country skiing—at the Winter Olympics in Sapporo, Japan. Then twenty-six years old, Beattie was also a Nordic Combined athlete, having competed years earlier during his time at the University of Denver in Colorado. He still skied as much as possible in his native Adirondacks, working odd jobs in and around Lake Placid to pay the bills—maple sugaring in the spring, greens keeping at area golf courses, helping out at a small oil company his father owned at the time.

Lamb and Beattie would be assisted by a trio of close friends that would act as the pair's support team. Harry Eldridge, director of the North Country School, and Roger Loud, the school's assistant director, would provide logistical support, delivering food and sleeping bags to lean-tos, cooking meals when necessary, and coordinating transportation to and from trailheads at the beginning and end of each day. Dinny Loud, Roger's wife, headed up "base camp," the Louds' home at the North Country School.

Eldridge, more so than anyone else, thought that Lamb and Beattie should add a third person to their roster. He liked the idea of any backcountry trip, and especially one of this magnitude, having at least three people to increase the margin of safety. Thus entered Patrick Griffin, a thirty-one-year-old Irishman who came to the United States four years earlier in 1968. Originally from Skerries, a small fishing village near Dublin, Griffin landed a job as a cook at the North Country School, where he also became an informal leader of outdoor activities. His students called him the "Iron Man"—at 6 feet tall and 170 pounds, he was the picture of athleticism, and was known for carpooling to the Elm Tree Inn in Keene for a happy-hour beer with his fellow teachers, and then running the 7 miles home, all of it uphill.

In the weeks leading up to the trip, however, Lamb backed out, leaving Beattie and Griffin—relative strangers—to tackle the High Peaks as a duo. "We were thrown together a bit," Beattie says. "We hiked the better part of a month together, but Pat was quite a bit older than me, and there wasn't a real cohesiveness between us." Nonetheless, the two men did share the common goal of accomplishing what no one else ever had.

The expedition was set to begin on Tuesday, June 20, 1972. In the weeks immediately prior, Griffin and Beattie set off on practice climbs of their routes, sometimes solo and sometimes together, and checked their hiking times against an elaborate spreadsheet that detailed the intricacies of their climbing schedule.

On Monday evening, June 19, Beattie's parents drove the two men to Corey's Landing in Tupper Lake. From there, the pair walked 4 miles of trail to the Ward Brook Lean-to, where they would sleep that night before setting off into the mountains the next morning. They fell asleep underneath clear skies, and overnight, the stars shone brightly, sharply visible above. Earlier during the day on Monday, however, they had seen a television report that indicated Hurricane Agnes was moving northeast out of the Gulf of Mexico. Born over Mexico's Yucatan Peninsula, Agnes was the first storm of the 1972 season—a rare June hurricane. She crossed the Gulf and made landfall over Florida's panhandle.

Silently, the men hoped that the hurricane would head out over the Atlantic Ocean, staying far enough south of the Adirondacks that the mountains wouldn't get much rain. "We planned a day to go, and we were going to stick to that," Beattie says. "We could see the hurricane coming, and figured we'd get wet one day and then we'd be fine." They wouldn't get their wish. Agnes barreled northward along the eastern seaboard, cutting through Pennsylvania, New Jersey, and New York, with her sights set on the Adirondacks.

Around 5:15 a.m. on Tuesday morning, June 20, Griffin and Beattie awoke to see heavy clouds butting up against Seymour Mountain, the first of the forty-six peaks. Sitting in the lean-to, they ate oats, nuts, and dried apples for breakfast, washing it down with cold milk from a thermos. Their daypacks were packed and ready to go—compass, flashlight, moleskin (for blisters), Band-Aids, extra shoelaces, hats, gloves, a windbreaker, candy bars, gorp (trail mix), and water bottles. They stashed their overnight pack filled with their sleeping gear behind the lean-to, where it would be picked up later that day by someone from their support team.

Shouldering their packs, the two men shook hands. "I said [to Pat], 'Well, let's get on with it and hope we make it,' " Beattie recalls. Tragically, Griffin wouldn't—although Hurricane Agnes would not be to blame.

They set off from the Ward Brook Lean-to at 5:45 a.m. Their plan that day—day one of five—was to climb seven mountains split between the Seward and Santanoni ranges in the western High Peaks. By Adirondack standards, the peaks of the Seward Range are very remote— miles from anywhere and without trails to their summits. They make up four of the twenty trail-less High Peaks. Climbers follow streambeds, ridgelines, compass bearings, and the occasional herd path to their tops.

The men knew that no one had ever attempted to climb the forty- six High Peaks in as few as five days, charging hard for as many as sixteen hours each day. But from the outset they believed it possible; they had carefully calculated a plan of attack that included input from many of their experienced friends. It was important to remember that they wouldn't need to climb every peak from bottom to top. By traversing from peak to peak along high ridges within a given range, they could minimize the elevation they'd lose and subsequently have to regain as they ascended each mountain.

One hour later, at 6:45 a.m., Griffin and Beattie reached the top of Seymour Mountain, where they signed the summit register, which was stored in a gray, weatherproof canister. As they ascended Seymour, Beattie hoped that they would have good visibility traversing from Seymour's summit to Seward Mountain. But luck was not on their side—clouds remained socked in all around them.

Acting as the navigator from Seymour to Seward, Beattie took the wrong streambed while descending to the col between the two peaks, which cost the men half an hour from their already tight schedule. They backtracked and regained the proper route.

The east side of Seward, which they soon encountered, was a dense tangle of weathered tree trunks toppled during a 1950 hurricane. It was slow going, weaving over, under, and around the mess of fallen trees. Griffin and Beattie, rather than following one another, traveled in parallel paths 20 to 60 yards apart, occasionally calling to one another to maintain contact and to debate about which way to go. For the most part, however, they didn't talk much as they climbed, breaking the silence only to discuss the route or complain about the incessant blackflies.

Soon enough, they made it to the top of Seward. The sun taunted them at times, but ultimately, clouds hung low over the Cold River Wilderness. As they continued on, finishing their climbs of the four Seward Range peaks, their clothes became wet from the condensation on trees as they bushwhacked at the higher elevations.

Griffin and Beattie then descended and crossed 5 miles of boggy flatland to the foot of Couchsachraga, the first of three Santanoni Range mountains they'd climb. On the top of Santanoni Peak, Beattie signed the summit register and left a note: "60,000,000,000,000,000 bugs."

"It was a very bad blackfly season," Beattie remembers. "It was so buggy on that first day."

They finished climbing the three Santanoni peaks and then dropped into the valley below, where they followed an old logging road and retrieved a pair of bicycles they had cached before the trip. From there they rode 2 miles to the road at Tahawus Village, where Harry Eldridge waited to pick them up. It was 8:45 p.m.

Roughly fifteen hours had elapsed since they had set out early that morning, and the two men were tired but in good spirits. They had covered 14 miles, most of it without trails, and had climbed 6,700 vertical feet. They were on schedule, and confident that they'd succeed in completing the trip if they didn't make any major mistakes.

As they drove back to the Louds' home in Lake Placid, Griffin and Beattie laughed as Eldridge told them how a bear had carried their overnight pack into the woods from the Ward Brook Lean-to. That night, they went to sleep full of a high-protein dinner and beer, compliments of Dinny Loud.

Everyone woke before dawn on Wednesday, June 21, at the North Country School. Griffin and Beattie each ate his own special, high-energy breakfast, the foods they thought gave them the best boost for the day: rhubarb for Griffin, tuna fish for Beattie. They would need the energy. The day's schedule was heavy—eleven mountains, 25 miles, and 10,000 vertical feet of climbing. Plus, it was pouring rain—the first of many torrential downpours, thanks to Hurricane Agnes.

Impatient to get started, Griffin rushed Beattie out of the house and into the Louds' Volkswagen bus for their transport to the trailhead. The pair forged out into the wilderness, climbing through the soaking rain that continued all day. Fortunately, the weather was relatively warm—around 60 degrees—and the heavy rain kept the bugs at bay.

The men climbed Allen first, and were then transported to Elk Lake, from which they'd climb Macomb Mountain, and then the Dixes, Dial, Nippletop, and the rest of the High Peaks southeast of the Adirondack Mountain Reserve property. Already, Beattie realized that the hardest and most stressful part of the endeavor would not be the physical or mental challenge. It would be Agnes. "It was around noon when we started up Macomb. It started raining and poured for the rest of the day, until 9:00 p.m.," he says. "It was an unnatural feeling—unless you're really out backpacking, you usually don't hike in the rain for that long [without taking shelter]. We didn't have rain gear really, and were soaked to the skin."

At 5:30 p.m., Roger Loud pulled into the parking lot at the Ausable Club at the Adirondack Mountain Reserve. From there he paddled in a rowboat southwest to a boathouse at the end of Lower Ausable Lake, where he planned to meet the men. By 8:15 p.m., the pair still had not returned. Concerned, Loud noticed that the lake had risen a foot in the time it took him to row the length of the lake. Questions began to run through his mind: Would the men get caught in the dark and be forced to spend the night out? If they did return sometime that evening, could they wake up early the next morning to continue their journey?

A few minutes later, Griffin and Beattie appeared out of the woods between Upper and Lower Ausable Lakes in good spirits and in apparent good shape, despite the less than favorable conditions. They climbed into Loud's rowboat for the ride back to the Ausable Club. As they rowed down the lake, Griffin and Beattie looked up at the abrupt cliffs along the lakeshore. Water was cascading over the rocks in sheets like they had never seen before. Back at the club, they piled into the Volkswagen and joked about how wet they were—their feet were like prunes and they teased one another about needing to check for diaper rash.

They returned to the Loud "base camp" for another hearty dinner and more cold beer, and to discuss their plan for the coming days. "If we can keep going at the rate we've achieved so far, in bad weather," Beattie said, "then we're not going to have any problems finishing this trip."

Finally, everyone turned in for the night around 11:30 p.m. As he climbed into bed, Griffin could hear the wind howling outside. He wondered if any leaves would be left on the trees by morning. Hurricane Agnes, it seemed, was reluctant to release her grip on the Adirondacks.

On the morning of day three—Thursday, June 22—the wind was calm and the sky clearing. Again impatient to get started, Griffin had to shake Beattie to wake him. Every minute the pair lost that morning would come back to haunt them at day's end. By the time they walked out the door it was 6:00 a.m., thirty minutes behind schedule. It was to be another tough day—25 miles again, 10,000 feet of vertical gain, and ten more mountains, including Street and Nye, the entire MacIntyre Range, and then Esther and Whiteface. The end of the journey still seemed far away, yet both men were determined that it could be done.

The weather held throughout the morning and much of the day, but by 5:00 p.m., clouds were closing in on the mountains once again. As Griffin and Beattie headed down past Heart Lake en route to the trailhead, they passed the Adirondack Mountain Club's Adirondak Loj. A cook stuck his head out into the deteriorating weather: "Where are you going now?"

"We're going over to do Esther and Whiteface," the men replied.

"Tonight?" the cook countered. "Don't you know Agnes is coming?"

The men couldn't believe it. They both thought the hurricane had already passed. In truth, it had, but now it was back. Agnes had circled over the Adirondacks, and the Northeast, for three days, drenching the mountains with torrential rain and battering the forests with howling 85-mph winds. By the time Agnes finally died—sometime around June 25—she had caused more than 120 deaths, including 24 in New York State, and caused damage estimated at $11.6 billion in 2005 dollars.

Incredulous, the pair hiked out to the parking lot where a car was left for them to drive to the nearby village where they'd meet the Louds. From there, the Louds drove the pair to the old Marble Mountain Ski Area to start their climb of Esther and Whiteface.

Along the way, Dinny handed each man a beer, and watched as Griffin painfully unfolded himself in the backseat of the car. Twenty minutes later they arrived at their destination, and to Dinny's surprise, both men, apparently rejuvenated from the short ride, got out without hesitation and disappeared into the gathering storm. As she sat in the car around 6:00 p.m., staring out the window up into the swirling maelstrom, Dinny could see that conditions were terrible, and knew the two men were up there somewhere, with two mountains and more than 10 miles to go before the day would be over.

At the top of Esther Mountain, Beattie wrote in the summit register: "This Crazy Trip is getting crazier all the time." The adventure had alternately been referred to as the "Stupid Trip" or the "Crazy Trip" ever since Beattie had first seen those words penciled onto Eldridge's calendar. Now, with the hurricane bearing down, it seemed the trip was indeed crazy, and a wholly different beast than when they had first envisioned the challenge.

Nevertheless, even on top of Esther, the weather still didn't seem that bad to Beattie. "It wasn't a threatening night when we started up Esther," he recalls. "We had daylight until almost 9:00 p.m.—that's one reason why we chose June as the time of year for the climb. The wind wasn't too bad going up."

Then the pair started up Whiteface from Esther, and things got really bad. Two trees snapped in the gale-force winds. Griffin and Beattie succeeded in making it to the summit. From there, in order to save time, they went straight down the ski trails at Whiteface from the weather station on the mountain's top. "It was quite intense," Beattie says. "Trees were literally blowing over and snapping off. Fortunately, we were in no danger being in the middle of a ski run."

During their descent, Beattie fell behind, his leg hurting from shin splints that had started to develop. His knee hurt badly, too. In the weeks leading up to the trip, Beattie injured his knee when a horse he was riding at the North Country School smashed him into a tree. Despite the pain, by 9:00 p.m., both men had reached the parking lot at the foot of Whiteface Mountain's ski area, and soon returned to base camp at the North Country School.

There, at the Louds' house, they again swigged more beer, and dined on steak and milk. They washed their clothes. The two men looked tired and grim. Beattie's leg still hurt, but he didn't mention this to anyone.

Dinny Loud woke at 4:00 a.m. on Friday, June 23, to cook breakfast. Beattie awoke soon after. Sometime around 4:30, Harry Eldridge arrived. He planned to hike 8 miles up Johns Brook Valley that day and meet the two men at the Snobird Lean-to (long since removed by the state in keeping with new wilderness regulations). That morning Eldridge plainly saw a growing weariness in the pair.

Out on the trail, Beattie realized that his leg had a serious problem—excruciating shin splints. Almost immediately, he fell behind Griffin. Beattie decided to continue onward to provide support and encouragement for his friend. If his leg became too painful, he would drop out entirely, Beattie reasoned. Up ahead, Griffin waited for Beattie on the summit of Mount Colden. On the top of Colden, the sky was clear. The men lay on the rocks, soaking up the sunshine. Both remarked how far away Tuesday now seemed, when they had first begun their journey.

Heading down Mount Colden's back side, Beattie's leg was bad, and he made the decision to bail out of the effort. But by the time he had reached the valley bottom, Griffin had already gone ahead. Beattie had no choice but to continue for now.

They met up again at the Uphill Lean-to on Mount Marcy's west side, where they discussed Beattie's leg. Griffin understood that Beattie could no longer continue. They agreed that Beattie would either head out to the trailhead at Heart Lake, head over to the Four Corners trail junction and wait for Griffin, or go ahead to the Snobird Lean-to where he, Griffin, and Eldridge planned to spend the night together.

The pair confirmed that Griffin's pack had a compass, a map, and some food. They shook hands, wished each other luck, and parted ways. It was 12:25 p.m. Together, they had climbed thirty-two mountains since Tuesday. For Beattie, the trip was over. For Griffin, there were still six more mountains left on the schedule for that day, with the full weight of the expedition's success or failure riding on his shoulders.

Griffin's plan was to bushwhack to Cliff, head up Redfield, traverse 1.5 miles through scrub conifer to Skylight, take the trail back to Four

Corners and then up Gray, and finally hike on to Mount Marcy's summit. From there he would descend toward the Snobird Lean-to, going over Haystack along the way.

With Griffin gone, Beattie sat at the Uphill Lean-to, trying to decide what to do. Between this expedition and his previous adventures in the Adirondacks, Beattie had climbed forty-five of the forty-six High Peaks. Only Gray remained, and he contemplated climbing it en route to the Snobird Lean-to. But the weather continued to deteriorate—it was overcast and beginning to rain once again. He hiked to the Four Corners Lean-to. By the time Beattie arrived, it was raining heavily, and he abandoned any thoughts of climbing Gray.

He waited "for a while" for Griffin, and while he sat there at Four Corners, two other groups of climbers came in out of the rain, including a pair of teenage boys. Huddled in the lean-to, Beattie tried to start a fire, but his matches were wet. None of the other climbers had matches. The teenage boys were heading home over Mount Marcy, they told Beattie and the others. "Pat wasn't really overdue yet," Beattie recalls, "but it had started to get nasty again." The wind had picked up once more—gusting to nearly 40 miles per hour—and Beattie thought it wisest to go over the top of Marcy with the others, rather than attempt a different route to the Snobird Lean-to, solo.

From Four Corners up to Marcy's summit, it is more than 1,000 vertical feet. Two-thirds of that climb weaves through alpine stunted woods, while the upper third of the route climbs over open slabs of rock on Marcy's bare summit cone, where only painted arrows mark the route. Climbers are exposed to the full brunt of winds howling over New York's highest peak, and to the climber's right, the mountain drops away 2,000 feet into the depths of Panther Gorge.

High on Marcy, strong gusting winds now estimated in excess of 60 miles per hour knocked one teen over. The trio hurried over the top of Marcy without stopping, and arrived at the Snobird Lean-to around 6:00 p.m. The boys continued on, leaving Beattie there. Eldridge hadn't arrived yet, and Griffin wasn't due until much later. Alone, Beattie huddled in the back corner of the lean-to and fell asleep.

The sound of children's voices roused Beattie from his sleep. The voices came from two of Harry Eldridge's daughters. Eldridge and his half-collie, half-shepherd dog, Teeny, were close behind. While the group waited for Griffin to arrive, Eldridge heated some goulash on a white-gas stove he carried with him. The four ate their dinner, saving a large portion for Griffin.

By 7:30 p.m. it was almost dark. The two girls bundled into their sleeping bags for the night. Beattie and Griffin draped sleeping bags over themselves and talked while they waited for Griffin. Beattie told Eldridge that he hadn't known Griffin well before the trip. It worked to their advantage, he explained, since they mutually deferred to the overall goal of the trip, instead of arguing over one another's judgment.

As they talked, Eldridge watched his dog, Teeny, who might hear and respond to sounds of Griffin in the storm long before the men did. But as evening wore on, there was still no sign of Griffin. For a time, Eldridge contemplated going out to look for Griffin on the trails, but with the combination of too many trail possibilities and the horrendous weather, he decided to wait. Besides, he reasoned, Griffin could have aborted his plans and headed out of the woods another way; or, he might have hunkered down in another lean-to or sought shelter from the storm in the woods. He was well prepared, and even carried a can of beer.

At long last, Beattie and Eldridge finally fell asleep around 10:00 p.m. The temperature at Snobird hovered around 40 degrees.

Everyone at the Snobird Lean-to woke early on Saturday, June 24. It was still pouring rain. Eldridge focused on getting his young girls and Beattie out to Keene Valley. They ate breakfast and headed down the mountain, detouring along the way over a trail they would have expected Griffin to follow. There was still no sign of their friend.

Back in town, no one had heard from Griffin either. His name was absent from all the area trail registers, and no one had had personal contact with him since he and Beattie had parted ways at Uphill. Eldridge drove a car to the Garden parking lot and left it there with dry clothes for Griffin. Then he returned to Lake Placid.

One hour later, Eldridge's telephone rang. It was Roger Loud. He was worried and wanted to head into the mountains that night to look for Griffin. If Griffin was hurt and immobile, waiting until morning would mean two brutal nights out in the High Peaks for their friend, Loud reasoned. A short time later, Eldridge, Loud, and four climbers from nearby Camp Treetops convened at the North Country School with overnight gear. The six men met briefly in Roger Loud's living room, then left for an 8:00 p.m. rendezvous with a New York State Department of Environmental Conservation (DEC) forest ranger who would drive them to Marcy Dam on a Conservation Department fire road.

They divided into three two-man teams. Their objective for that night was to get as far into the mountains as possible in the vicinity of Griffin's expected location. The next morning, each pair would methodically search a pattern that would slowly narrow Griffin's possible location. Two teams set off for the Lake Colden Interior Outpost, cradled between Mount Colden and Algonquin Peak above

Avalanche Pass. The other team went to the Feldspar Lean-to between Colden and Marcy.

Early on Sunday, June 25, one pair climbed Gray; another Redfield. Eldridge and Loud struck out on the trails, eventually destined for the Uphill Lean-to where they were all scheduled to meet at noon. By the time Eldridge and Loud arrived, the party that had climbed Gray already had a fire going. There had been no sign of Griffin on Gray, but the Redfield team found his name in that mountain's summit register, along with a comment about being cold.

One team set out to search the bushwhack route from Redfield to Skylight; one person was sent down to the Lake Colden Interior Outpost; the remaining three went to Four Corners to wait for the Redfield-Skylight team. While the three waited at Four Corners, sitting on a log, an independent group of three climbers came down from Marcy. No one had to ask what they had seen.

After crossing from Redfield to Skylight, Griffin had started up Marcy's summit cone from Four Corners, several hours behind Beattie and the two teenage boys. By then the wind was stronger, and the rain was lashing at the rock and at Griffin. Then, 150 yards below Mount Marcy's summit—the thirty-sixth of the forty-six peaks in the endeavor—a heart defect Griffin never knew existed claimed his life.

Upon hearing what the climbers had discovered while descending from Marcy's summit, Eldridge immediately climbed up the peak, found Griffin's body, and covered it. Over the next seven hours, he shuttled back and forth between Marcy's summit and Four Corners, leading a rescue team up to the body, meeting up with the Redfield-Skylight searchers who had not yet returned to hear the sad news, and helping to carry the litter that transported his friend off the mountain.

Roger Loud, meanwhile, had arrived at Marcy Dam. The actions of the rescuers, and their hurried conversations, gave Loud a feeling of dread in the pit of his stomach. He sensed the worst. Then, two climbers brought news of a dead man up on Marcy, and Loud knew. For two hours, he cried alone on the corner of the ranger cabin porch.

At the North Country School, Dinny Loud received the news by telephone, but she refused to believe it until positive identification of Griffin had been made.

Beattie sat at home, wondering where Griffin might be, when a friend telephoned with the news.

A coroner later determined that Griffin had died from a massive heart attack, and that the strain of the expedition had caused his circulatory system to deteriorate over four days to that of an eighty-year-old man. He passed away sometime between 6:00 and 9:00 p.m. Friday night.

"You know, I somehow figured it was all over," Beattie told reporters months later. "Something told me, as I sat there trying to puzzle out what had happened, that Pat hadn't made it." Would Beattie ever try to finish what he and Griffin started? "Yes, I would like to. I think it can be done. And I would like to try, in memory of Pat," he told a writer in 1973. "I am, in fact, looking for someone to climb with, someone who lives here and knows the mountains. To do something like this you have to appreciate what the mountains are; a lot of people just look at them but don't appreciate them. I would have to find a climber with the physical ability first, and then the mental makeup. Someone like Pat."

The weeks and months following Beattie and Griffin's attempt saw a range of reactions from the outdoor community and greater public, from harsh criticism of the expedition's motivations to praise for their valiant attempt. "Why must we set transient records? What is accomplished by running up and down peaks in record time?" questioned one reader. "The great justification for climbing at all is the feeling of joy at the beauty one can see from the tops of the beautiful Adirondack peaks."

The most hurtful of all, however, came from someone close to home. "The mountains are there and they are meant to be climbed," wrote Glenn W. Fish, former president of the Adirondack 46ers, in a letter to *The New York Times*. "However, they are also to be treated with respect. Attempts to climb them in record time create little respect for climbers and none for mountains." Fish, Beattie says today, actually supported the expedition—he offered the men use of his hunting camp at the base of Allen. "Then he writes a scorching letter saying we should have never been up there," Beattie says. "We were going, 'Thanks a lot.' It was definitely strange of him to be fairly adamant [in his letter] that we shouldn't have tried it."

And yet, Griffin's death, for sure, was a tragic fluke—a function of a cardiovascular flaw revealed by the strain of the attempt, but in no way caused by it. One can only wonder if the criticism would have been so harsh and so prevalent had both men survived.

Beattie never made another attempt to climb the forty-six High Peaks in successive days with the idea of capturing a speed record. Several people stepped forward and offered to try with him, but ultimately, his marriage one year later, and a host of personal reasons, held him back from giving it another go.

But in July 1972, one month after Griffin's death, two climbers succeeded in climbing the forty-six High Peaks in seven days.

In the years since, attempts at Adirondack speed records have continued, and in June 2002, the standing record toppled once again. Ted "Cave Dog" Keizer succeeded in smashing the previous record by climbing the forty-six High Peaks in less than four days. Thirty years old at the time, the Brown University graduate and self-titled bum completed the feat in 3 days, 18 hours, and 14 minutes.

Supported by a group of sixteen friends and family members aptly named the Dog Team (who are based in an also aptly named motor home, called The Kennel), Keizer worked on just fifteen minutes of sleep per day and battled deep mud en route to his record. At 10:29 p.m. on Thursday, June 27, he dove for the Whiteface summit marker as the fastest 46er ever, beating the previous 1977 record of 4 days, 18 hours, and 18 minutes by more than a day, and having trekked over 140 miles and climbed 140,000 vertical feet of Adirondack wilderness.

At once notorious and heralded for his speed hiking attempts, Keizer's success on the forty-six Adirondack High Peaks added another notch to a belt that today includes speed records for Colorado's Fourteeners, New Hampshire's White Mountain Four Thousand Footers, New York's thirty-five Catskill Mountains over 3,500 feet, and Vermont's Long Trail.

Ironically, though, Keizer may not have been a success in the Adirondacks without insights provided by Beattie. In late summer 2001, the two men spoke, at which time Keizer revealed his goal to attempt the forty-six High Peaks that fall. Beattie cautioned against the timing of such an attempt, highlighting that conditions in the mountains that time of year would be cold and wet, exposing Keizer to the very real threat of hypothermia. "I think he must have listened to me," Beattie says today, "because he did it early the next summer. He's a very strong person."

The desire to set speed and time records in the mountains, it seems, is part of human nature—or at least an inherent characteristic of a particular subset of outdoor adventure seekers like "Cave Dog." But will his record last? Only the passage of time will reveal the answer. In the meantime, one thing does remain certain: Whether in the Adirondacks, on the rock walls of Yosemite, or the icy flanks of Mount Everest, humans will continue to strive to be the first and the fastest.

7

OF ICE AND MEN: ICE CLIMBERS AVALANCHED OFF CHAPEL POND SLAB

Shallow men believe in luck. Strong men believe in cause and effect.

—Ralph Waldo Emerson

The slab . . . does present some problems and dangers. Avalanches sometimes sweep from the more benign-angled slopes above and have taken more than one unsuspecting party to the ground.

—Don Mellor, *Climbing in the Adirondacks: A Guide to Rock and Ice Routes in the Adirondack Park* (1995)*

On Saturday, March 8, 1975, three ice climbers—Peter Gough, Tony Patane, and Ken Martin—stood at the base of Chapel Pond Slab in Keene Valley and looked up at the 700 vertical feet of ice running down its face. None of them had ice-climbed in the Adirondacks before, and none of them knew that anything was out of the ordinary on this particular day. A few short hours later, that blissful ignorance would change their lives in a way they'd never forget.

Adirondack ice is known as some of the best in the Northeast, and in the country. The thick flows, beautiful frozen waterfalls, and

* This information was originally published by Adirondack Mountain Club Inc. (ADK). This copyrighted material is used with the permission of ADK, www.adk.org.

challenging multi-pitch routes have lured ice climbers for decades to classic destinations like the cliffs and gullies around Chapel Pond, Wilmington Notch, Pitchoff North, and Poke-o-Moonshine. Ice climbs at such destinations have become immensely popular, and though misadventures are the rare exception, rather than the rule, Adirondack ice has been home to more than one accident, and death, over the years.

In January 1988 a twenty-six-year-old ice climber from Long Island, New York, was leading the second pitch of Multiplication Gully, Wilmington Notch's classic climb. He was 30 feet above his last ice screw, attempting to place another piece of protection, when he fell, tumbling nearly 70 feet and smashing into a ledge before finally being stopped by his belayer. He was left paralyzed with a neck fracture.

Eight years later, in February 1996, a sixteen-year-old ice climber from Quebec was left stranded high in Chouinard's Gully above Chapel Pond after something went wrong during a rapel and his forty-six-year-old climbing partner fell 220 feet to his death. Without ropes, the teen was forced to await rescue by several local climbers, including Ron Konowitz, who four years later would survive being caught in an avalanche on Wright Peak while backcountry skiing (chapter 16).

Finally, in a highly publicized accident in February 2002, an ice climber from Toronto, Ontario, was killed when a large section of ice pulled off the rock face of Poke-o-Moonshine while he was leading the ultra-classic route, Positive Thinking. He fell to the ground below, and although members of his climbing party attempted CPR at the base of the cliff, he was pronounced dead at the hospital.

But in 1975, those three ice climbers at the base of Chapel Pond Slab had no expectation of misadventure, and no reason to believe they'd get a whole lot more than they had bargained for.

Just one month earlier, in February, Peter Gough and his wife had arrived in upstate New York from his native New Zealand. Gough, then twenty-eight years old, was a new doctoral student at the University of Rochester, where he planned to continue his work in the field of optics as an electrical engineer. The slim, 5-foot-11 Kiwi was an experienced and accomplished ice climber. He started climbing when he was just sixteen, and in 1970, five years before he landed in New York, Gough succeeded in completing the hardest ice climb in New Zealand at the time—a 6,000-vertical-foot route up the imposing Caroline Face of Mount Cook. By 1975 he had also logged several first ascents and new routes on high-altitude peaks in the Peruvian Andes, and had worked summers in New Zealand as a mountain climbing guide.

Years earlier, while back in New Zealand, Gough had crossed paths with an American climbing guide from Syracuse, New York, who was in the country on an exchange program. When Gough later arrived in Rochester he called the guide, who had long since returned to New York, and asked if he knew anyone who went ice climbing. The guide recommended his friend, Ken Martin. By coincidence, Martin's mother was a Kiwi—she had left New Zealand in 1946 as the war bride of an American Marine stationed overseas—and the connection between Gough and Martin was immediate.

Though not of Gough's caliber, the then twenty-nine-year-old Martin was also an experienced ice climber who had attempted the Grand Teton and other routes in the West. He had recently started ice climbing with Tony Patane, a Morrisville State College employee who lived in Clockville, outside of Canastota, New York. Patane was by far the least experienced of the three climbers. He had started climbing only two years prior, and the bulk of his experience consisted of what he describes

as "mild winter mountaineering and camping in the Adirondacks."
Even so, he and Martin had completed a winter ascent of Left Gully
in Tuckerman's Ravine on Mount Washington in New Hampshire, and
the New Year's Day immediately before their Adirondack ice climbing
adventure, he and Martin had also succeeded in a winter bid to summit
Katahdin in Maine.

Having never met one another before, let alone climbed together,
Gough and Martin talked on the phone, planned an ice climbing weekend
in the 'Dacks, and resolved to meet at the front door of a rest stop on the
New York State Thruway at 9:00 p.m. on Friday night, March 7, 1975.

Gough and his wife arrived in one car, Martin and Patane in
another. The two vehicles caravanned as they drove north, destined for
Keene Valley, where they planned to climb the standard route up Chapel
Pond Slab. It would be Gough's first time in the Adirondacks. Only one
week earlier, he had succeeded in securing his medical insurance in the
United States.

The standard ice route up Chapel Pond Slab was first climbed by
Adirondack legend and pioneer Jim Goodwin in 1936. Together with
his partner, Bob Notman, Goodwin cut steps in the ice the whole way
up, using a long-shafted ice ax and belaying from chopped platform
stances. Decades later, world-renowned climber Yvon Chouinard
arrived in Keene Valley sporting new ice climbing equipment like front-
point crampons and technical ice tools, forever changing the face of ice
climbing in the Adirondacks, and lending his name to new, harder routes
like Chouinard's Gully. Ever since the advent of technical ice climbing
equipment, routes like Chapel Pond Slab, while still committing, no
longer posed the challenge they once did, and climbers like Gough and
Martin, and Patane as well, could expect a pleasant day on the ice.

Gough, his wife, Martin, and Patane arrived in Keene Valley late Friday night. Overnight the temperature dropped below freezing, but still remained warm by ice climbing standards. A hard, heavy snowfall dropped big, fat flakes that quickly accumulated to impressive depths. When the climbers arrived at the base of the slab Saturday morning, with temperatures already hovering dangerously in the mid-20s, they looked up at the climb and saw nothing that gave them pause.

"The biggest mistake that we made was that not one of us had any idea of what normal conditions were," Gough recalls. "When we rolled up and saw that everything was covered in snow, we all made the assumption that it was the way it always was. People that had been there a lot would have recognized that the snowpack wasn't stable."

"It was no day for ice climbing," Patane says in retrospect. "We were really stupid for climbing."

At the base of the climb, Patane, who was the least-experienced climber, tied into the ropes in the middle climbing position, with Gough and Martin on either end. In this way, Gough and Martin, who were more experienced, would "swing leads," taking turns doing the harder and more dangerous lead climbing while Patane followed them up. They planned to complete the climb in four pitches, or roughly, four rope lengths.

They approached the ice by angling up across a steep apron of snow at the base of the slab. As they ascended, they kicked off small slough avalanches, but nothing substantial or serious enough for anyone to give notice. From there they set off up the left side of the ice onto the technical portion of the climb, headed for a birch tree that would serve as the first belay. The ice was in good condition, Patane remembers.

Once at the birch tree belay, the trio of climbers traversed out right onto the slab, aiming for the base of a steep bulge of ice where it squeezes through a constriction in the rock. That bulge is the crux of the climb, and once above it, the climb's angle slowly eases back as you crest the top of the climb, still climbing mostly over ice.

Gough, Martin, and Patane reached the upper portion of the route without any difficulty. Soon, they found themselves on the final summit slab, a low-angled rock face covered in snow, just 50 feet from the finish of the climb. They were still roped together, but walking almost side by side on the nontechnical terrain. They joked with one another, and were about to cut into the trees at the top of the climb and traverse to the descent gully when they suddenly heard a crack and a dull thud.

The climbers could see a break in the snow some 15 to 20 feet ahead of them—the snowfield had fractured right down to the black ice on the rock underneath. Then they heard a scraping noise as the entire slab of snow started to slide. Patane thought, "Oh, shit—this can't be happening."

All three men, acting on mountaineers' instincts, dropped into self-arrest position to stop their fall. It was useless. "It's not much use when what you are self-arresting on is also falling at the same rate that you are," Gough says. "Our instinctive reactions were all exactly right, except that the slab we were on was moving . . . there was not a lot we could have done about it. The whole top just slipped off, with us on it."

Down below, Gough's wife sat in a car parked next to Chapel Pond, reading a book. Every now and then she would glance up and look out the car window to monitor her husband's progress as he, Martin, and Patane climbed higher. At one point, they were very near the top. When she looked up again, they were gone.

Returning to her reading, she assumed that they had stepped into the trees and out of view. Suddenly, she heard yelling and screaming, but dismissed it. The noise, she figured, was coming from another group of climbers at the base of the route. What she couldn't see were Gough, Martin, and Patane, out of sight below tree level, dangling from the lower portions of the slab. She went back to her book.

When the summit snowfield started to slide, and the climbers dropped into their self-arrest position, Patane was on his stomach facing uphill. Gough and Martin were nearby in identical positions. They all remember going over the top . . . and then falling.

"I started sliding and bouncing . . . each bounce was a bit longer than the last one," Patane recalls. He tumbled and somersaulted until his head faced downhill. Each time he struck the ice he was thrown back into the air for longer and longer periods of time. Then he hit the ice bulge. His chest impacted first. The force of the hit whipped his head forward and slammed it into the ice. Then his left foot hit, and his leg snapped.

"I remember hitting the ice bulge and breaking my leg. And I remember hitting my head. I was awake when I hit," Patane painfully recounts. "Then I got launched big-time and passed out in the air."

Somewhere nearby, Gough's body was also being battered against the ice as he fell. At one point his crampons caught on the ice, twisting his legs and breaking both ankles. He also sustained a boot-top fracture—a break in the lower leg just above the cuff of a boot. His left foot pointed backwards.

On the face below, four other climbers—John Palmer, David Beech, Gene Casper, and Barbara Wilt, all students from Paul Smith's College—were strung out across the trio's fall line, making their way up the lower portion of the route, unaware of what was happening above.

Suddenly, Gough, Martin, Patane, and a mass of snow came

slamming down into them. Palmer and Beech were thrown from their stances on the ice. Then a miracle—or perhaps, more accurately, many small miracles—happened. Everyone stopped falling.

The ice screws securing the college students to the face held. The ropes from the two independent groups of climbers tangled. A loop of rope between Gough and Patane wound itself around Barbara Wilt's ankle and then up and over her shoulder. A carabiner on one of the men's harnesses amazingly clipped through the other team's rope.

"It was bloody amazing," Gough recalls. "I mean, we'd fallen three pitches, bouncing, and to be suddenly stopped on the rope . . . I am alive because this girl just happened to be in the wrong place at the wrong time."

When everyone miraculously stopped falling, seven climbers in total lay strung out across the ice face, dangling from a mess of ropes and in varying states of injury.

Gough, who never lost consciousness, hung from a length of rope wrapped around Wilt's ankle, his body weight dislocating her knee and pulling her leg so far behind her as the rope looped up over her shoulder that her crampons poked her in the back.

Nearby, Patane was unconscious, hanging from Wilt and the tangle of ropes.

Martin was out of sight from the other climbers, suspended somewhere on the other side of a rib of rock and ice.

They were all suspended 100 feet off the ground.

Down on the ground below, a third group of climbers—French Canadians—were at the base of the slab getting ready to climb when they saw Gough, Martin, and Patane slam into Palmer, Beech, Casper, and Wilt. They immediately went into action, climbing up to the injured climbers to start the rescue effort. Meanwhile, one of the French Canadian climbers remained below and ran to the road to get help. There he found Gough's wife reading in the car. Despite his Quebecois French and her Kiwi English, they somehow managed to communicate, and rushed into Keene Valley to call for help.

David Ames, a thirty-two-year-old DEC forest ranger in Keene Valley, received the call. Ames and the Keene Valley Rescue Squad immediately responded, setting out for the slab. By the time they arrived, the French Canadians had already set up a rope rigged to a birch tree up on the face that was used to raise and lower the rescue litter.

As Ames approached the base of the climb, avalanche debris was more than 12 feet deep. Looking up at the slab, he could see the two groups dangling, twisted together. "Everybody stopped [falling]. It was just amazing," he says.

Back on the ice above, Wilt, despite her dislocated knee, and her companions were in relatively good shape. Gough, Martin, and Patane, on the other hand, were all badly hurt. Patane, in addition to his broken leg from impacting the ice bulge, also had a punctured lung and was coughing up blood. Gough's ankles and left leg were broken. Martin couldn't feel below his legs, and possibly had a broken back.

Gough, recognizing that he was the least injured of his climbing party, knew he would be rescued last. He wanted to take his weight off of Wilt, who was in excruciating pain. He placed an ice screw and anchored himself to the face. Then, realizing that he would be hanging there for a long time while rescuers helped the others, Gough splinted his own two feet together using one of his ice axes and a roll of tape that he carried.

Patane, who had blacked out during the fall, regained consciousness when he heard the voices of rescuers coming up the slope. He had fallen the farthest—more than 300 vertical feet. As Ranger Ames climbed up to Patane, he could see that like Gough, Patane was hanging badly on Wilt. He reached Patane and placed an ice screw to secure the injured climber, preparing to finally take the weight off Wilt's leg so she could be lowered. Ames looked at Patane: "I've gotta cut your rope." Patane quickly retorted: "Oh no, you're not cutting my rope!"

"I didn't blame him," Ames says today. "He had just come down 300 feet . . . so we tied him into the ice screw, and I also kicked my crampon into the ice and he held onto that so we could get to Barbara [Wilt]." Rescuers lowered Wilt, and then Patane.

Rescuers reached Martin next, and finally were prepared to go for Gough. As they approached him with the litter, he insisted on helping himself. "Leave me alone, I'll do it myself," he told them. Gough pulled himself into the litter on his belly, and the rescuers strapped him in just as he lay.

The climbers were transported in waiting ambulances to a nearby medical clinic (long since closed) in Keene Valley. There, Peter Gough was treated by a doctor who shared his last name. (From the 1930s through the 1950s, Dr. Gough had been a major participant in the informal search and rescue days, alongside Jim Goodwin.) Gough the doctor wanted to put a cast on Gough the climber's leg. To do so, medical technicians would need to cut Peter Gough's boots off to access his broken leg and ankles. He refused. The boots, which were brand new, were slated to be used for an expedition to Patagonia that November, just six months later, and Peter Gough wanted them to remain intact.

While this debate between Gough and the medical technicians raged on, Patane and Martin lay in another room at the same medical clinic. "I remember Peter yelling, 'You're not cutting the goddamn boot off!' " remembers Patane. In the end, the medical technicians pulled the boots off of Gough's feet, despite what must have been incredible pain.

Meanwhile, doctors realized that both Patane and Martin needed more advanced medical attention. They were flown to Vermont Medical Center in Burlington in a Plattsburgh Air Force Base helicopter. During the flight, Patane had more and more trouble breathing. He had torn the pleura in his chest, a membrane lining that covers the lungs. One lung had partially collapsed, and his chest was filling with fluid and air.

When the helicopter landed in Burlington, a doctor stood waiting in the parking lot. As the helicopter doors opened and Patane was offloaded at the medical center, the doctor rushed forward, pulled Patane's shirt back, and stuck a scalpel into his chest to release the pressure.

Incredibly, everyone survived.

Patane and Martin both spent three weeks at Vermont Medical Center. Martin, it turns out, had a cracked pelvis, not a broken back. He was released from the hospital and sent home two days before Patane, but was rehospitalized a short time later when the pelvis became infected. Normally 175 pounds, he had dropped to just 138.

Patane, in addition to his punctured lung, had broken both the tibia and fibula in his left leg. He was out of work for five weeks, and never climbed again, although he continues to hike, camp, and kayak.

Peter Gough spent the months from March through August laid up in plaster. In August, doctors placed pins in his ankles and leg, including several longer, temporary pins to hold all his bones in place while he healed. In November, just one week before the Patagonia expedition, Gough had the long pins pulled out and went on the trip. One person died on the expedition during a fall into a crevasse on a glacier, but Gough went on to continue climbing around the world. His climbing finally tapered off after the year 2000, when arthritis set in in his feet and inhibited his ability to climb.

"It always slides off of there, but it usually doesn't bother anybody," Ranger Ames, now retired, says of the snowfield atop the Chapel Pond Slab ice route. "I had never heard of something like this happening. It's steep enough that it's not usually avalanche-prone."

"They just picked the wrong day . . . that really was it," he says looking back. "It had to be an awful ride down through there. It would be a good nightmare. One of the guys said to me during the rescue, 'No doubt about it—we were up there and we came down.' "

8

MARCY'S MIGHT: THE SEARCH FOR STEVEN THOMAS

Greatness begets popularity, whether it be of hero, potentate or mountain. So Marcy, highest of them all . . . lures a yearly host of devotees to its summit.

—*The Adirondack Forty-Sixers* (1958)

To want to climb the highest is human nature, so Mount Marcy will always be a big attraction.

—Gary Randorf, "One Man's Forever Wild," *A Century Wild* (1985)*

Early April is a deceptive time in the High Peaks of the Adirondacks. In the valleys below, spring is in the air. Grass shows on the lawns and daffodils are in bloom. But the pleasantness of town belies a winter still fiercely holding on in the mountains above.*

"It's a common thing when people come from other areas," says retired DEC forest ranger Gary Hodgson of people's misperception of mountain conditions. "In town things don't look so bad, but as you gain elevation, the snow gets deeper and deeper, and although the days are pleasant, at night it gets really cold."

* Courtesy of Neal Burdick, editior. *A Century Wild.* Saranac Lake, N.Y.: Chauncy Press, 1985 (out of print).

Such was the scene on Monday, April 12, 1976, when six students from Onondaga Community College in Syracuse headed high into the mountains destined for the northern flanks of Mount Marcy. Their names were Bruce Weaver, Bob Bromley, Mark Seymour, Jim Thackaberry, Ken Sherwood, and most notably, Steven Thomas. Around 3:30 p.m. that afternoon, nineteen-year-old Thomas walked away from the lean-to where the group was making camp for the evening, and was never seen again.

One day earlier, on Sunday, Steven Thomas was eating breakfast at his family's home on Kayuta Lake north of Remsen, New York, just outside the far southwestern border of the Adirondack Park. His mother, Mary, made pancakes, while she silently worried that, with the exception of friend Bruce Weaver, Steven was about to go camping with a group of people he didn't know. As he prepared to leave for the camping trip, his father asked if he had a compass. Yes, Steven replied. In the years since, however, the Thomas family has accounted for all their compasses, and believes that, in truth, Steven probably didn't have one that day.

Steven left Kayuta Lake that day with Bruce and Ken Sherwood. The three drove to Lake Clear where they met up with the other half of their group: Mark, Bob, and Jim. Steven and Bruce left together in one car and drove to the Adirondak Loj trailhead at Heart Lake south of Lake Placid, some 37 miles from Lake Clear. They parked their car and hiked the 2-plus miles to Marcy Dam, where they spent the night in a lean-to. Steven carried his usual navy blue North Face pack.

On Monday, he and Bruce continued hiking, heading to the lean-to at Indian Falls, where they planned to meet up with the remaining four members of their group. Steven wore a blue bandana on his head, a yellow rain jacket, blue wool sweater, red-and-white-checkered shirt, white wool long underwear, blue jeans, and boots. That afternoon, as the others made camp, Steven brewed Darjeeling tea on his stove and hung his backpack in the back right corner of the lean-to. Everyone kept shuffling and moving around to keep warm in the extreme cold.

"You want to go for a walk?" Steven asked Bruce. Bruce didn't want to go, and neither did any of the others. Steven left camp alone, walking toward Upper Plateau in the general direction of Mount Marcy's summit, carrying nothing but his knife. He left his pack and his snowshoes behind at the lean-to. Steven headed out of sight up the trail, and disappeared, it seems, into thin air.

Darkness set in that Monday night around 7:00 p.m. It was a bitterly cold evening. The temperature dropped to just 10 degrees. Hard-packed snow clamped down on the forest floor. A crisp wind blew across the mountaintops above, and a full moon shone in the clear sky.

By 10:00 p.m., the other members of Steven's group began to get worried. Bruce and Bob went out to search. Despite the full moon, they carried flashlights anyway. As they climbed higher, the pair battled 55-MPH wind gusts. With the 10-degree raw temperature, the wind chill plummeted to a bone-chilling minus-40 degrees. Although Steven never said he was heading to the top of Mount Marcy, his companions assumed that's where he went. But Bruce and Bob never succeeded in making it to the top. Blowing ice crystals forced them back, and the howling wind absorbed their voices. They returned to the lean-to to await dawn.

At daybreak on Tuesday, April 13, the five men split into two search teams. One group went to Bushnell Falls and then looped back along another trail. The second group went to the top of Marcy. Neither group found any trace of Steven. When they all returned to the lean-to later that day, some rested and regained their strength while others hiked out to Adirondak Loj to notify the State Police of Steven's disappearance.

Although they couldn't have known it at the time, the twenty-four hours the five college classmates spent circling around camp looking for Steven would later hamper more formal search efforts. "It left signs from them all over the place," says Gary Hodgson, a retired DEC forest ranger who led the search efforts for Thomas. This complicated finding and following any tracks that might have been left in the snow by Steven.

By Wednesday morning, April 14, the formal search for Steven Thomas was slowly getting under way. The first helicopter, from the DEC, arrived on the scene to search Mount Marcy from the air. Soon, a second from the State Police, and eventually, a third helicopter from the air force, would join the search. Details of Steven's disappearance were few. Amazingly, the Thomas family was not notified of Steven's disappearance until Wednesday night when the telephone rang at their home in Remsen, more than twenty-four hours after Steven was first reported missing. The Thomases immediately packed their gear and left for Lake Placid in Steven's 1965 rusting red and pink Ford Falcon.

They spent a fitful night at a Lake Placid motel, and early Thursday morning, April 15, they waited at the airport nearby to participate in the search for their son and brother. Robert Thomas, Steven's father, flew in one of the helicopters. Looking down on the High Peaks, their upper flanks still caught in the icy grip of winter, he called them "as formidable as some Alaskan peaks I am familiar with." Despite growing search efforts, Thursday came and went without any sign of Steven.

Friday, April 16, was a difficult day for searchers. Forest rangers called the conditions on upper Marcy "extreme." The snow was 5 feet deep on average, and significantly deeper in hollows, crevices, and at the bases of cliffs. The weather was hostile, with high winds and low visibility in the High Peaks region. Veteran helicopter pilot Ace Howland flew rangers up over the area between Indian Falls and Marcy's summit, conducting an aerial search. Helicopters also dropped search teams, including seven additional forest rangers, on the ground to commence tight grid searches around Little Marcy, Ausable Lakes, Johns Brook Valley, and the Feldspar and Opalescent drainages. But the fate of Steven Thomas remained a question mark, and pessimism slowly crept in among the searchers.

A day later, on Saturday, April 17, helicopters followed Marcy Brook from the Dam to its source high on the mountain, and then flew over the shoulder of Marcy to Panther Gorge. They had perfect visibility that day, and could see animal tracks on the snow covering the brook from several hundred feet in the air. They also saw tents, and hikers walking along the cliffs of the High Peaks. Between fifty and one hundred searchers participated in the effort. But still, no sign of Steven.

The search slowed on Sunday, April 18, in observance of Easter, but picked up with renewed vigor on Monday morning, April 19. The headline of the *Adirondack Daily Enterprise* read FATHER STILL HOPEFUL HIKER WILL BE FOUND. Steven's father, Robert, remained optimistic, maintaining that searchers would find his son "walking." It was the seventh day of the search. Specially trained German shepherd search dogs were flown in to assist. Some of Steven's friends from home arrived to aid in the search. Don Blum, one friend from Remsen, signed the trailhead register simply, *Find Steve.*

By the eighth day of the search—Tuesday, April 20—rumors began to circulate that the search was dying down. Forest rangers, meanwhile, insisted that only the search dogs had been taken out to rest, and that the main search continued. But a day later, on Wednesday, April 21, intensive search efforts ended. What started as a search lasting days had now moved into weeks, ballooning to more than a hundred searchers at its most intense, and now contracting into almost nonexistence. After two weeks of searching, the state-led search finally concluded officially.

The Thomas family refused to give up hope, and continued their own search with what at times approached single-minded obsession. They were an almost constant presence in the High Peaks in the weeks and months following Steven's disappearance, and would return every year thereafter on and around the anniversary of his disappearance to continue their efforts to discover any clue that might hint as to what happened to their beloved Steven.

In their quest to uncover Steven's fate, the Thomas family and friends helped to resolve a number of other adventures gone awry. On June 13, 1976—two months after his brother's disappearance—Robert Thomas Jr. discovered the camping gear and personal effects of a Massachusetts man named George Atkinson Jr. who had been missing for more than three years. On March 15, 1973, Atkinson signed the trail register at Marcy Dam, indicating that he was climbing solo and headed to the top of Marcy. Like Steven, he never came back from the mountain. He was reported missing on March 20, but he hadn't been seen since days earlier when two groups of hikers reportedly saw him near the Indian Falls Lean-to one afternoon. By the time forest rangers received the call that Atkinson was missing, the High Peaks had been blasted with a horrendous snowstorm, and searchers assumed Atkinson must have gotten lost in the terrible weather.

"By the time of the search, the mountains were blanketed with feet of new snow," recalls retired Ranger Hodgson. "You could have walked right over the top of him. In fact, there's a good chance that somebody did." More than three years later, while looking for his brother, Robert Thomas discovered a shotgun and a jacket while searching in Panther Gorge. His find sparked a flurry of activity combing the wall of the gorge that also found a sleeping bag, boots, hat, jacket, glasses, and wallet containing Atkinson's ID. One month later, in July, searchers found the missing man's body, ending an old unsolved mystery. But still, the question of what happened to Steven Thomas remained unanswered.

Five years after his disappearance, in 1981, the Thomas family and friends returned once again to look for Steven. This time they were accompanied by Ed Hale, a former editor for the *Lake Placid News* who covered Thomas's disappearance. The family was there, yet again, to "trace a cold trail warmed by stubborn devotion," Hale wrote for *Adirondack Life* in 1982.

The group included Robert Thomas Jr., Steven's older brother, and Marilyn, his sister, who carried the very pack that Steven had left behind in the lean-to the night he disappeared. It has become an annual ritual for them, and despite their mission, it is a cheerful event—they've come to love the Adirondack wilderness to which they've returned repeatedly, looking for their brother. "We always stay at the lean-to where Steve stayed," Sue Corrigan, a friend of Steven's, told Hale. "The last tea my brother had was this Darjeeling," Robert added, brewing a pot on his backpacker's stove. "Steve was here just five years ago today."

By his own estimate, by 1981, Robert had walked more than 2,500 miles and climbed to Marcy's summit more than 600 times, each time dropping down into a different drainage, gorge, gulch, or river that could funnel a lost hiker like his brother. Sometimes, he would repeat the process as many as five or ten times in a day . . . going up, coming down, and then going back up again.

Robert went on to live in Lake Placid for a number of years, working as a stonemason and spending a lot of time in the mountains looking for his brother and enjoying the outdoors and the Adirondack wilderness. And although he no longer lives in the North Country, a short time before he moved away, he helped to provide closure to one final misadventure. In the winter of 2000, six backcountry skiers were caught in an avalanche on a slide on Wright Peak (chapter 16). One person died, and it was Robert's dog who located the body buried under the snow.

What really happened to Steven Thomas? The simplest answer is that no one really knows. Even so, family and friends have their theories. One month before his Adirondack disappearance, Steven had returned from an extended trip out West, a part of the country he clearly loved and wished to return to. In the weeks between his return and his Adirondack trip, Steven was aloof, hinting at some set of secret plans he had in his head. Perhaps, some speculated, Steven might have returned to the West.

The theory didn't persist for long. "As far as I'm concerned, he's still on the mountain," Robert said in 1982. The continued uncertainty about Steven's fate has haunted the Thomas family over the years. At one point, a young man from upstate New York with Steven's name and age was injured in a shooting in West Virginia. The man wasn't Steven, but did he know him and use his name?

Ultimately, no one knows what happened to Steven Thomas—his disappearance has remained an unsolved mystery. Perhaps the Adirondacks will one day reveal clues as to his fate. Or, more likely, the mountains will keep their secrets and people will be left to wonder what really happened. "There was not a single thing," remembers Gary Hodgson. "Never a track. Not an article of clothing. It was like he just left the world."

9

RUNNING THE HUDSON RIVER GORGE

The Hudson is born among the clouds . . . and in the mountain
meadows and lakelets near the top of Tahawus, almost five thousand
feet above the level of the sea. It is cradled in the awesome chasms
of Indian Pass, the Panther Gorge, and the Gorge of the Dial. After thus
rising upon its highest mountain peaks, it crosses in its wild course
down the southern slope of the Wilderness no less than four immense
mountain chains that all seem to give way at its approach . . . .

—Nathaniel Bartlett Sylvester, *Historical Sketches of Northern
New York and the Adirondack Wilderness* (1877)

In October 1977 two friends from Staten Island, New York, got the idea
to paddle the Hudson River Gorge in a borrowed canoe. Well, actually,
that's not quite what they had in mind.

They were twenty-one-year-old Jim DeGaetano and twenty-
six-year-old Bob Henry. "I remember most of it like it was yesterday,"
DeGaetano says through a stereotypically thick New York City accent.
"We were on an adventure."

Henry had hunted extensively throughout the Adirondacks and
loved the region, often hiking as many as 15 miles in search of remote
locations where he'd be sure to find solitude (though not necessarily

game). "In all the years I spent hunting, I never shot a deer," he jokes. "I never even squeezed the trigger."

Regardless, Henry thought that it made a lot more sense to try hunting in some equally remote location, but rather than hiking, to instead use the convenience of a canoe to access the wilderness. Together with DeGaetano, Henry devised a plan to scout out a suitable location prior to the opening of hunting season where they could return later in the year. As he scanned the contours of a topographic map, Henry's eyes fell squarely on a remote stretch of the Hudson River between Newcomb and North River.

With the very basics of a plan laid out, Henry borrowed a canoe from his uncle, who lived in Lakewood, New Jersey. It was a red, 17-foot fiberglass boat, handmade and custom-built for his uncle by a man in Tom's River. "I asked Bob, 'Have you ever canoed before?' " says DeGaetano. "And he said, 'Oh yeah, sure.' He asked me the same thing. I said, 'Yeah, when I was a Boy Scout.' " In truth, both men had relatively little experience in a canoe, and none whatsoever in white water.

They planned to put in at Newcomb and take out at North River—a journey of some 25 miles. And, they planned to complete the journey in a day. Most groups take at least two.

The Hudson River flows 275 miles from its source at Lake Tear of the Clouds high on Mount Marcy to its terminus in New York Harbor alongside Manhattan. Of its entire length, 25 miles—DeGaetano and Henry's route—might be the most revered among outdoor adventure seekers, and certainly white-water paddlers. The 25-mile stretch is split between the Upper Hudson River and the Hudson River Gorge. From Newcomb, the Upper Hudson flows gently south-southwest for 12 miles to its remote junction with the Indian River, a Hudson tributary.

It is an inviting stretch of river, but one that leads directly into the turbulence of the Hudson River Gorge as the river turns abruptly and marches eastward. For the next 13 miles, the river becomes an expert-only paddlers' paradise packed with a series of difficult Class V rapids with powerful hydraulics and high, standing waves.

Henry wasn't concerned, however. "I didn't think it was gonna be such a major issue that time of year," he says in retrospect. "Obviously, fall is not spring, and I assumed—and I use that word loosely—that this was gonna be a piece of cake. And even though we weren't canoeing experts, I assumed that this river was theoretically at the low point, and we'd be able to make the trip without a lot of grief."

He was wrong. "Periodic releases from Indian Lake maintain high water levels through June, and in September and October," says the Adirondack Regional Tourism Council's booklet *Adirondack Waterways*. "Open canoes should not be used here except by experts at mid-summer water levels."

The two men, it seemed, would be tempting fate at every turn.

Five people in total drove from Staten Island up to the Adirondacks—Bob Henry and his wife, Jim DeGaetano, and DeGaetano's boss and his wife. DeGaetano's boss and the two women stayed in a cabin near Newcomb while Henry and DeGaetano prepared to set off on their adventure. They packed the canoe with garbage bags stuffed with an extra change of dry clothing, in case they got wet.

"Bob brought a topographical map that he supposedly knew how to read," DeGaetano says. "By his map, there are rapids up to Class V [on the Hudson], but we weren't going to reach them because there was supposed to be a railroad bridge, and that's where my boss—who stayed back with the girls—was going to meet us at an overpass." But Henry and DeGaetano were mistaken—the railroad overpass doesn't intersect the Hudson until after the most violent rapids.

When they put in up near Newcomb, the water was deceptively calm and serene. "It was like a mirror," DeGaetano recalls. The men had life jackets, but decided not to wear them. "It was so calm we didn't think anything of it," DeGaetano continues. They headed south floating on the river, enjoying the sunshine of a beautiful fall day.

Shortly after they set off paddling downriver they saw a mist rising from the river ahead, and heard a rumbling noise—the first rapids. It was a relatively minor Class II and the first of a number of tests that would only grow harder with each rapid. They negotiated it without much difficulty. "This is nothing . . . it ain't so bad," thought DeGaetano. Even so, "it was our first taste that maybe we were getting in over our heads," says Henry. "But we got through it, and that probably was the incentive to keep going."

Then they hit Ord Falls, a Class III rapids early in the journey. Ord is the first major challenge for inexperienced canoeists on the river, and predictably, many of them dump here trying to navigate the rapids. DeGaetano and Henry, for their part, flipped. Their canoe capsized and their gear went floating away down the river. The two men dragged the canoe to shore and regrouped.

"We decided that whenever we hear rapids, we'll walk [the canoe]," DeGaetano explains. They got back in the boat and resumed their paddle, pulling ashore and walking the canoe in the water along the edge of the river each time they encountered rapids. Miles downstream, they found their garbage bags full of their gear at a bend in the river. The men changed into a fresh set of dry clothes and resumed their journey on the river.

As the day wore on, DeGaetano became impatient and concerned. "Where's this bridge, Bob?" he asked. The trip was taking too long. DeGaetano thought the pair should camp out overnight while they were still dry. They could build a fire, he suggested, and maybe someone would come looking for them since they were due out that night, or they could simply head out on their own the next day.

Henry refused. He had to return the canoe to his uncle as soon as possible, he insisted. "We'll make it," Henry reassured DeGaetano. "It's only down the river a little farther." In truth, they hadn't yet reached the halfway point of the trip, but they continued on.

Their process of lining the canoe—standing on shore and sending the canoe downriver while holding fast to a bowline—continued each time they approached a major rapids. Slowly, the canoe was coming apart, beginning to crack and break as it banged into rocks while being lined through the rapids. "We reached a point where we realized that the canoe was no longer going to be our way out of there," Henry says.

Soon, the sides of the river started rising up into steep cliffs, and it became impossible to walk along the shore ushering the canoe through. The men knew that soon they'd reach Cedar Ledges Rapids, and beyond that, Blue Ledge Falls, one of the Hudson's most infamous rapids. After Blue Ledge, the river plunges into the depths and bowels of the Hudson River Gorge. It is a stretch of narrows with powerful rapids and canyon walls rising high on both sides, miles from any roads or the nearest civilization.

DeGaetano and Henry were forced back into the disintegrating canoe, where they'd have to try and negotiate rapids bigger and meaner than either of them had ever faced before. The next major rapids they encountered did them in. "It was right out of the movie *Deliverance*," DeGaetano remembers.

Both men were tossed from the canoe and sent into the tumbling rapids without life jackets or helmets. The canoe smashed up against some rocks and broke "into a million pieces." Henry disappeared downriver. DeGaetano managed to hang onto one of the paddles, and knew enough to float on his back with his feet facing downriver—standard white-water position.

"I don't know how far we floated downriver," DeGaetano says. Eventually, he swam ashore. DeGaetano called for Henry but couldn't find him. "I thought I was alone because nobody answered," he recalls. "I kept walking farther downriver and looking, thinking maybe I'd find his body. And then he finally answered."

Henry had floated nearly a mile farther downriver. Both men flopped onto shore, soaking wet.

As evening approached, the cool October weather changed. It started to rain, and with darkness falling, switched to snow, then to sleet, and back and forth again. It got darker and darker. The men had no matches. Their Bic lighter ran out of fluid. Their gear was gone, washed away downriver. They only had the wet clothes on their backs, and the oar DeGaetano had held onto when they last wiped in the rapids.

The men continued walking downriver, assuming they were much closer to the takeout than they actually were. Eventually, cliffs once again forced them up off the shoreline. Henry started limping badly—the cold water had aggravated an old leg injury.

"It was getting so dark that you couldn't see your hand in front of your face," DeGaetano recalls. As the cliffs pushed them farther and farther up off the river, and as total darkness set in, the only way the men knew they were heading in the right direction was a break in the trees overhead where the river cleaved the forest, allowing them to see a half moon in the sky above.

At one point they saw a larger break in the trees, and the river got noticeably wider. They assumed it was the Indian River flowing into the Hudson.

DeGaetano led them through the forest, using the paddle as a "feeler" stick to probe for trees and rocks and other obstacles obscured in the darkness in front of them. Henry followed close behind. As the men walked along the top of the cliffs, suddenly the oar dropped into space. At their feet was an unseen precipice of unknown depth.

"Bob, freeze!" DeGaetano said. All night, Henry had been bumping into DeGaetano, and DeGaetano feared that his friend would bump into him again and knock him over the cliff. They stepped back from the void and continued on, all the while becoming more and more fatigued, and colder with every step.

Finally, they decided to stop for the night. The two men piled pine boughs onto the freshly fallen snow to try and insulate themselves from the cold ground. They huddled together to conserve body heat. It didn't work. They couldn't sleep and couldn't keep warm. "I thought we were going to freeze to death," DeGaetano remembers. They realized that they needed to keep moving, and so they walked on through the night.

At one point DeGaetano thought he saw lights—possibly flashlights—on the other side of the river. With any luck they could even be searchers looking for the lost men. He and Henry called out, but the sound of the river drowned out their voices. They sparked the empty lighter's flint, hoping someone would see, but no one did.

By dawn the next morning they had walked a number of miles farther downriver. A wet, slushy snow fell from the sky, and the men trudged through snow and mud, slipping and falling as they jumped over streambeds and slick logs.

Henry reached a point where he could no longer move efficiently because of his leg. "I can't walk," he said to his partner. DeGaetano looked back at his hurting companion. "Bob, I'm gonna keep going," he said. "I don't wanna die here. I don't want to freeze. I'll go get help and come back. Just follow my tracks and stay along the river. I'll find somebody."

DeGaetano powered ahead, walking and walking, eventually getting miles beyond Henry. DeGaetano was forced to stop every two minutes to rest, and to wring out his socks in an attempt to dry out his feet. He was almost in tears.

At last, he reached his end. DeGaetano dropped to his knees and cried out, "God, help me get through this!" Amazingly, somebody answered.

A forest ranger stood on the banks of the river directly across from DeGaetano. "Are you from the canoe trip?" the ranger yelled across the rushing river. "Yes! It's me! Look, I've got this oar!" DeGaetano called back.

Both DeGaetano and Henry attribute the ranger's presence on that shoreline to nothing short of Divine Providence. The odds of DeGaetano and the ranger—both in the middle of the wilderness—stepping out of the forest onto the banks of the Hudson River directly across from one another, and where they could see and hear each other over the roar of the rapids, were simply too incredible to explain away as mere coincidence.

The ranger instructed DeGaetano to continue walking downriver. It was too dangerous to cross there, but a little farther down, a group of Boy Scouts were camped out on DeGaetano's side of the river, looking for the missing pair of canoeists. "Everybody's out looking for you!" the ranger shouted.

The night before, DeGaetano's boss had called the forest rangers when the two men failed to return from their river adventure. Rangers immediately started a search and rescue mission that night. Just one year before, two other men had attempted an almost identical trip and they had died. No one wanted a repeat performance. Volunteers from three counties showed up to participate in the search for the two men.

Acting on the ranger's directions, DeGaetano forged ahead, and soon came upon the Boy Scouts. They were packing up their camp, almost ready to leave, when DeGaetano burst out of the woods. The boys ran over to him with blankets. "I swear it was like somebody kissed me," he says. "It was the best thing I've ever seen. They threw a blanket over me and were giving me Hershey bars and peanut butter sandwiches."

DeGaetano explained that Henry was still in the woods, a few miles upriver. A group rushed to reach him. Two miles upriver, they found Henry struggling through the forest. He had covered maybe 1.5 miles in four or five hours. As he stumbled through the woods alongside the river, he later explained, he nourished himself by consuming wild mushrooms. Fortunately, he didn't get sick. "The ranger, after questioning our sanity for coming down that stretch of the Hudson River in an open canoe, asked me if I got sick from eating the mushrooms. I told him, 'No!' 'So,' he said, 'you know the difference?' I said, 'Yeah.' I didn't tell him that I was only eating the ones that looked like they were on the cover of a can of mushrooms at the grocery store. That was my guiding light. I didn't want to have to say that I didn't have a damn clue, really."

With both men located, rescuers were able to evacuate them to a waiting ambulance where a priest sat ready to read the men their last rites. "They all expected us [to be] dead," DeGaetano says. "They were looking for bodies. They didn't find one piece of the canoe . . . it just splintered." In actuality, both men had fared well, suffering primarily from slight hypothermia. They were taken back to a local ranger station and changed into dry clothes. Somewhere along the way, the paddle that had been DeGaetano and Henry's trusted companion went missing.

"I wish I had that oar . . . I would frame it," DeGaetano says. "Thank God for the oar . . . that's all I can say. I really believe that thing saved my life."

Henry's uncle, understandably, was "severely disappointed" over the loss of his canoe. "I reimbursed my uncle for the canoe, but that didn't solve the basic situation that I had lost his canoe," Henry says. "Needless to say, I was not popular at family gatherings for a while."

Today, DeGaetano and Henry both still live on Staten Island, where Henry, ironically, is a tugboat captain on the Hudson River in New York Harbor. "I'm still looking for that canoe every time I go across the harbor," he says. "I would at least expect pieces of it to come down the river."

"I have to give 100 percent credit to the rangers and the people they work with to look for lost folks, and to drag our sorry asses out of the woods," he continues. "In our defense, we were never lost. We always knew where we were—we were in the river or next to it. But there was a point where I physically didn't know if I could have gotten out of there on my own, and Jimmy reached a point where mentally and physically, he felt beaten down by the whole thing. But luckily, he picked the right spot to holler for help . . . . Another 100 yards up or down the river and there could have been an army of people on the other side of the river and they never would have heard him.

"It's not as though we could turn around and paddle back upriver. We were in for a penny, in for a pound. It's a very impressive river . . . . People have no idea—they would never connect that little babbling brook from up in the Adirondacks to what we have here in New York City. The river has my full respect.

"[That experience] hasn't turned me off to the Adirondacks," he concludes. "It's just made me respect it a little more."

10

DEADLY ALLURE: MOUNT COLDEN'S TRAP DIKE

It is the momentary carelessness in easy places, the lapsed attention, or the wandering look that is the usual parent of disaster.

—Albert F. Mummery, *The Quotable Climber* (2002)

On the morning of Saturday, March 11, 1989, five friends—thirty-six-year-old Linda Hepburn; her boyfriend, Art Portmore; Patrick Clark; Peter Osborne; and Mike Douglass—arrived in Avalanche Pass at the base of Mount Colden, ready to attempt the Adirondacks' premier winter mountaineering route (and one of the classic slide climbs by summer)—the Trap Dike. What they didn't know as they started up the route is that one of them wouldn't come back alive.

Mount Colden's Trap Dike is considered *the* historic Adirondack climb, notes Don Mellor in his climbing guide, and is the birthplace of Adirondack rock climbing. The route follows an eroded dike of gabbro intruded into the mountain's typical anorthosite granite, so prevalent throughout the Adirondacks. Differential erosion has carved away the dike, leaving Colden with a deep cleft running down its face, a chasm with towering walls, and an obvious climbing route from Avalanche Pass to the summit slabs above.

137

Starting at a debris cone at the mouth of the Dike, the route climbs a series of steep rock steps alongside a waterfall before exiting right onto slabs that lead directly to Colden's summit, 2,000 feet above the pass. In winter, the same route is used by mountaineers, the dike filled with snow, and the waterfalls frozen into blue walls of ice.

Hepburn, Portmore, and the others stood at the base of the Dike, preparing to climb. Hepburn, actually, didn't plan to join them for the climb. With relatively little experience, she planned instead to watch from below as the others climbed. But conditions in the Dike were good, and she accompanied the others as far as the first frozen waterfall.

She was not totally inexperienced. Hepburn had hiked and climbed with boyfriend Portmore during the previous summer in the Canadian Rockies, gaining a slowly increasing comfort level on steep snow. Even so, the Trap Dike was a more difficult climb than she had ever attempted. Her strong performance on the steep pitches low on the route, however, led the other members of her climbing party to believe that she'd have no problem on the lower-angled summit slides above.

Hepburn successfully bypassed the first frozen waterfall, taking a snow-filled gully to its right. She soon arrived at the second, and highest, waterfall, and succeeded in climbing past it as well. The whole group of five continued upward, exiting from the Dike onto the slabs above. There they found about 1 foot of snow covering the slide, overlain by an icy crust due to rain the previous weekend. In some places, there was only a thin layer of weak ice covering the rocks. For the most part, though, the conditions allowed for comfortable and efficient climbing with crampons, and by kicking steps.

Portmore, the most experienced member of the group, led the

way up the slide. Hepburn followed, and then the others. By this time, Hepburn, inexplicably, no longer had her ice ax. She had laid it down while back in the Trap Dike and had forgotten to pick it up again when she continued climbing.

Douglass brought up the rear of the group. He found Hepburn's ice ax and tried to bring it to her, but the group had become too spread out and he couldn't relay the message forward. Then, around 1:00 p.m., Douglass heard a scream and saw Hepburn sliding headfirst down the slide. She slid about 100 feet before being stopped by a small island of trees on the exposed slab of rock, ice, and snow.

Douglass was the first member of the party to reach her. She was unconscious, and had a broken leg, abdominal injuries, and an obvious injury to her head. He covered her with warm clothing and administered what first aid he could.

When they saw the accident happen, Osborne and Clark immediately headed up and over Colden's summit—the fastest route— to get help. Simultaneously, a skier below on the frozen Avalanche Lake saw Hepburn fall and had already gone to get help by the time Osborne and Clark reached the top of Colden.

The skier ran into Dave Dohman, the caretaker at the Lake Colden Interior Outpost, on "Misery Hill" above the Avalanche Lake Lean-tos around 1:10 p.m., ten minutes after Hepburn's fall. Dohman skied back to the Outpost and called for a rescue. It was 1:30 p.m.

The DEC alerted its Backcountry Rescue Team, which was specially trained for rescues on technical terrain. The responders included local climbers Don Mellor, Jeff Edwards, and Mark Meschinelli, as well as Mark Ippolito, a physician's assistant at Placid Memorial Hospital, and Peter Wallace, a staffer at Adirondak Loj.

Using snowmobiles, the rescuers reached Avalanche Lake and climbed to the accident site by 4:45 p.m. But Hepburn was already dead. She passed away sometime around 2:30 p.m.

Mount Colden's Trap Dike was first climbed in the summer of 1850 by Robert Clarke and Alexander "Sandy" Ralph. Both men were nephews of the owner of the Tahawus Iron Works, and had recently become employed there as managers. That July, while Clarke was visiting from his permanent home in Cincinnati, Ohio, the two men decided to climb Mount Colden by way of the Trap Dike. The mountain, and the Dike, had never been climbed before.

Clarke and Ralph set out around 5:00 a.m. carrying bread, pork, and tea. They also carried a teapot and cups, blanket, compass, spyglass, ax, rifle, and a bottle of brandy known affectionately as "the Admiral." They walked the forest path along Calamity Brook—the same path widened to transport Henderson's body out of the wilderness in 1845, and used by Cheney to guide Headley to the top of Marcy in 1846 (chapter 1).

From there the men headed around Lake Colden, and by 10:00 a.m., they had reached the base of the Dike. Clarke and Ralph left most of their equipment there at the base and started the climb. They set off into the Dike, dark rock walls rising on both sides. Almost immediately, they encountered the steepest rock of the climb—a series of rock steps up which climbers scramble, usually, although not always, without ropes.

Then, after 300 feet, by their estimate, the men exited to climber's right out of the Dike onto smooth rock slabs—the Colden summit slides—keeping to the edge along vegetation when possible, and stopping every now and then to rest. The upper slides are not difficult by modern rock climbing standards, but they are still a serious place to be, and one where a fall would be extremely bad. The exposure is impressive and exhilarating (and intimidating to the uninitiated rock scrambler or hiker).

The pair made it to the summit, the rock falling away 2,000 vertical feet to the lake below. It took them one and a half hours to climb from bottom to top. In so doing they recorded the first ascent of Colden—at 4,713 feet, the eleventh-highest peak in the Adirondacks—and of the Trap Dike route itself.

Clarke and Ralph spent an hour and a half on the summit, admiring the view, relaxing, examining the unique alpine vegetation, and marveling at an eagle that soared overhead. Eventually, they descended—probably by a different route—and circled back around to the base of the Dike where they retrieved their gear. They shot a deer on the shores of Lake Colden, and spent a comfortable night camped beside a huge fire. In the morning, they caught fresh trout for breakfast, and then leisurely made their way back to the Iron Works.

In the 150-plus years since it was first climbed, the Trap Dike has lured climbers, scramblers, and hikers up its enticing route in ever-increasing numbers, the masses drawn to the route for its exposure, aesthetic line, commanding views, and unparalleled wilderness locale. And for just as long, men and women have ventured onto the semitechnical terrain of the Dike and found themselves stuck, unable to ascend higher on steep rock, and unable to descend the way they came for fear of falling on the challenging terrain.

For local climbers like Ed Palen, the owner of Adirondack Rock and River, a climbing guide service, rescuing these individuals has become an almost routine affair. As recently as the summer of 2004, two separate pairs of hikers were rescued in as many months on the Trap Dike.

On September 20, around 11:40 a.m., forest rangers received a cell phone call from two men: thirty-seven-year-old Bill Jirouele from Ohio and forty-six-year-old Tom Hirsch from Fairport, New York. The men had reached a point halfway up the Trap Dike when they got stuck. Forest rangers and rescuers flew in by helicopter, and by 4:40 p.m., the men were safely back on level ground. They decided to continue their stay in the backcountry.

A month and a half earlier, on August 8, thirty-one-year-old Ken Bielmeier from Lancaster, New York, and thirty-nine-year-old Kevin Bielmeier from Connecticut were climbing the Trap Dike when they took a wrong turn, ending up on bare rock slides too steep on which to risk moving. Rangers rescued the men, safely lowering them in climbing harnesses and returning them safely to the ground unharmed.

The Trap Dike can be a wholly different beast in winter, when conditions transform the climb into the Adirondacks' premier mountaineering route. It wasn't until 1935—eighty-five full years after its first summer ascent—that Jim Goodwin and Ed Stanley, using long ice axes and ten-point crampons, succeeded in logging the first ascent of the Trap Dike in winter. It was the hardest ice route in the Adirondacks at the time, having denied the attempts of a group from Yale the previous winter. A year later Goodwin and Bob Notman raised the standard of ice climbing again with their first ice ascent of Chapel Pond Slab (chapter 7).

In the years since, numerous parties have had serious winter mishaps on the Trap Dike.

On March 21, 1987, Jean Grenon and Paul Junique, both thirty years old, were struck by a wet snow avalanche while ice climbing the Trap Dike. The avalanche flushed them out of the Dike and swept them to its bottom. During the fall, Grenon's crampon caught on the ice, causing a spiral fracture of his right leg, but also preventing him from being carried all the way to the bottom where he would have been buried under the accumulated avalanche debris.

Nearly six years later, on February 13, 1993, thirty-four-year-old John Wylie and twenty-eight-year-old Glen Hauser, both from Ontario, climbed the Trap Dike. Conditions were less than favorable. Heavy snow in the Dike and on the slide above slowed their progress. They finally succeeded in reaching the summit as darkness fell. Descent proved equally difficult, and the men opted to spend the night in a snow cave just below the mountain's summit. They descended early the next morning, meeting up with a rescue team just above Marcy Dam that was heading up to look for them.

Most recently of the notable Trap Dike winter incidents, on December 19, 2004, Fred Vishnevsky (a middle-aged climber from Englewood Cliffs, New Jersey, attempting his fifth winter ascent of the route) and sixteen-year-old Alan Glick from New Jersey set out to climb the Trap Dike. They left South Meadow around 6:15 a.m., and attempted to ski the DEC fire road to Marcy Dam. Conditions weren't good for skiing, and the pair abandoned their skis after only half an hour. They hiked the rest of the way to the base of the Dike, arriving at 10:00 a.m.

The pair started up the climb carrying 75 feet of rope and six ice screws, expecting lots of ice and not much snow. They weren't disappointed. Vishnevsky and Glick bypassed most of the lower section of steep ice by climbing through snow on its right. In short order, they reached the main frozen waterfall, which stood a little over 60 feet tall. Their short rope was just long enough to reach the top. Above, one final

30-foot pitch of ice remained, but they chose to bypass it by climbing up snow on the left in order to save time.

Around 2:00 p.m., they left the Dike and started climbing out onto the upper slabs. By 3:00 p.m. they had reached a landmark known as "cave rock." The slab was glazed over in hard ice that was covered with just 2 inches of crunchy snow. The pair continued climbing higher until Vishnevsky was 100 feet below the final 200-foot pitch of steeper rock, and 300 total feet from the finish of the climb. Glick was 75 feet below him. It was 4:10 p.m.

Then, Glick lost his footing and fell, sliding and tumbling 400 feet down the slab. Vishnevsky, who was looking up at their route, didn't see Glick fall, but he heard the teenager scream twice, with as much as three seconds elapsing between yells.

Vishnevsky immediately removed his backpack, pulled out two headlamps, a face mask, and a neck gaiter, and began downclimbing to Glick. Fifty feet above Glick, Vishnevsky found one of the teen's ice tools (each climber carried two) with a glove still holding onto its shaft. Thirty feet above Glick, he found one of the teen's boots with the crampon still attached, stuck in some brush.

Finally, ten minutes after the accident, at 4:20 p.m., Vishnevsky reached his injured climbing partner, who was caught against a small tree. Fortunately, Glick was wearing a helmet, which had protected his head, but he didn't come away unscathed. As he fell, his boot had caught on a tree, ripping the boot off his foot and injuring his leg. The crampon on his other leg, meanwhile, had managed to puncture his now-exposed foot sometime during the fall.

Glick—having slid 400 feet and having had his fall arrested by a small tree while remaining relatively uninjured—was lucky to survive.

But now, the two climbers would have to summon their inner drive and experience in the mountains to self-rescue from the situation.

After checking Glick's injuries, which were remarkably minor, Vishnevsky called for help on his cell phone, dialing 911. He told the dispatcher that they were mobile, and that they would attempt to reach Colden's summit and go down to Lake Arnold. They didn't expect anyone to come for them that night, he explained, since it was snowing heavily, but if he didn't call back in the morning, searchers should send a rescue team into the woods for them.

Glick and Vishnevsky then moved off of the slide and into the comparative safety of the trees and brush, swimming through deep snow as they fought their way up the mountain. Three and a half hours later, they reached a trail 200 feet north of Colden's summit. The pair immediately began their descent and arrived at Lake Arnold around 8:30 p.m. As they circled the area, searching for the trail that would lead them home, they met up with two forest rangers, the first of eight rescuers in total who had been dispatched when Vishnevsky first made his cell phone call.

The rangers gave Glick a fresh pair of mittens, and the four men hiked out to Marcy Dam, all the while with Glick enduring extreme pain in his knee. From there, Glick and Vishnevsky enjoyed a snowmobile ride out to South Meadow.

Back home in New Jersey, Glick visited an orthopedist, and an MRI determined that he had torn both the anterior cruciate ligament and the medial collateral ligament in his knee. On February 18, 2005, he went into surgery to have the damage repaired.

Five weeks after the accident, Vishnevsky's backpack (which he had left on the slab when he downclimbed to rescue Glick) was found by a ranger who, on a whim, had descended from Colden's summit to see if the pack was still there. It was, and the backpack was returned to Vishnevsky, all contents accounted for, including his chocolate candy.

In the end, Glick and Vishnevsky's close call stands as a stark reminder that, despite one's level of experience, Colden's Trap Dike has the ever-present potential to quickly turn dangerous, or deadly, regardless of its mountaineering allure.

11

SOLO: A LONG-DISTANCE HIKER'S FINAL DAYS

Nature is so pitiless, so unresponsive, to a person in trouble! I had read of the soothing companionship of the forest, the pleasure of the pathless woods. But I thought, as I stumbled along in the dismal actuality that, if I ever got out of it, I would write a letter to the newspapers exposing the whole thing. There is an impassive, stolid brutality about the woods that has never been enough insisted on. I tried to keep my mind fixed upon the fact of man's superiority to nature: his ability to dominate and outwit her. My situation was an amusing satire on this theory.

—Charles Dudley Warner, "Lost in the Woods,"
The Adirondack Reader (1964)*

Sometime around 3:00 p.m. on June 5, 1990, David Boomhower stepped onto the trail and into the woods, beginning a long-planned hike on the Northville-Placid Trail (NPT). Built in 1922 and 1923 by the Adirondack Mountain Club, the NPT—whose accepted end-to-end length varies from 117 miles to as many as 133 miles—winds its way northward, starting around Northville near the southern terminus of

---

* Excerpted from *The Adirondack Reader*, edited by Paul Jamieson and published (first edition) by MacMillan in 1964. This copyrighted material is used with the permission of Paul Jamieson. Subsequent editions of *The Adirondack Reader* published by Adirondack Mountain Club Inc. (ADK), www.adk.org.

the Adirondack Park on the shores of Great Sacandaga Lake and ending in the village of Lake Placid amid the High Peaks. Most hikers today—including Boomhower in 1990—begin their trek not in Northville, but in the nearby town of Benson, in order to eliminate some early walking on roads before reaching the trails that head off into the wilderness.

Boomhower's plan was to finish the journey ten days later, on June 15. On his first day he covered 8.3 miles, reaching the Silver Lake Lean-to before dark. There, like so many hikers before and after him, Boomhower probably sat along the shores of the lake and listened to the cries of the iconic bird of the Adirondack waterways—the loon. Then, before turning in for the night, he signed the trail register, noting that it had been "a beautiful day."

On day two, his feet were sore, but otherwise Boomhower was in good shape. He continued north, stopping along the way to take a bath in Mud Lake, where he shampooed at the lakeshore, and then dried himself using a wool sock. "This is the essence of camping life," he thought. Later on along the trail, he passed a gigantic beaver dam. Looking toward the sky, he noted a constant threat of rain. Ten miles later, around late morning, he reached Whitehouse on the Sacandaga River.

The next day—day three of a planned ten—Boomhower intersected Route 8 between Piseco and Oxbow lakes, near 3,050-foot Buckhorn Mountain. Route 8 cuts east-west across the southernmost tier of the Adirondack Park, meandering from Hinckley Reservoir at the southwestern corner of the Park to the town of Speculator on Lake Pleasant. Boomhower used his rare brush with civilization to mail a postcard to his sister and her family, addressed "All you Pollocks."

Then, by June 8—day four—he was deep in the wilds again. Hiking along, he passed Spruce Lake, and then, the remote West Canada Lakes.

By now he had already covered 40 miles on the NPT, with fewer than 100 miles to go. Uncharacteristic of notoriously weight-conscious long-distance hikers looking to shave pounds off their pack weight, Boomhower carried a bulky Coleman lantern and a heavy container of fuel.

That morning his physical condition had ominously changed. He had no energy, his hiking speed had slowed, and he stopped to rest often. But despite noticing such changes, Boomhower continued on at what he still considered to be a "decent" pace.

Around 9:00 a.m. he signed the trail register at West Canada Lakes, and less than an hour later, met another hiker—Paul Wilbur from Lake Pleasant. Wilbur was fishing near Cedar Lake Dam, and when the two men met, Wilbur noticed that Boomhower's pack was askew, with tent poles protruding out at odd angles. During his chance meeting with Wilbur, Boomhower didn't say he was ill, and didn't ask for help. But it would be the last time anyone saw him alive. Boomhower never came out of the woods.

Thirty-eight-year-old David Boomhower lived in Latham, New York, a suburb of the state capitol, Albany. A seventeen-year veteran of the United States Postal Service, he worked as a postal clerk in the nearby town of Colonie and spent evenings and weekends as an assistant scoutmaster for Troop 537 of the Brunswick Boy Scouts. Although he spent his days inside sorting mail, Boomhower longed for a trip that would take him away from everyday life and into a dramatic wilderness landscape. He had grand plans to trek the desert and the jungle; to hike the Grand Canyon; and to join an outing club trip to the Amazon.

In the end, though, Boomhower finally settled on something closer to home—he would solo-hike the Northville-Placid Trail from end to end.

He was a moderately experienced outdoorsman, having done numerous two- and three-day trips in the Adirondacks, although this was likely to be the longest undertaking he had ever attempted. He was also a careful planner, and eagerly spent many nights in his living room sorting gear for his trip. Boomhower even came up with his own "survival recipe"—a combination of peanut butter, chocolate, nuts, and Cracklin' Oat Bran cereal that he pressed into empty margarine containers.

As the date for his departure approached, friends wondered whether or not the trip was actually an escape from the pain of Boomhower's recent divorce from Krista, his wife of seven years. Krista had remarried, and her new husband was Boomhower's best friend, Jim Lombardi. In the six or so months immediately following the wedding, the trio—Boomhower, Lombardi, and Krista Boomhower-turned-Lombardi—lived an uncomfortable existence under the same roof. Finally, the Lombardis asked Boomhower to move out, and he set off into the wilderness, perhaps planning to never come back, many speculate.

Boomhower's sister Judy discounts such a theory, and says that her brother did not commit suicide due to depression. In the days and weeks leading up to his trip, she noted that he had seemed cheerful, enthusiastic, and motivated. According to another of Boomhower's sisters, Joan Craney, he had trained for the trip for six months, jogging 50 to 60 miles per week, lifting weights, and consulting a nutritionist. Then, just prior to the trip, he cached a food supply at the Lake Durant Campsite, four miles south of Blue Mountain Lake village.

Although we will never, in all likelihood, know Boomhower's real plans when he walked into the Adirondack wilderness, we do know this: On June 5, 1990, friends dropped him off at the southern trailhead for the NPT in Benson, and Boomhower headed into the woods for the last time.

Two days after he was due out of the wilderness—on June 17—Boomhower's family still had not heard from him. Concerned, they alerted the DEC. Forest rangers immediately initiated a hasty search on the trails, sending out "strike teams" of fast-moving rangers to cover the trails quickly in hopes of finding Boomhower himself, or any obvious clues as to where he might be.

Their initial investigation revealed that he had signed every trail register north, up to and including the one at West Canada Lake, about 40 miles north of Benson. That last register entry was dated June 8—the same day Boomhower had bumped into fisherman Paul Wilbur—but Boomhower never signed the next trail register at Wakely Dam, some 16 miles farther along the trail.

His apparent disappearance prompted a formal and intensive search effort centered around a 9-mile stretch of the NPT between Cedar Lake, where Wilbur last saw Boomhower, and Cedar River Flow. Just four days into the search, searchers had already combed 30 square miles of wilderness. They searched rugged off-trail terrain surrounding the NPT, thinking that Boomhower may have strayed into the wilds during a bushwhack, and could possibly be on the move looking for a way out, or for a way back to the trail.

Then they found a clue. Search teams discovered footprints near Little Moose Lake, west of Cedar River Flow, that they believed belonged to Boomhower. But searchers were wrong. The footprints didn't belong to the missing man.

And despite the rangers' assumption that Boomhower was likely on the move, those closest to him disagreed. "He would have pitched his tent and waited," Boomhower's ex-wife, Krista, told the Albany *Times Union* on June 22, 1990. "He would realize someone would be out there looking for him." She was right, but what she didn't know was that Boomhower had pitched his tent miles away in a corner of the wilderness where no one was looking, and that he was fighting to survive.

The search for David Boomhower continued for three more weeks, involving scores of forest rangers and as many as two hundred volunteers, but they still had "not found a shred of evidence," forest ranger Frank Dorchak told reporters.

Then, on Sunday, July 8, the intensive search concluded, and a day later, on July 9, the search was downgraded to "ongoing," with the DEC willing to respond to any new leads but unprepared to continue its previous efforts. In the days following, newspapers implored readers: Anyone who might have had contact with a lone, male hiker in the Cedar River Flow area, or even possibly farther north along the NPT, should call the DEC.

Boomhower's family, including his sister Judy and her husband and son, continued searching for weeks and months. By mid-September, they, too, grew weary of searching without any sign of him. It was a perplexing and frustrating end. Investigators had already ruled out foul play as a possible outcome, and everyone expected that Boomhower was out there, lost somewhere. They just didn't know where.

"He had just gotten his life really together," one of Boomhower's sisters told reporters. "He was planning several trips and just bought a new car."

In total, seven aircraft and 286 people—including five psychics—spent more than 13,000 hours looking for Boomhower, but his disappearance remained a mystery and the search, both formal and informal, went into relative dormancy.

October 20, 1990, was opening day of big-game hunting season in the Northern Zone of the state. Hunters headed into the woods throughout the Adirondacks. One small group started in from Lewey Lake, south of Snowy Mountain and Indian Lake village. They hiked westward on the Sucker Brook Trail and then, destined for Cellar Mountain, moved off-trail.

One hunter became attracted to a red object in the trees. It was a red United States Postal Service sweatshirt hung on a stick. Looking more closely, he then saw a tent pitched near Sucker Brook. Thinking that the equipment had been abandoned, he continued on to the brook itself and discovered a badly decomposed human body—David Boomhower.

The hunters investigated the macabre scene further. Boomhower's gear was scattered around a campsite he had evidently used for some time. The remains of several fires were nearby, possibly used by Boomhower to signal for help.

It was more than five months since Boomhower had expected to finish his trip, and from where the hunters stood, the NPT lay many miles to their west, on the opposite side of a small mountain range. Their discovery of his remains provided closure to a months-old mystery, but it also prompted more questions than answers . . . until they found a diary with his body that recorded his final days in excruciating detail. It was a small, lined notebook that started, "Day 1 . . . June 5."

After passing Paul Wilbur near Cedar Lake Dam, Boomhower continued north. His food was running low, and he didn't believe that he could make it to his resupply cached at Lake Durant. Then, he made a fateful decision to leave the NPT and try to get out of the wilderness. As he followed the trail, and the Cedar River, north between Lamphere Ridge and Round Mountain, he turned east, leaving the NPT, and started up toward the Colvin Brook Lean-to.

His journal entry on day five read: "Colvin Brook Lean-to . . . I never expected to see this place." He was on the Sucker Brook Trail, a spur trail that he believed would provide a shortcut to civilization, which would offer the opportunity to renew his food supply, or if he chose, to call off the trip entirely. Despite its name, the Sucker Brook Trail actually follows Colvin Brook. The trail's namesake actually lies several miles to the east, just south of the trail's continuation on the opposite side of a ridgeline, where Sucker Brook eventually flows into Lewey Lake. This nuance would puzzle Boomhower in the weeks to come.

From the Colvin Brook Lean-to, it is almost 7 miles to the Lewey Lake Campsite on Route 30. From there, Boomhower planned to hitchhike the 8 miles to the village of Speculator. But he wouldn't make it.

"Rotten weather and too light rations have driven me from N-P. Am really feeling the effect of inadequate nourishment," he wrote in his journal. He pondered why the Sucker Brook Trail actually follows Colvin Brook, and mentioned a weakness that suddenly overcame him while hiking the day before. "Started yesterday when I had to change [hiking] style to cover ground . . . maybe I'm getting old."

He left the Colvin Brook Lean-to and headed east, soon discovering the miseries of the Sucker Brook Trail. The trail follows Colvin Brook so closely that a hiker must ford the stream fourteen times. Boomhower called it the "soak-foot trail." After 3 miles, the trail at last leaves the stream and climbs 1,200 vertical feet up a steep slope. There, the trail crests a 3,300-foot-tall mountain range before dropping into the Sucker Brook drainage on the range's eastern flanks. Forest ranger Tom Eakin called it "probably the most remote country left in the state . . . it's just one huge, remote piece of real estate."

There, atop the mountain range, the intermittent red trail markers are hard to follow. On the far side of the ridge, and only 3.5 miles from Lewey Lake, Boomhower made a fatal wrong turn. At the saddle between Cellar and Lewey mountains, the trail contours north before heading east as it drops off the ridge. Boomhower never contoured north with the trail, instead dropping straight down into the upper reaches of the Sucker Brook drainage where he made his camp 30 feet north of the brook and just a quarter-mile—though he didn't know it—from the trail.

The next morning Boomhower made another journal entry. "Day 6 . . . Lost Day 1 . . . June 10 . . . camp close to where trail was but cannot find trail. Nothing to do now but wait it out, rest, stay calm, go about normal upkeep chores [hygiene]. Sure hope someone will inquire after 10 days . . . . Sure hope I get some sustained sunlight to dry out things. Going to pray a lot too." But at that point, Boomhower wasn't expected to come out of the woods for at least five more days, and he was already running low on food and well away from his expected route of travel.

"Hung colored, red clothing at major access points in all four directions leading into camp," he wrote before crawling into his dome-shaped tent for the night. Months later, and much too late, that same red clothing would lead the unsuspecting hunter to Boomhower's camp.

On the morning of day seven it was pouring. "Day 7 . . . Lost Day 2 . . . June 11 . . . Bad news! Still raining . . . 4 days now. Can't even start a fire to dry things out," his journal continued. "Good news: The sleeping bag has dried out . . . . Got a snail today. Nice change of pace for . . . [unreadable] . . . 8 days until I'm sure searchers have . . . [unreadable] . . . out."

His homegrown survival mix apparently gone, Boomhower had already transitioned to eating plants and insects. Later that day he wrote: "Discovered the joys of eating insects. Simple enough . . . [unreadable]

. . . the tent flap, let them in, close the flap, and eat them. Favorites, blackflies, sweet, unknown, tiny teardrop-shaped bug, crunchy . . . . They are a protein source and with the clover for greens, I just may have a sustenance diet . . . ."

While he waited for an end to the rain, Boomhower pondered his options: Should he wait to be rescued? Should he sit and regain his strength for a few days? Should he immediately strike out for Route 30? Which way should he go?

At one point, he did try to make a move. "Bad news. Effort to get out via Sucker Brook didn't work," he wrote. "Didn't intercept trail either. Sure would like to know why Sucker Brook Trail apparently never goes near Sucker Brook . . . ."

Boomhower soon grew dizzy from hunger, and the tent started to leak, wetting his sleeping bag, which he was no longer able to keep dry. "Day 11 . . . Lost Day 6, June 15 . . . . Rained again last night," his journal continued. "In a little while will start the fire . . . . Hope to God somebody . . . contacted the rangers after day 10 passed."

But the search would not begin for another two days—on June 17—when Boomhower's family reported him missing. Weeks later, the search would end while he was still alive.

"Where the hell is anybody?" Boomhower wrote. His journal continued: "Day 20 . . . Lost Day 15 . . . June 24 . . . thought I would try to go down the brook to get to the lake, but not strong enough to go far. This is my last escape effort. Either I'm found here or I die here . . . ." Despite his journal entry, however, Boomhower would make additional attempts to save himself.

By now, the search was already under way, but teams were looking near Cedar Lake and Cedar River Flow along Boomhower's intended travel route, as many as 8 miles away. He had written in a trail register that he planned to stick to the NPT. No one had expected him to attempt a shortcut to Lewey Lake Campsite via the Sucker Brook Trail.

But the circumstances of Boomhower's disappearance raise a number of questions. For Boomhower, why did he expect to be found in a remote off-trail location far from his intended route of travel, especially when he had indicated that he planned to stick to his route? For searchers, given that Boomhower reliably signed every trail register he encountered, why, when he failed to sign the next trail register, didn't forest rangers send out teams on the trails that diverge from the NPT between Boomhower's last register entry and the next register?

As Boomhower struggled to survive, he wrote that he kept seeing a plane with pontoons flying overhead. It haunted him, as it seemed to pass above in the sky each passing day. He couldn't have known that it was ferrying searchers to Cedar Lake. Each night he lit his Coleman lantern and left it under the trees as a beacon in the night. But rescuers, including the airplane pilots, never saw it since they didn't fly their search aircraft at night.

"Day 21 . . . Lost Day 16 . . . June 25 . . . . I'm going to move around as little as possible," Boomhower's journal continued. "Stay as warm and dry as possible . . . and keep a firm grip on life for as long as possible."

The rain did not let up for three more days. Finally, on June 27, the weather broke. Boomhower dried his sleeping bag and boots in the sunshine. He wrote that he regretted missing a relative's birthday, and that he was too weak to walk. "All I can do is hold on, using my lantern as a beacon on the brook bank until it runs out of fuel. Very dizzy today," he wrote.

The next day—June 28—was also sunny. "Nice day again but no plane," his journal continued. "But then again, I've never been sure that plane was connected with me or not.... Sure wish I had some indication I was being looked for ... if I'm still here on the 4th, I'll probably hear celebration from the lake. If so, I'll just take some extra clothes and make a do-or-die go for it ...."

Boomhower referred to the annual Fourth of July fireworks at the Lewey Lake Campsite, but thanks to more bad weather, the celebration was canceled for the first time in years.

While Boomhower fought to stay alive, the massive search for him combed the wilderness, grid by grid, less than 10 miles away. Each night, Boomhower's sister Judy spent the evening in her car at search headquarters at Wakely Dam, roughly 12 miles away from her missing brother. She urged rangers to continue looking.

"Am resting all day today .... Won't matter," Boomhower wrote on June 30. "No longer believe anyone will come. Survival is up to me ...." He felt constantly dizzy and weak, and hadn't written about food—insects, snails, edible plants—for more than a week. A day later, on July 1, his journal exhibited uncharacteristic anger and profanity: "Big rain most of yesterday ... Just waiting for a clear day so I can see the morning sun and go for broke. Lantern ran out last night. Not that it apparently did any good anyway. I wonder if anyone has died out here waiting, believing in that 'stay calm and help will arrive' bullshit."

Two days later he wrote: "Day 29 ... Lost Day 24 ... July 3 .... Well, I got my sunny day but it did me no good. What a laughably, if this were a laughing matter, short distance before I collapsed, and had to crawl; 12 steps, rest, 10 steps, rest, back to camp. I'm too weak to save myself ...

this is a good time to die but I can't imagine that . . . . All I can do is stay warm. Go dormant."

Boomhower scribbled the word HELP on his tent using a piece of charcoal. The next day he listened for the fireworks that never actually happened, and despaired at not having strength enough to even get out of his sleeping bag. "Nothing new or noteworthy," is all he wrote.

By then the search was over two weeks old, and his sister and other family members were circulating flyers with his picture and a list of his equipment.

On July 5—one day after the canceled Fourth celebrations— Boomhower wrote on the last page of his notebook: "Very difficult sleeping nights. Somewhat groggier than normal. Can't take ten steps now without stopping."

His journal continued on the pages and margins of his Adirondack Mountain Club guidebook: "Just what happened? I didn't bring enough food, ran out, and also encountered string of bad weather. Took [unreadable] trail, the only one [unreadable] seen on map to reach Lewey Lake Campsite. Phone home. Somehow got lost off that . . . [unreadable]. I'm surprised they haven't found me . . ."

Boomhower's gear lay in disarray around his campsite, and he had written a will and good-bye letters to his family. Even so, he still hadn't totally given up. Sometime during the second or third week of July, he tried to get out but never went far, and was possibly getting confused about how long he'd been lost.

"I am David Boomhower," he wrote. "I have been lost here 55 days. To save myself have gone down the brook . . . voices . . . receiving no cooperation. I can expect no assistance from anyone else. I guess it's a good time to die. The world has got to be such a place [unreadable] . . .

it is too far away from me. I am proud of the way I die . . . not frightened. Good-bye, Uncle Dave."

There was one more entry still—Boomhower's last. "Approx. Aug. 3 . . . . If you [unreadable] searching, go down the [unreadable] close to [unreadable]. P.S. Not likely to get far, violently ill from beaver fever [giardiasis]." If Boomhower's date was correct, he had been alive long after the search for him had ended.

Months later, the hunters discovered Boomhower's body facedown in the small brook less than 30 feet from his camp. He had seemingly slipped on a log and fallen into the creek bed, and was believed to have died from hypothermia or drowning.

In the years since, including 2005, Internet discussion forums—especially the Northeast-specific Views from the Top—have played host to lively discussions about Boomhower's fate and what went wrong. Comparisons to Chris McCandless have been frequent. McCandless—whose fate was described in Jon Krakauer's *Into the Wild*—died alone in the Alaskan wilderness, his body found four months later by a hunter. Perhaps Boomhower was after a similar experience, sucked into self-destructive behavior.

Others say that Boomhower didn't carry a good map, causing him to overlook or miss the fact that there is a ranger station at Wakely Dam, just 6 miles farther along the Northville-Placid Trail from the point where he diverged onto the Sucker Brook Trail. Others questioned Boomhower's motivations for keeping a journal and sitting in one place for more than a month.

Ultimately, speculation remains just that, and we are left with only what we know—that a man died alone in the woods.

"The story still boggles my mind," wrote one poster after visiting the area where Boomhower spent his final days. "The woods are real open and the brook is easy to follow. It should have been no more than a one- to two-hour walk from there to the road . . . . It was sobering to realize just how disoriented one can become through hunger and fatigue. What seems easy, and skills we take for granted under 'normal' conditions, become difficult and life-threatening in just a few hours or days."

12

WITHOUT A TRACE: THE DISAPPEARANCE OF THOMAS CARLETON

I then turned to go back, but, alas, had not the slightest idea of the
course I had traveled; and the sun now being down, and the high
trees blotting out everything but a little space of sky overhead, I was
utterly at a loss which way to go.

—J. T. Headley, *The Adirondack: Or, Life in the Woods* (1849)

It was Columbus Day Weekend of 1993, and as with most holiday
weekends in the Adirondacks, the mountains and trails were swarming
with people. Among the masses was Thomas Carleton, a forty-four-
year-old prison psychologist from Skaneateles, New York, in the Finger
Lakes region of the state. He was an experienced outdoorsman, and
when he walked into the woods alone that Saturday, October 9, no one
expected that he wouldn't walk back out.

Like so many headed into the High Peaks, Carleton parked his
car at the Adirondak Loj trailhead south of Lake Placid and hiked into
the mountains. But as he passed the sign demarcating the High Peaks
Wilderness Area boundary, he neglected to sign the trail register, and
hadn't left an itinerary with anyone back at home. His plan was to be
gone for two nights. The 5-foot-11-inch man with dark blond hair, blue

eyes, a thick mustache, and eyeglasses wore a red wool cap, maroon parka, olive-drab hiking pants, and possibly blue windbreaker pants. He carried a sleeping bag, but no tent or stove.

As Carleton trekked deeper into the forest, the weather took an ominous turn. The warm, sunny morning that had greeted hikers gave way to rain, and eventually snow later that night. A strong cold front passed through, dropping overnight temperatures into the teens. The sudden change caught many people, and no doubt Carleton, by surprise.

When he failed to return home on Monday, Columbus Day, his wife reported him missing. The forest rangers predictably went into action. Most searches are resolved within the first twelve hours of when the call comes in, they knew. It was a critical window of opportunity, and they hoped for a quick resolution of the search on the holiday weekend. But they wouldn't get so lucky.

Rangers had almost no information to go on. They located Carleton's car at the Loj trailhead, but this discovery offered little help. It did center the search over the High Peaks, but it was an enormous area to cover, encompassing 100 square miles—256 miles of marked trails, miles more of unmarked trails, and more than two dozen of New York State's highest peaks. Unlike other trailheads, such as the one for Giant of the Valley, the Loj trailhead could lead almost anywhere: to Indian Falls, up Street and Nye Mountains, Mount Jo, Algonquin Peak, Mount Colden, Lake Arnold, Mount Marcy, Phelps, over into Johns Brook Valley. Searchers essentially didn't know where to start looking.

They struck out on the trails hoping for a lucky hit, but they found no sign of Carleton. He had walked into the wilderness and vanished without a trace . . . or so it seemed.

At the Loj, rangers transformed the parking lot into Incident Command, Ground Zero for the search operation. In order to keep the Loj relatively uncrowded and manageable, the nearby North Elba Fire Department served as a staging grounds where searchers could drink hot coffee and eat breakfast in the morning, pick up bag lunches for the day, and then ride in buses to be dropped off at Incident Command.

The search for Thomas Carleton was about to balloon into one of the largest search and rescue operations in the history of the state. Like the search for David Boomhower three years before (chapter 11), and the search for Steven Thomas decades before that (chapter 8), it would be remembered as one of the Big Ones.

The Adirondacks have long made a habit of swallowing people whole. Sometimes the mountains reveal their secrets . . . eventually. But just as often we are left to wonder what really happened.

On August 10, 1951, E. F. Crumley, a pharmacist and former mayor of Fort Ann, disappeared while camping and fishing near Bear Brook between Raquette Lake and Blue Mountain. More than nine hundred people participated in the unsuccessful seventeen-day search for the sixty-nine-year-old man. Then, more than six years later, Frederick House, a hunter from Cicero, New York, who participated in the original search, spotted part of a rubber raincoat in the forest. Upon closer inspection, House also found a small metal box, a tie clasp, and five small bones. The next day he guided Orren Lanfear and his son, Jerry, to the site, where they also dug up fishing tackle, two medicine bottles and a vial, two pencils, buttons from a shirt, and an empty .32 Winchester special caliber shell. Paul Crumley, the missing man's son, identified the tie clasp as his father's, and noted that the man always carried an empty shell casing of that kind, which he used as a whistle in the woods. Finally, an old mystery was resolved.

A decade later, eight-year-old Douglass Legg walked away from the 13,000-acre estate near Newcomb where his family was staying and was never seen again. More than four hundred people volunteered in the search for the boy, which became the longest-running search and rescue operation in the Adirondacks at the time. In addition to the forest rangers, searchers included volunteers from local communities and from the Legg family's suburban Syracuse neighborhood, air force pilots, ninety-seven Marines, twenty-five army soldiers from Fort Drum, and twenty-nine mountain rescue specialists—part of the Mountain Rescue Association—flown in from California by the Legg family at a personal expense of more than $9,000. Despite the efforts, Douglass was never found.

Adirondack lore, especially from the 1950s onward, has long recounted the story of a man—Howard Gilroy—who rode his bicycle to the Santanoni Great Camp and then headed up to climb Santanoni and Panther peaks. He never returned, and his mysterious disappearance became something of a ghost story told 'round campfires late at night: Don't go up into the Santanoni range lest you stumble across his dead body. Then, sometime during the mid-1990s, someone did just that, when they discovered his body high in a drainage between the two mountains.

Not all such disappearances have ended so tragically. During the summer of 1942, a thirteen-year-old boy was discovered alive after spending five days in the woods, eating berries for sustenance and sleeping under the trees come nightfall. Twelve years later, a hunter trekked twenty miles off-trail through the forest after becoming separated from his group in a fog, eventually making his way out of the woods after spending an uncomfortable night without food or fire.

Around 7:00 p.m. on Wednesday night, October 13—less than three days after Carleton was reported missing—the telephone in the Benoit household rang in Queensbury in the southern Adirondacks. Peter Benoit, then president of Lower Adirondack Search and Rescue (LASAR), answered the phone.

LASAR had been founded a little less than three years earlier in the wake of the search for David Boomhower. Brothers Jim and Bill Cranker got the idea in August 1990 after participating in the Boomhower search as independent volunteers. Realizing that the southeastern Adirondacks hadn't sent a response to Boomhower's disappearance, they decided to try and organize a search and rescue team there. Using a fire department's bylaws as a model, and with five additional people on board to make seven total founding members, they placed a small ad in local newspapers calling for members. In November 1990, they signed LASAR's charter with twenty-five names. They met monthly in Warrensburg, initially in the basement of one member's home.

Two years later, in December 1992, Benoit was elected president. He had joined the team as a charter member after participating in the search for a family friend, Dr. David Clark. Clark was an ophthalmologist from Glens Falls who went missing on Buck Mountain and was eventually discovered dead from hypothermia. It gave Benoit a deep-seated passion to help others through a group like LASAR. Then, in October 1993, less than a year after he had been elected president, Benoit received the phone call from the forest rangers, asking him to activate LASAR for the Carleton search. "Get your team ready," a lieutenant told Benoit. They would be needed the next morning.

As Thursday dawned, Incident Command revealed a frenetic mix of forest rangers, Army 10th Mountain Division helicopter transport crews, volunteer search teams (including LASAR), and independent searchers from New York and Vermont. Amid the controlled chaos, Benoit's LASAR crew was instantly recognizable in their trademark blaze-orange hats, team patches, and Silva Ranger–model compasses hanging from their necks.

The LASAR contingent included seasoned veteran Joe "Coach" Iuliano, a physical education teacher and former wrestling coach from South Glens Falls. He was a muscular, dark-skinned Italian with a thick, black handlebar mustache who carried himself with an air of military authority. A helicopter pilot stepped through the crowd and paced up to Iuliano's imposing figure. "Have you had chopper training?" he asked. "Yeah," Iuliano responded flatly. "Good," the pilot countered. "Put your crew together and follow me."

Iuliano and four other LASAR members piled into the back of a pickup truck for the short ride to Lake Placid Airport, where a helicopter was waiting. As the search team prepared to load into the chopper, the pilot tossed each man a pair of instep crampons. "Here—you're going to need 'em," he said.

They piled into the chopper, its engine roared to life, and soon, they were speeding south over the treetops en route to 5,344-foot Mount Marcy. Approaching the mountain, the pilot's voice crackled over the radio: "I can't land on top of Marcy, but there's a plateau there below the summit. I'm going to come down as close as I can and then you're going to have to jump off!"

Slowly the chopper descended, but suddenly, the tops of the tallest spruce trees began to shatter, splintering as the rotor blades collided with them. The helicopter hovered over the shoulder of the mountain, unable to land, or even to approach close enough to unload its crew.

Pointing to a lone tree, the pilot yelled over his shoulder to Iuliano: "You're going to have to go and cut that tree down!"

Iuliano slid the chopper's door open, eased out onto the skid, and jumped to the ground far below, landing in deep snow. The rotor wash was terrible, causing an intense wind chill and stirring up a whiteout of blowing snow. Iuliano had little more than a knife with which to cut the tree down (carrying a folding saw became standard team practice after the search). The process seemed to take forever, with the chopper hovering overhead, but finally the tree fell.

The pilot carefully brought the helicopter in until one skid almost touched the mountainside. The search crew unloaded, crouching together in a group off the front left of the chopper in view of the pilot. The chopper then pulled back, turned, and floated away out of sight down a valley. They were left alone on Marcy's upper ramparts. The team brushed themselves clean of the blown snow and then mobilized. It was time for the real work to begin. It was time to find Carleton.

Carleton's wife and friends had told searchers that he had a tendency to hike older and more abandoned trails, rather than the newer and better-maintained ones. Iuliano's job was to lead his crew on a search that would scour the old trail network on Marcy. The group spread out in a line and advanced down through the forest, looking for clues—a footprint, eyeglasses. They contoured around the mountain through dense blowdown, methodically searching. But late that night they hiked out to the Loj under the power of headlamps, having found no sign of Thomas Carleton.

"We're going to need a lot of luck to find him," said ranger Tom Oatman, who was leading a crew elsewhere on Marcy that day. "It's a big country, and he didn't leave us many clues."

Elsewhere in the mammoth search area, scores of other teams were also looking for any hint of the missing man. One such team was led by Pat McGinn, a white-bearded high school science teacher from Warrensburg. His team was charged with searching the thick woods around the Rocky Falls Lean-to on the way to Indian Pass, a tight passageway through the mountains bounded by precipitous cliffs, including Wallface.

Rangers hypothesized that when the weather turned for the worst, Carleton may have tried to hike out through the pass to Newcomb. The pass was also the "place last seen"—search-speak for the last confirmed sighting of the missing man. A group of hikers told searchers that they thought they had seen Carleton at the lean-to over the Columbus Day weekend. The only problem was, other groups also reported having seen Carleton simultaneously at locations miles apart. Carleton, it seems, had become a ghost. He was everywhere and nowhere all at once.

Benoit remembers overhearing a conversation between forest rangers at Incident Command. Not a single footprint from Carleton had been found that indicated he had set foot on the trail beyond that lean-to, they said. In fact, except for hikers' sightings of Carleton on the trail, forest rangers and searchers found no trace of Carleton whatsoever.

Benoit, for his part, spent weeks on the Carleton search. With his own consulting business at the time, he had the flexibility to take the time off of work and devote himself to the search. Also, as the newly elected president of LASAR—a position he would hold for eight years—he felt compelled to provide on-site leadership for his team.

The search took him all throughout the High Peaks region. He was flown into the Lake Colden Interior Outpost, where he then searched Mount Marshall, using an altimeter to hike concentric circles of elevation contours around the mountain. He combed the shoulder of Wallface Mountain near the ponds above Scott's Clearing and Indian Pass Brook. And he remembers getting picked up by a helicopter near Calamity Pond, and on the way back to Lake Placid Airport, suddenly corkscrewing down into Indian Pass where the chopper touched down a skid in Scott's Clearing. Two searchers and a search dog burst out of the woods and charged into the already full chopper, forcing one crew member to clip into the helicopter and stand on the skid outside the open door for the flight back to Lake Placid.

Helicopters proved an invaluable resource on the search, inserting search teams throughout the High Peaks day after day, and then picking them up in clearings in the forest at day's end. Sometimes, if search teams couldn't reach a clearing to meet their helicopter, they'd be forced to spend the night out and resume searching the next morning.

By Friday, October 15, area newspapers, as with the Boomhower search, implored anyone who might have had contact with Carleton on the trails to contact DEC.

The search continued, and on Sunday, October 17, more than fifty searchers went back into the forest yet again, this time searching Mount Jo, Johns Brook Valley, and other areas. They checked off-trail locations where hikers go for views and overlooks, twenty-four separate lean-tos, campgrounds, and even outhouses.

"Any one pinprick on the map could be where he is," forest ranger Pete Fish told reporters. But that pinprick proved increasingly difficult to locate, assuming Carleton was even in the Adirondacks at all.

Like Benoit, Ron Konowitz spent nearly a month looking for Carleton. Konowitz was a teacher from Keene Valley and a longtime member of the region's search and rescue and outdoor communities.

He had rescued a stranded ice climber in Chouinard's Gully above Chapel Pond (chapter 7), and was a direct participant in an avalanche on Wright Peak (chapter 16). He was a consummate outdoorsman, highly experienced in backcountry skiing, ice climbing, and more or less any other outdoor pursuit in the Adirondacks. He knew the mountains better than almost anyone, including many of the forest rangers.

During the earliest days of the search for Carleton, Konowitz was flown into Colden's Interior Outpost, where he headed up trail-less peaks, including Cliff and Redfield, to retrieve the summit registers (which have since been removed) and record the names entered on dates from over the Columbus Day weekend. Perhaps he'd find Carleton's name, or if not, he would at least have the names of people who were in the woods at the same time. Forest rangers could then question them about whether they had seen the missing man.

Meanwhile, forest rangers pored over the trailhead registers. Carleton's name was absent from both the trailhead and summit registers, but rangers were still hopeful they'd be able to track down people who might have seen him. It was a monumental task. The registers were crammed full of names thanks to the popular holiday weekend, and in a time when the registers didn't offer a place to leave a phone number, locating and contacting people who signed the registers proved exceedingly difficult.

Like other searchers, Konowitz was flown into various insertion points throughout the High Peaks, where he looked high and low for Carleton, including in the ice caves of Indian Pass. But unlike many other searchers who eventually started to go home and return to their everyday lives, Konowitz stayed on when clues finally started to trickle in.

Search dogs followed Carleton's scent from the Loj parking lot past Marcy Dam—as expected, traveling off the main trail—and up TR Peak. "The places we were looking there were so thick, it's plausible someone could fall and break their leg and be there, and not be seen or found, or just get lost," Konowitz remembers. Then, a possible sighting of Carleton on top of Algonquin shifted the search westward, toward Indian Pass. Not long after that, the discovery of a newspaper in a fire ring near Lost Pond (in the vicinity of Wallface Ponds), and an account from someone who heard a tapping sound from high on the south side of the pass, further focused the search around Scott's Clearing and Indian Pass.

An Ithaca, New York, couple positively identified Carleton as the person they had met at the Scott's Dam Lean-to on the Indian Pass Trail. Carleton had told the couple that he planned to go through the pass and camp at the Wallface Lean-to. When they indicated that that was their plan as well, he seemed disappointed that he wouldn't have the lean-to all to himself. Around the same time the Ithaca couple offered their account, one of Carleton's coworkers came forward with the information that Carleton said he was going through the pass and then would "get off the trail."

He never did show up at the Wallface Lean-to, and no other hiker on the Indian Pass Trail that weekend reported having seen him. Maybe, some speculated, rather than travel to the Wallface Lean-to, Carleton had instead opted to take a more direct, but trail-less, route to Duck Hole, farther to the west via the Wallface Ponds and then Roaring Brook. Toward the end of the search, Konowitz remembers, everything was focused around Indian Pass up near MacNaughton Mountain, which separates Indian Pass and Wallface from Duck Hole. This is country so thick that even searchers lost some of their equipment in the course of looking for Carleton in the drainages on the side of the mountain.

As days turned into weeks, and hope of finding Carleton alive (or at all) continued to fade, rumors about his fate began to circulate in coffee shops, around town, and among the tight-knit search and rescue and outdoor communities. He was in Montreal with an illicit girlfriend. He was with Elvis. He had been abducted by Martians. He had faked his own disappearance and moved to another part of the country to start a new life. He was locked up in a Chicago psychiatric hospital after having a nervous breakdown and being institutionalized. Even the most plausible of these has never been substantiated.

And like the Boomhower disappearance, there was rampant speculation of a possible suicide. During the search forest rangers admitted that Carleton had probably been carrying a .357 Magnum pistol, ostensibly for protection against rabid animals. But Carleton's car was conspicuously devoid of dry clothes or anything else a hiker might leave there for the drive home. Even so, DEC considered Carleton's a simple case of a missing hiker. There is always such speculation (of suicides), noted Lieutenant Marone, but that rarely turns out to be the case.

Slowly, search crews—both those that had already gone home and those that remained—grew more and more discouraged. Winter was settling in to the High Peaks. The nights were cold, and the rugged terrain grew more inhospitable with each passing day.

Finally, on October 31, forest rangers officially suspended the search. It was more than three weeks after Carleton had started his trip, and more than nine thousand man-hours had been spent looking for him. Later that winter, in one final effort, rangers flew low over the search area in helicopters looking for coyote tracks in the snow emanating out from a central point in the forest. If such tracks were found, perhaps the animals were traveling to and from a carcass, and just maybe, that carcass would be Thomas Carleton.

Despite the promising clues that at last trickled in toward the end of the search, the effort to find Carleton ended without ever having found the man himself. But then, more than ten years later, a group of hikers stumbled across some old hiking and camping equipment on MacNaughton Mountain. A team of eight forest rangers went in to the wilderness to investigate, and while they didn't find Thomas Carleton, they did find the equipment the hikers mentioned, and they did confirm that the equipment belonged to Carleton.

So it seems that searchers were on the right track when they focused on MacNaughton in the last days of their search efforts back in 1993. But despite the promising find ten years later, no one knows what really happened to Thomas Carleton, and perhaps, no one ever will. Only time will tell whether the mountains will one day divulge their secrets and end one of the Adirondacks' longest-running unsolved mysteries, or whether Thomas Carleton will be remembered as the man who vanished without a trace . . . almost.

13

BLOWDOWN! A ROGUE MICROBURST DESTROYS FOREST
AND TRAPS HIKERS IN THE WILDERNESS

The quantities of fallen timber scattered throughout the forest in
every direction—huge trees lying across each other, presenting an
endless succession of barricades and impenetrable thickets—arrest
the traveler at every step.

—J. T. Headley, *The Adirondack: Or, Life in the Woods* (1849)

Fifty-year-old William Moskal Sr., his eighteen-year-old son, William
Jr., and nephew, eighteen-year-old Thomas Moroney, often camped in
the woods together. They'd pick a place and go hike to it. And in early
July 1995, their chosen destination was High Falls, a popular spot along
the Oswegatchie River surrounded by virgin, old-growth white pine
forests, tucked away in a remote corner of the Five Ponds Wilderness
west of Lows Lake and southwest of Cranberry Lake. If the trip went
well, they also had hopes of climbing 2,261-foot Cat Mountain, a short
side trip to the east off their out-and-back route.

On Friday, July 14, they started in the town of Wanakena, where
the Oswegatchie River empties into Cranberry Lake. They hiked
southeast, and then south, along the trail, skirting the end of Dead

Creek Flow, an arm of Cranberry Lake that juts out to the southwest. At a trail junction just below Glasby Pond, they turned southwest—turning east would have led them to Cat Mountain—and followed Glasby Creek downstream as it flowed between Roundtop and Threemile mountains en route to the Oswegatchie. They reached a section of wilderness known as The Plains, and turned south-southeast again, finally arriving at the High Falls Lean-to on the Oswegatchie River.

They set up their camp at the lean-to, with Moskal Sr. inside, and his son and nephew sleeping on opposite sides of the fire pit outside. Across the river, a group of Boy Scouts who had canoed into the wilderness made their camp. A larger group of young Canadians carrying Coleman stoves and bottles of red wine also made themselves comfortable in the woods near the High Falls Lean-to.

Moskal Sr. cooked a spaghetti dinner over the campfire and invited the Canadians to join his trio for dinner, if the Canadians were hungry. The Canucks obliged, and "devoured everything we had," Moskal Sr. says. The Canadians were famished from hiking double-digit trail miles that day with their heavy equipment and comfort items. Moskal Sr. invited them to share the lean-to, as well, but they declined that offer, camping instead down by the riverbank above the falls. Later that night, everyone went to bed.

In the predawn hours of Saturday, July 15, 1995, while Moskal Sr., his son and nephew, the Canadians, the Boy Scouts, and dozens of other hikers, campers, and canoeists slept in the Adirondack wilderness, a rogue storm boiled up over the night sky. Meteorologists called the storm a *derecho* (also known as a microburst), taken from the Spanish, meaning "direct" or "straight." It refers to the storm's winds, which blow in a straight line, as opposed to storms with twisting winds, like a hurricane or tornado. The term was first coined by Gustavus Hinrichs in 1888, though it wouldn't gain general acceptance until the 1980s, roughly a century later.

The rare storm system is notoriously difficult to predict, and particularly devastating. It is a big, fast-moving, long-lived storm, characterized by a line of intense thunderstorms and highly concentrated wind bursts that often exceed 100 miles per hour, marching through the atmosphere as if in file. It even generates additional storms ahead of itself, accelerating its own propagation well beyond ambient wind speeds, moving as a convective wave through the atmosphere. On the ground, the derecho is evidenced by separate but strikingly similar swaths of damage. Such storms are common in the midwestern United States, where they often spawn tornadoes. But in the East, such storms are infrequent. No matter. The derecho of July 15, 1995, was about to establish itself as possibly the largest in the recorded history of the eastern United States.

In the days leading up to that Saturday morning—especially July 13 and 14—the atmosphere in New York State was very moist and very unstable. The dew point hovered near 80 degrees. Temperatures in Albany, the state capital, reached 99 degrees. In the air above, there was moderately strong low-level wind shear (change in wind speed with altitude), but there were no strong fronts or other weather systems in the region.

Hundreds of miles away, over Ontario, Canada, a large group of thunderstorms moved to the northeast along a weak cold front. They probably generated a column of ascending warm air that provided the derecho with its initial energy source, scientists speculate. Once started, the derecho was able to feed itself, in essence acting independently of the atmosphere around it. As the thunderstorm complex grew, strengthening downdrafts created a squall line. All the pieces were falling into place for the formation of a full-fledged derecho.

Radar detected that the whole storm system tracked at 50 MPH. But mid-level winds were only 30 to 35 MPH. The storm system was moving faster than the atmospheric winds, indicating that it had become a convective wave. The beast was born.

At 2:00 a.m. on July 15, SELS, the Severe Storm Forecasting Center (now known as the Storm Prediction Center), warned of a possible derecho exiting Georgian Bay on Lake Huron. At 3:00 a.m., the Center added a warning that the derecho may hit New York State directly, and the National Lightning Detection Network showed a very heavy concentration of lightning associated with the storm. Around 4:30 a.m., the storm crossed Lake Ontario and moved within the range of Doppler radar weather stations at Rome and Bern, New York.

The radar image displayed a classic *bow echo*—a boomerang-shaped radar signature—130 miles long, with particularly intense wind and rain at its northern end, aimed directly at the northwestern Adirondacks. There, the wind speed shifted from near zero to more than 100 MPH in a span of less than 10 miles from the leading edge of the storm to its most intense core. The Center issued a severe storm warning, and cautioned that the storm could be potentially life-threatening.

Twenty minutes later, at 4:50 a.m., the northern end of the squall line was about 10 miles from the Lewis-St. Lawrence-Hamilton county lines. The storm was traveling at 50 MPH, and generated 3,500 lightning strikes per hour—roughly one per second. Observers reported that the lightning was so intense, the sky had a yellow glow. Winds gusted well over 100 MPH, and sustained winds exceeded 77 MPH, the maximum local

Mount Colden's Trap Dike.

Ken Martin leading a pitch on Chapel Pond Slab shortly before the climbers were avalanched down the face.

Ice climber on Positive Thinking
at Poke-o-Moonshine.

Chapel Pond Slab in
summer.

Forest rangers during a mock swift-water rescue on Chicken Coop Brook.

Collage of forest rangers during high-angle ice-rescue training.

Forest rangers using a helicopter and hoist to conduct ice-rescue training exercises.

A forest ranger guiding a litter down a vertical cliff face during the rescue of a rock climber.

Forest rangers during high-angle rescue training.

Members of Lower Adirondack Search and Rescue during cold-water and ice-rescue training.

The wreckage of Bill and Mary Black's airplane after their crash into the mountainside.

Gothics.

Ethan Marcello trekking across frozen Avalanche Lake before the storm's arrival.

The view out of Dalhaus and Marcello's lean-to the morning after the nor'easter.

Ethan Marcello fights through deep snow during the heart of the storm.

Cairn below summit of Haystack.

Doppler radar stations were set to measure. Violent downbursts from the intense line of thunderstorms began to blow down conifer forests in continuous bands.

Then, at 5:11 a.m., the leading edge of the bow echo entered the Oswegatchie drainage. In the next twelve minutes, it would flatten twelve to fifteen thousand acres of trees in the basin, or approximately 18 percent of the total area.

Early Saturday morning, Moskal Sr.'s group woke to the sound of heavy winds blowing through the forest. To the northwest, the sky exploded with flashes of lightning and crashes of thunder. "All of a sudden, we started hearing these thumps, thumps, thumps," he says. "It was actually the trees falling down . . . big trees in the woods." Moskal Jr. and Moroney were both camped in individual one-man bivy tents outside the lean-to. They were concerned. "I told them not to worry, that they'd be fine," Moskal Sr. remembers. As the senior adult, he didn't want to make anyone nervous, and gave the appearance of calm for the sake of the others. But Moskal Jr. and Moroney were too worried to stay outside the lean-to, and they clambered under its protective roof with Moskal Sr. It would prove to be a wise decision. Trees continued to fall all around them, and by the time the wind died down and the trees had at last stopped falling, both tents were crushed beneath large trunks, completely destroyed.

The Canadians, too, had abandoned their tents and gear and huddled in the lean-to with the others. They lost all their gear beneath the fallen trees, but thankfully, no one was injured.

As they all hunkered down in the lean-to, Moskal Jr. noticed that the roof was leaking. A large tree had fallen on the lean-to as well, and had punched a gaping hole in the roof. Moskal Jr. climbed up and stuffed a rain poncho over the hole to halt the leak and shield them all from the rain. "If it wasn't for the lean-to," Moskal Sr. says in retrospect, "we probably would have had a lot of injuries." In the area around the lean-to, massive trees lay fallen like weak matchsticks. The forest was entirely toppled over in the same direction—with the treetops pointed southeast.

Throughout the northwestern Adirondacks, the accounts from survivors were much the same. Alice Broberg, from the Onondaga Chapter of the Adirondack Mountain Club, was part of a canoe camping trip that weekend. The trip was meant to be a reprieve from an intense summer heat wave, but the forest was just as hot, and Mason Lake, on whose shoreline they were camped near Indian Lake, offered the only opportunity to cool off. Friday afternoon, Broberg paddled across the lake to a flat rock popular with swimmers, watched a pair of loons, and returned to camp.

It was clear that night, with the moon and bright stars filling the sky overhead. Tall trees stood all around, and the insects were graciously absent. Even at night it was too hot to sleep inside her sleeping bag, so she lay on top of her bag inside the tent. At 4:30 in the morning she woke to the calls of the loons. Outside the tent, she watched the moon disappear behind "white fluffy clouds." The treetops fluttered in a gentle breeze.

Suddenly, from the northwest, thunder and lightning exploded over a nearby mountain. Heavy rain and wind, and intense thunder and lightning, "hit all at once." She zipped up the open door of the tent, and ran to check on the group's gear and canoes. Wind and lightning lashed at the forest. Splintering trees broke all around her. As she cinched the cooking-gear bag closed, the top of a big hemlock came crashing down alongside her. She ran back to the tent and huddled under a beach towel, shivering, not from being soaking wet, but rather from the realization that her tent offered little protection.

She spent a terrifying hour in the tent, listening to the violent gusts of wind. When she at last emerged from her nylon sanctuary, the southeast shore of the lake was "a wall of uprooted tree root systems 10 to 20 feet tall."

At Jo Indian Island on Cranberry Lake, Noah Weber estimates that the storm lasted for about one and a half hours. The "night was lit up as if it were day," he recalled. The lake is "normally quite a placid lake, but that night its surface was covered with whitecaps crashing against the shore," he recounted. During the storm he heard the cracking of tree branches and the crashing of his group's aluminum canoes. When he paddled into town the next day, the power was out, and people told him he had been in a tornado.

At Lake Durant State Park, Nancy Dill remembered how "the thing came all at once." The wind came in waves, with pronounced lulls between each gust. Each front of wind was louder and more violent than the last. All the winds came out of the west, she recalled. When she peered out the half-open door of her tent, she saw trees "whipped around like in a hurricane." She was reminded of her mother's words from a life lived in the Midwest: "If it sounds like a freight train, that's a tornado!" Dill heard four distinctive "freight trains," with two minutes between each one. From her tent, she could hear nothing above the roar of the wind, not even trees snapping. But she could hear things—heavy things—falling around the tent. Dill instinctively put her arms up over her head. "Those moments were truly frightening," she said. At one point she realized that something was butted up against the door of the tent. It turned out to be a red maple, 14 inches in diameter, with one of its branches pinning down a corner of the tent. And then, "quite suddenly, it was all over and very quiet." Amazingly, the tent wasn't ripped or punctured. She wriggled out the front door. "Only then, as I looked around, did I realize the severity of what had taken place," she recalled. Whole trees were snapped in two or uprooted, and one car near the campsite was buried beneath a pair of trees.

Just as quickly as it came, the storm went—at least for the northwestern Adirondacks. But the derecho wasn't yet finished. At 5:36 a.m., the gust front crossed Raquette Lake. Nine minutes later, at 5:45 a.m., the leading edge of the storm crossed into Warren County in the southeastern Adirondacks. The storm had by then weakened, if only slightly, and a section of the bow echo east of Indian Lake had broken away from the main section, taking with it some of the storm's energy.

Between 6:30 and 7:30 a.m., the northern part of the storm crossed Lake George and then passed into Vermont, where it caused sporadic blowdowns. The southern part of the storm, meanwhile, passed over Albany, and then into Massachusetts and the Taconic mountains. At Albany International Airport, radar measured sustained winds over 50 MPH for a period of fifteen to twenty minutes, with a 73-MPH wind gust, the second highest ever recorded at that location. Lightning detection systems recorded 2,000 strikes per hour, with a five-minute rate of 3,000 strikes per hour.

Finally, the rogue microburst passed over Rhode Island and dissipated somewhere over the Atlantic Ocean. The storm lasted three hours—for the Adirondacks, at least—and left a swath of destruction seldom seen before, or since.

Later that Saturday morning, Moskal Sr. walked down to the

river to check on the Boy Scouts, camped on the opposite side. They were fine, they said, with no injuries, though they had lost some of their canoes and ended up tying logs together as makeshift rafts, floating out with their equipment over the next several days.

Back at the lean-to, a forest ranger appeared virtually out of nowhere—or at least out of the blowdown—and inquired about the status of everyone present. Convinced that they were all okay, he continued on his way to check on other campers in the woods, running over and under the mess of fallen trees "like a chipmunk," says Moskal Sr.

Faced with the day ahead of them, Moskal Jr. contemplated going up Cat Mountain, not yet realizing the extent of the devastation. "No," Moskal Sr. countered. "I think we should go back to the truck." The slow, tedious hike out took them two days. The trail was more or less gone, hidden beneath the blowdown. The trio weaved their way through the forest. Halfway back to their truck, darkness fell, and they made camp beneath a large, freshly fallen tree trunk, crammed into their one remaining tent and sharing their food and water.

Continuing on the next day, they stumbled into other dazed hikers and campers also caught by the storm. The whole massive group moved into a clearing and built a smoking fire, and placed sheets of aluminum on the ground to reflect light skyward toward aerial search teams. A helicopter came into view overhead, and made several trips to transport everyone out of the woods.

On the "outside," Moskal Sr. discovered that most of that region of the Adirondacks was without power. The local fire department was coincidentally hosting a field day at Star Lake High School, where the helicopter dropped off its loads of survivors. Kielbasa and other hot sandwiches were passed around to the campers. Moskal Sr. found a telephone repair man working on restoring service to the local communities, and Moskal convinced the man to patch him through to his wife to tell her they were okay.

Shortly after the storm, Moskal Sr. saw the yellow poncho his son had stuck in the roof of the lean-to published in a photograph taken from a helicopter flying above the area immediately after the storm. One month after the microburst, Moskal Sr. and Jr. canoed back in to the Five Ponds Wilderness along the Oswegatchie. They thought about going as far as High Falls to try and retrieve some of their gear, but decided it wasn't worth the effort. That next Christmas, Moskal Sr. received a GPS unit, in case he ever found himself in need of navigating through near-impenetrable blowdowns again. He and his son printed up T-shirts in honor of the storm and their experience. Now, they remember it as "the good old days," like veterans retelling a favorite war story.

"I didn't understand the whole scope of what was going on," Moskal Sr. says in hindsight. "All of a sudden these trees started to fall down. I could hear things going on in the woods . . . big kabooms . . . as the wind knocked the trees over."

From the DEC's perspective, first notification of the disaster came at 8:00 a.m. on Saturday, July 15, but the true extent of the storm's damage was not fully realized until midmorning, when reports came in from throughout the area. DEC initiated an immediate rescue response headquartered at the Star Lake firehouse, with assistance from the county fire coordinator, local fire and ambulance crews, New York State Police, highway departments, and local governments. Communication was all but impossible due to extensive power outages and phone service disruption, and the fact that all of DEC's radio repeaters—which relay signals from their radios throughout the mountains, except for the one on Whiteface Mountain—were also out of service.

Rescue efforts continued throughout the day and into the evening on Saturday, using two DEC helicopters and one from the National Guard in Rochester, New York, with plans to formally establish Incident Command at Star Lake at 7:30 a.m. on Sunday morning.

Sunday, July 16, brought much of the same, trying to locate people throughout the Five Ponds Wilderness, and evacuating them via helicopter, or with assistance on foot. Two rangers were dispatched to High Falls—the area hardest hit. While a triangular swath of the western Adirondacks was hit hard by the storm, a more concentrated nucleus just southwest of Cranberry Lake, and centered around High Falls, was literally obliterated. On day three of the rescue effort—Monday, July 17—the air rescue was suspended due to weather. By then, everyone was out of the woods except for a group of ten that was missing near Lake Lila. They were later located from the air, and found to actually be a group of six. Within two and a half hours of being spotted from the air, they were successfully evacuated from the forest.

In total, 61 people were rescued with ground support; another 31 were rescued via helicopter; and 114 people hiked out of the forest on their own.

Blowdowns from rogue storms like the 1995 derecho have happened before (1950) and since—most recently with Hurricane Floyd in 1999, which caused widespread blowdowns and eighteen new slides. That October, post-Floyd, a group of Middlebury College students, faculty, staff, and alumni hoped to summit all forty-six Adirondack High Peaks on the same day. The event was orchestrated by Jeff Philippe, community outreach coordinator for the college's Mountain Club, who got the idea from other colleges that have tried the same thing before.

St. Lawrence University has consistently been the most successful. Their event, known as Peak Weekend, started in 1983, and they try every year around the end of September or beginning of October. They succeeded in 1987, and in 2002 continued a streak of success that greeted the new millennium. Then, in 2005 they attempted yet again, this time in honor of the school's 150th anniversary, but only logged forty-three of the forty-six.

Middlebury planned its 1999 attempt to coincide with the celebration of the college's 200th anniversary. They called it the Bicentennial Summit Extravaganza, and tackled the challenge with bold ambition. Middlebury would attempt the forty-six Adirondack High Peaks, the five 4,000-foot mountains in Vermont, plus mountains throughout the world that would be attempted by students studying abroad. Over four hundred people participated in the event, but even before it started, Philippe realized they wouldn't succeed. In the Adirondacks, intense blowdown from Floyd blocked roads and trails, and ultimately prevented many teams from reaching their destinations, or in some cases, even the trailhead. But they did top out on Vermont's five 4,000-footers, plus thirty-six of the forty-six Adirondack High Peaks. Abroad, Middlebury had representation on roughly twenty summits and quasi-summits, including Mount Fuji in Japan, Mount Omul in Romania, Ben Nevis in Scotland, and on the Great Wall of China.

Early estimates of the 1995 microburst suggested that 126,000 acres of forest had moderate to severe damage. That number was later revised and increased to 143,000 acres, making the microburst the second most damaging windstorm on record for New York State. Longtime Adirondack residents compared it to the Great Blowdown of

1950—the most damaging windstorm on record—which badly damaged an incredible 424,000 acres of forest, including some 250,000 acres of forest preserve, with 25 to 100 percent blowdown.

In all, roughly 16 percent of the trees in the areas hit hardest by the storm were blown down. In the Five Ponds-Lows Lake area alone, the DEC estimates that over 50,000 trees fell, including a virgin timber stand atop Pine Ridge, one of the best-known old-growth remnants from the Adirondacks' pre-logging era. By September later that year, more than 600 miles of trail in the Five Ponds Wilderness were still inaccessible.

But despite the destruction, devastation, and loss in human terms—the storm claimed five lives, including four campers who were killed by falling trees, and caused up to $200 million in damage by one estimate—it wasn't an ecological disaster. The forest has lived on (even many of the toppled trees survived), and the Adirondacks remain as "forever wild" as ever.

14

MAYDAY IN THE SAWTOOTH MOUNTAINS

There are two critical points in every aerial flight—its beginning
and its end.

—*Alexander Graham Bell* (1906)

Around 11:30 a.m. on Wednesday, August 7, 1996, an Aerofab Lake
250 Renegade plane took off from the waters of Lake Champlain near
Burlington, Vermont. The Lake 250 is an amphibious plane, capable of
taking off and landing on both land and water. The six-person seaplane
manufactured by Laconia, New Hampshire–based Lake Aircraft is
more than 29 feet long, with a 38-foot wingspan. The Renegade's belly
provides its buoyancy on the water, with a shape like the deep V of a
boat's hull. Pontoons near the end of each wing provide balance. Its
single 250-horsepower engine is mounted on a pedestal that extends up
above the cockpit.

On board were then husband and wife, forty-four-year-old Bill
and thirty-eight-year-old Mary Black. Bill had earned his pilot's license
in 1971 while a student at the University of New Hampshire. Two years
later he earned his commercial pilot's license, and a year after that, his
instrument rating. Bill spent the summers preceding medical school

doing air taxi work for a Maryland-based outfit, running flights between eastern Maryland and Baltimore and Washington, D.C. He went on to become a family practice physician, but still flew an impressive 200 to 400 hours per year.

The Blacks spent Tuesday night in Burlington where they had been for two days with Bill's parents, who were starting a trip from Lake Champlain to the Great Lakes in their motorboat. Bill and Mary, for their part, were kicking off a weeklong summer vacation. As was their habit, it was an unstructured holiday, with no real plan for where to go and what to do. "We had the floatplane and clothes, but no agendas," Bill says. "It was my ideal summer vacation."

Bill had purchased the airplane the February before in California, ferried it home to Dublin, New Hampshire, and had spent the next six months earning his seaplane rating. The airplane was in perfect condition, he thought. One week before the long-awaited vacation with Mary, he "spent several afternoons . . . honing my newly acquired skills in varying conditions, no doubt irritating the inhabitants of the many lakes around where I lived with multiple landings and takeoffs." It was to be his first flying vacation, and he "wanted it to go off without a hitch."

And so on Wednesday morning, he and Mary took off from the waters near Burlington with a full tank of fuel—90 gallons—on what was turning into a warm August day. On a whim they turned west and flew toward the Adirondacks, which had tantalized the couple from their view across Lake Champlain in the days prior. "The only thing between the Adirondacks and heaven was a gentle blanket of haze," Bill remembered. It was to be his first return to the Adirondacks since his childhood. As they left Vermont behind, "I remember thinking how reassuring it was to be in an amphibious aircraft as we crossed over Lake

Champlain," Bill says. He and Mary meandered in their Renegade over the mountains, passing just north of Lake Placid. Then, around 1:30 p.m. in the afternoon, their plane disappeared from radar over mountainous terrain 10 miles to the south.

Every year, general aviation pilots—basically everyone except for commercial airline pilots and those for shipping outfits like UPS and FedEx—log more than 20 million hours of flight in planes across the United States. And also every year, thousands of those planes crash. In 1996, for example—the same year Bill and Mary Black disappeared from radar in their Lake 250 Renegade—there were more than 1,900 plane crashes, with 361 of them fatal. Even so, aviation had been getting safer year by year. In the twenty-year period from 1985 until 2004, the number of crashes had steadily dropped from more than 2,700 to 1,600.

The Adirondacks, however, have been a veritable Bermuda Triangle for pilots. Ever since the crash of American Airlines Flight 166 in 1934 (chapter 4), planes have been crashing, and disappearing, in the mountains, valleys, and lakes of the Adirondack North Country. For example, in the decade of the 1970s: In June 1972, four people survived the crash of their airplane on DeBar Mountain and were rescued alive; in November 1973, a plane missing for eleven months—since December 1972—was discovered deep in the woods near Ragged Lake. In March 1974, air force captain Robert Rumberg ejected from his F-106 plane, and despite searchers' locating the plane within hours, Rumberg remained missing, and was later found dead; a month later, in April 1974, rescuers found the pilot of a chemical spray plane alive in the Sentinel Range after crashing into the mountains. Then, two months after that, in June 1974, forty-five-year-old Lewis Morgan died when his twin-engine Beechcraft, en route from Watertown to Burlington, reported he was going "to hit a hill" and crashed in the Adirondack wilds southeast of Tahawus. Finally, in January 1979, three college students at the beginning of a ski vacation died near Lake Placid when their plane crashed; it wasn't discovered until months later.

With a full tank of fuel—enough for roughly five hours of continuous flight—Bill and Mary Black thought they'd fly over the Adirondacks, perhaps land on an inviting lake, take a quick swim, and then circle around and head up to Maine. After passing north of Lake Placid, Bill started a wide, slow, counterclockwise turn that would bring them over the Saranac Chain of Lakes and toward the 3,700-foot Sawtooth Mountain Range south of Saranac Lake. The remote range runs in a west-to-northeast arc just northwest of the High Peaks, northeast of the Seward Range, and southeast of the Ampersand Mountains, with a number of creeks and streams that tumble out of the Range and flow northward into the Saranac River and Saranac Chain of Lakes.

Bill scouted for potential landing sites—suitable lakes—from the air. As was his practice, he would look for a lake of sufficient size, without too much traffic, and with the proper winds. Then, he would descend and do a low-altitude flyover above the lake, scouting more closely for an approach direction for landing, and ideally, looking for a sandy beach on a lee shore. If things looked good, he could then circle around and come in for a landing.

But that Wednesday he was having a hard time finding a candidate lake. Finally, he found one at the base of the Sawtooth Range. He flew over Oseetah Lake, just south of the village of Saranac Lake, and descended to about 600 feet above the surface of Pine Pond, which sits just southwest of Oseetah. He decided that conditions weren't right. The winds were gusty, and the shoreline was a little too rocky for his taste. He initiated a circular climb to a higher altitude. There was one final lake—Ampersand Lake—that he wanted to try, over a ridgeline to the southwest.

He flew up the valley, slowly gaining altitude to crest the ridge and reach the lake on its other side. "The Ampersand Mountains and the Sawtooth Mountains loomed off our nose, and my goal was to traverse one of the passes between these to make our way over to Ampersand Lake," he recounted. It was a flight like on any other day, and nothing seemed out of the ordinary. "I only worried about which mountain pass to choose," he says.

The valley floor rose up beneath the Blacks faster than their plane climbed, but that wasn't unusual. "Flying a seaplane, you get used to flying fairly close to the trees," Bill explains. He at last reached a point, however, where he wanted more altitude. He pushed the throttle and the variable prop angle forward, checked his mixture (the balance of air and fuel that provides for the best engine performance at a given altitude), and started what he thought was a climb. But in reality, "not a whole lot happened," he says. "[The engine] didn't make the right sort of noise." Normally, the prop would have spun faster, but it didn't, even though gauges on the instrument panel indicated a change in engine pressure.

Bill's stomach tightened as he tried to make sense of how his plane was reacting. He was initially focused on the motor and his gauges, flying deeper into the valley between the mountains. "At some point I decided I had spent too much time looking at the motor and not enough time looking outside, and I was flying up into a tighter area than I wanted," he remembers. He started a turn to the left, with the plane's power at full. As the nose of the plane came around, he was forced to tighten his turn to avoid an area where the mountain "bulged out."

Then he realized the plane was starting to stall, with rising terrain on three sides. At that point, "I was close enough to the ground that I didn't dare take my eyes and attention into the cockpit," he later told a Federal Aviation Administration safety inspector. The yoke began to feel mushy, he said. Then the plane's stall warning horn sounded. Bill adjusted the throttle and lowered the nose of the plane, trying to recover from the stall, but again the warning horn sounded. The plane went into "a fairly severe pre-stall buffet," he says. Halfway through the turn, Bill realized he wasn't going to be able to make it without climbing higher . . . something that was impossible to do with the airplane about to stall.

"It was at that point that I realized I did not want to stall and crash," Bill says. "It was preferable to me at that point to put the nose down and do a controlled entry into the tree canopy. [I didn't want to] continue what I considered to be a wasted effort trying to salvage the turn. I turned to my wife and said, 'Mary, I am very sorry, but we've got to put the airplane down right here.' "

Bill felt terribly apologetic to his wife for "putting her through it." Yet, he never felt they were in mortal danger. "It was odd . . . at the time, I was completely and utterly confident that we would survive this," he says. "But at the same time I knew it was going to be rough." Bill credits his confidence to his training as a young pilot, when he flew under the tutelage of an air force instructor and "regular son of a bitch." "I thought he was a jerk, but thank God he was," Bill says. "He required me to repeat emergency procedures so routinely . . . that when it came time to make the 'go–no go' decision in the air, it was very natural. It was something I was ready to make, and I knew what I had to do. There was no ambiguity at that point."

Quickly running out of both territory and altitude, and with "nothing responding," the Blacks' Lake airplane entered the tree canopy going 93 miles per hour, roughly 100 feet above the mountainside. Just before entering the trees, Bill reached down and turned off the master switch. With several hours' worth of fuel left, he didn't want to go up in a blazing fireball on the mountainside. At the last moment, rather than pulling up to stall into the tree canopy, he instead pushed the nose of the plane down to land in "a more favorable area." The last thing he remembered was the sound of the leaves and branches brushing the wings, and thinking to himself, "Well, there goes the paint job!"

The impact with the trees tore off one wing and spun the plane 180 degrees, so that it slammed into the mountain essentially going backwards, hitting the north side of Sawtooth #1 near Cold Brook. The reinforced belly of the plane—strengthened for water landings—survived the impact with the trees, protecting Bill and Mary.

Sometime between the moment when they first entered the trees and when they struck the mountain, Bill and Mary both blacked out. They regained consciousness around the same time, though neither knows for sure how long they were out. Remarkably, they were both in relatively good shape. Mary had a cut on her forehead that bled badly for a time, but was mostly superficial. Bill was worse off, with several broken ribs that made it difficult to breathe. "We were both somewhat pleased to see that we'd survived," Bill says today. "She looked like hell because of the blood coming down her forehead, but she was actually in pretty good shape."

The smell of fuel motivated them both to get out of the plane. Bill and Mary climbed out of a gaping hole in the top of the airplane where the engine and its pedestal used to be. The couple started walking downhill in hopes of following a stream out of the woods and back to

Pine Pond, but after 200 yards, Bill realized he couldn't continue with his broken ribs. They climbed back up to a relatively flat area sheltered in the trees away from the airplane and assessed their situation. The forest there was so thick that just 50 feet from the plane, they lost site of the wreckage.

Mary returned to the wrecked plane and retrieved what she could—basically, their bags. Bill was frustrated and inwardly angry that he was virtually incapacitated by his ribs and couldn't do anything. Despite still having their bags, the Blacks had no food, water, signal flares, or backup communication with which to call for help. Mary returned again to the plane, this time with instructions from Bill on how to send out a mayday. She gathered their position coordinates from the plane's GPS system, tuned the transponder, and then set the communication radios to 121.5 megahertz, the civilian aircraft emergency frequency. Mary started the distress call, but the couple soon realized that they were actually transmitting the coordinates of Saranac Lake Airport, their last GPS waypoint. Not wanting to create confusion for rescuers, they abandoned the distress signal.

Three hours had passed since they crashed, and they hadn't heard any sign of rescuers on their way. The couple was unsure which ridge they were on, and so Mary climbed uphill, hoping for a better view. Half an hour later she returned with little to report.

The couple decided to separate. Bill would stay where he was while Mary would descend the mountain in search of help. She was reading the book, *Reviving Ophelia*—"a great, big, fat thing," Bill remembers. They agreed that she would tear out pages from the book and stick them on the branches of hemlocks and other trees as she hiked through the forest. If she found help, rescuers could backtrack to Bill, and if rescuers found Bill first, they could follow Mary's "bread crumbs" and locate her. "I tried to give her a Stephen King novel I was sick of at the time," he says. "But she said, 'I'm going to take my *Reviving Ophelia*.' "

Just before they temporarily parted ways, Bill asked Mary to return to the plane and ensure that the Emergency Locator Transmitter (ELT) was activated. The ELT sends out an electronic distress signal that rescue teams can track to the crash location. It was located directly behind the pilot's seat, but had broken away during the crash. Not knowing what to look for, Mary couldn't tell whether it had activated or not, and the couple had no idea whether anyone would be able to find them.

And so Mary set off downhill into the woods with a sweater and their chart, while Bill made himself as comfortable as he could. "It was difficult for both of us to find a way to say good-bye without having it sound too final," he recalled. "I listened to the sound of her footsteps fade too quickly into silence."

Bill covered himself with a beach blanket to shield his body, and his open cuts, from the voracious blackflies. He prayed for Mary's safety. With little more than his toiletry kit, "I just sat there and made myself comfortable . . . . I kept myself busy . . . looking into the trees and flossing my teeth . . . that's all I could do."

At the DEC offices in Ray Brook, forest rangers received a call that a plane had gone down, and sent out an aircraft to try and locate the source of the ELT signal. There was "some guy in the woods," ranger Robert Marrone recalls, "but we had no clue where he was." Bill, in fact, was at around 2,900 feet on the north side of Sawtooth #1.

Late that night, long after the batteries in Bill's flashlight had died out, he started hearing the drone of an airplane in the skies somewhere overhead, "around the treetops, flying what sounded to be a search pattern." Bill had heard planes all day, but this one was different; a single-engine aircraft that sounded like a Cessna, possibly a model 172. "It was late that night or early the next morning . . . . I could hear someone flying a [grid] pattern back and forth, and that was the most reassuring thing I had heard and it was just wonderful."

Early the next morning Bill waited patiently for the fog to burn off, which it finally did around 9:30 a.m. Then, close to 10:30 a.m., he heard the sound of a helicopter approaching. Forest rangers had located the ELT signal and were homing in on Bill's location. Soon, the chopper appeared overhead, "so close that the woods filled with the sweet smell of jet exhaust," Bill said. He hobbled into a small clearing and waved his arms as best he could. Forest ranger Gary Hodgson rappelled down out of the helicopter to the crash site, wearing hand-sewn moccasins he had made himself, "looking like Daniel Boone," Bill recalls.

Hodgson and the helicopter crew alike—pilot Dennis Miller and forest ranger Fred Larow—were surprised to see anyone alive. Hodgson had never seen anyone survive a crash as catastrophic-looking as that one, he told Bill. The veteran ranger cut down two smaller trees to clear a wider opening in the forest, and the helicopter sent down a "basket" from its winch. Hodgson fitted Bill into a harness, and the men were hoisted into the helicopter.

Around the exact same time, Mary had also been rescued. The previous night she had followed a streambed—Cold Brook—and spent the night in the forest. In the morning, she resumed her march to civilization and stumbled across a father and his two boys fishing where Cold Brook empties into the Saranac River, west of Oseetah Lake. Mary came across the children first, "looking like death warmed over with all the crusty blood on her," Bill says. The children ran to get their father, who realized that the woman needed help. They shuttled her across the lake in their motorboat to his parents' summer home on the Saranac River, off Kiwasa Road. Then they took her to the Adirondack Medical Center at Saranac Lake, where she received treatment for her injuries and called the State Police.

At the time, Ranger Marrone was confused. "I get a call on the radio from [forest ranger Fred Larow in] the helicopter, saying they've found the plane back in off of Sawtooth. Then, as I'm talking, I answered the phone—a woman who was in a plane crash was out on Route 3," he recalls. "I'm thinking, 'Wait a minute . . . there must be two different plane crashes here. There's no way she could be on Route 3, and the plane be way back in on Sawtooth at the same time. What the hell's going on?' "

But it was Mary. She had made it out, right around the same time that Bill was being flown to the same hospital.

Bill spent two nights in the hospital, and another six weeks nursing his broken ribs back to health. Not long after, he went back to flying, but he didn't get another Lake. "I went back to the airplane that I trusted absolutely implicitly," he says, "which was a Bonanza," one of the most respected high-performance single-engine airplanes around.

In 2000, Bill and Mary divorced, and Bill has since remarried and moved to South Carolina. In 2004 he sold his airplane, and he has given up flying, at least with him in the pilot's seat. "I was flying less and less," he says. "And I just feel that that's more dangerous than it is sensible.

"It was an unfortunate experience, but it worked out relatively well," he says of the crash. "To this day I don't really understand why that thing [the Lake] refused to climb and what went wrong . . . the FAA tried to find out . . . but there wasn't enough left [of the airplane] to make testing possible."

15

TRAPPED: RISING WATERS AND NO SAFE WAY OUT

Awfully savage and wild are the mountains that enclose this placid sheet of water.

—J. T. Headley, *The Adirondack: Or, Life in the Woods*, (1849)

Climbing [the Adirondack peaks more than 4,000 feet high] in winter was a different proposition. Adirondack villages generally battened the hatches with the first hint of snow, and paid scant attention to the icy High Peaks, beyond admiring them from a good safe distance.

—*The Adirondack Forty-Sixers* (1958)

In early January 1998, four college students from SUNY Geneseo in western New York State got the urge to go snowshoeing. The four friends—twenty-five-year-old Chris Baldyga, twenty-one-year-old Matt Baker, twenty-two-year-old James McCaughey, and nineteen-year-old Ian Thomas—planned a two-night camping trip in the High Peaks. Starting from the Upper Works trailhead to the southwest, they hiked north past Flowed Lands to the McMarten Lean-to on the south side of the Opalescent River, just before it flows into the waters that connected Flowed Lands with Lake Colden. It was the only lean-to on the south side of the river, though there were several other shelters on the northern banks.

They started their trip on Sunday, January 4. The days leading up to the trip had been very cold, and the ground was covered in several feet of snow. When they started their trip, however, it suddenly got very warm. Then it started to rain. "We saw a lot of things melting," McCaughey recalls. The four young men snowshoed around, and on Tuesday, did a day trip up Mount Colden. From the summit they saw nothing save for the clouds and the rain. On their return to the lean-to, they crossed over a swinging bridge that spans the Opalescent River. "We didn't see anything unusual at that point," says McCaughey.

It was early afternoon, and although they had originally planned to stay for one more night, they opted to hike out early and get back to their cars that evening. They regrouped at the lean-to, sorting their packs and changing into dryer clothes. McCaughey was in the midst of changing— wearing just his socks and long polypropylene tops and bottoms—when he heard the gurgling sound of flowing water. He peered around the corner of the lean-to and saw water in all directions, flowing right toward them, coming up fast enough for them to watch it advance.

"There's water coming!" McCaughey yelled. They quickly gathered their gear scattered about outside the lean-to and threw it into the shelter. Then, three of them—McCaughey, Thomas, and Baker— moved to higher ground. McCaughey, who got caught in the midst of his wardrobe change, had just enough time to put on his boots and escape the water's advance. The others were fully dressed.

With 5 or 6 feet of snow on the ground, the height of the snow surface was higher than the floor of the lean-to, and as the water swirled around the structure, the lean-to filled like a bathtub. "Whatever this is, it will pass," the trio thought from their stance on marginally higher ground in front of the lean-to. "It'll cut a channel and drain out." Baldyga, meanwhile, had clambered up onto the higher beams of the lean-to to escape the water. Now, the divided group found themselves cut off from one another.

When the three men stepped away from the lean-to with Baldyga still inside, they didn't have a plan, and didn't expect to need one. But with the rising water quickly pushing them farther away from their friend, they attempted a quick conversation before communication was no longer possible. They knew there was the Interior Outpost at Lake Colden, and had seen smoke coming from its chimney earlier in their trip, so they knew it was manned. The four men decided that the three not in the lean-to—McCaughey, Thomas, and Baker—would go to the cabin and get help for Baldyga. By then, he was perched on the roof of the lean-to. "I'll be fine," he told his friends. "Go get help."

They didn't know it, but they were in the midst of the beginnings of an ice storm and flood event that would go down as one of the worst in the history of the northeastern United States and southeastern Canada. An unusually warm and moist tropical air mass dropped a record 2 to 6 inches of rain. But cold, below-freezing temperatures at the surface near ground level caused the rain to freeze on contact, producing ice accumulations 3 to 4 inches thick on trees and most everything else throughout the Adirondacks. To compound the situation, the rain, when it didn't freeze, combined with a rapidly melting snowpack to cause record flooding, which the men were now experiencing firsthand.

The three men left Baldyga behind at the island of a lean-to and headed west. It was tough going. The water had turned the 5-plus feet of snow into "bottomless slush," says McCaughey. It was exceedingly difficult to walk through, and wet underneath the surface. Almost immediately, the trio became soaking wet and freezing cold. "We realized that we needed to get out of the water," McCaughey continues.

They reached a point in the forest where they could see north to the Opalescent River. It looked completely covered in thick snow. Though water flowed around the men, it appeared that the water remained below the snow surface in the river channel near the Opalescent itself.

The Opalescent River drains mighty Mount Marcy, the state's tallest peak, collecting the accumulated runoff of the mountain's northern and northwestern flanks. As it then flows south between Marcy and Mount Colden, it is joined by Feldspar Brook, which drains the mountain's western and southwestern flanks, and whose highest point is Lake Tear of the Clouds, the source of the Hudson River. Then Uphill Brook joins the Opalescent, adding still more runoff from the mountain's southern flank. The river then tumbles due west en route to Lake Colden and Flowed Lands. But on this particular day, somewhere just before it reached that destination, an ice jam formed, causing the massive amount of rain and snowmelt to back up and flood the surrounding forest.

"We were looking, and there was nowhere to stand," McCaughey remembers. "But we had to move." They decided to try and cross the river, hoping it was firm enough in the middle to stand on without someone breaking through. It was a risky decision, but they felt they had little choice. Before they could tackle the main river, however, they first had to cross a smaller, narrow, shallow-looking rivulet right in front of where they stood. The channel of water only looked to be 1 or 2 feet deep.

McCaughey was the unlucky first to attempt the crossing. He took a step and plunged into bottomless icy water, submerged fully over his head. With a burst of adrenaline, he kicked and swam his way to the surface, but his boots were long gone, sucked away by the current. He made it to the other side of the channel and pulled himself ashore. "I was pretty shaken up," he remembers. "I turned back and saw [Ian and Matt] looking quite white in the face, having watched me disappear into the freezing water."

Now between the first channel and the main river, McCaughey attempted to cross the Opalescent itself, while the other two looked on in case he plunged in again. "Very carefully and gingerly, I stepped out onto the river," he says. "It felt like solid enough snow, so I very tentatively crawled out across it." Miraculously, he made it across without falling in again. Safely on the opposite bank, he turned and waved to his companions.

On the north bank of the Opalescent is the main trail that would lead McCaughey to the Interior Outpost. And fortunately, at least at that point, it had been packed down by other snowshoers. Still, he was wearing only socks, and wet ones at that, and his feet were frozen. Worried about frostbite, McCaughey knew that "the best thing to do was get there [the Outpost] as quickly as I could." So he ran down the trail, and remembers a strange mix of emotions, "being really afraid—wondering what was going to happen—and also being amused that I was running down the trail in my underwear and socks."

From the north bank of the Opalescent, the trail heads west over the Lake Colden Dam, and then turns north as it goes up and over a rise and back down to the Beaver Point Lean-to on Lake Colden. There, the lake lies straight ahead, and the trail swings to the left. When the men had passed that point earlier in their journey during a side trip to Avalanche Lake and Pass, Lake Colden was still frozen. And despite the current conditions, it still looked as if it might be possible to walk across, which would have been the most direct route from where McCaughey stood to the Outpost. But "having had the experience I just had with water," he says, "I wasn't going to try it."

He tried to go left along the trail, but now the snow was longer packed down, and his legs started post-holing, punching down into the snow. He couldn't feel anything, and it was very slow going. That's when he started yelling for help.

Lake Colden Interior Outpost caretaker Mike Sheridan was hunkered down in the cabin. It was a "really rainy, gnarly day," he remembers. To keep himself busy, he had stepped outside to do some routine maintenance, clearing the helipad near the cabin.

McCaughey had resorted to crawling on his knees and elbows to prevent him from sinking into the snow. Each time he encountered a clearing toward the lake, he yelled, "Hello! Hello!" Sheridan heard him. "The more I heard, the more I realized it was a frantic call for help," he says. Looking up toward the Beaver Point Lean-to, he saw a figure fighting through the snow.

"The lean-to's been flooded. Three of my friends are stuck back there—and I'm crawling down the trail in my underwear," McCaughey called out.

"Well, continue to make your way toward the cabin," Sheridan responded. And so McCaughey did.

As McCaughey got closer to the cabin, Sheridan met him with an extra pair of snowshoes.

"There's an ice jam and flooding at the lean-to," McCaughey explained, "and some of them made a run for it, but one person was unable to get out."

Sheridan and McCaughey returned to the cabin, where Sheridan radioed DEC Dispatch and alerted them to what was happening. Forest rangers asked Sheridan to go out and assess the situation. He grabbed his gear and headed out right away, leaving McCaughey alone in the cabin. It was late afternoon. "I was there by the fire with my feet up," he says. "They started to thaw out, and I realized that they were still going to be feet and I was going to be okay. But of course, sitting there safe in the warm cabin, I was very worried about the other guys."

Not long after McCaughey had crossed the main channel of the Opalescent, the ground on which Baker and Thomas stood started to vanish and "turn into mush." It was impossible to stay at their location, so they decided to try and follow McCaughey. They moved upstream looking for a place to cross, and waded through the smaller channel, in up to their shoulders. Then, while crossing the main channel, one of them broke through and had to get pulled out by his partner. Finally across the river, they started hiking the trail to the cabin.

Sheridan, when he struck out from the cabin, was unable to go straight across the lake. There was too much water. He took the trail instead, where he met Baker and Thomas on their way to the Outpost. "They were soaking wet," Sheridan recalls, who sent the pair on to the cabin and continued on his way to check on Baldyga at the lean-to.

"Crossing the Opalescent was sketchy," Sheridan remembers. "It was a raging torrent." At the swinging bridge, the narrow bridge walkway itself was covered in 3 feet of snow, and below, a "huge wave train" threatened. Sheridan couldn't get to the lean-to, despite his snowshoes, because he post-holed up to his thighs in water. "This huge area was like a giant slushy," he says. "It looked like snow, but it wasn't." It was getting dark and foggy. Finally, Sheridan got close enough to the lean-to to make voice contact with Baldyga. They shouted to one another across 50 feet of water.

Back at the cabin, McCaughey, Baker, and Thomas were reunited, and traded stories and wondered about their friend. Sheridan had left a radio on in the cabin so the men could monitor his conversations with rangers. "We were very happy to hear that he [Sheridan] reported that 'the subject [Chris] tells me he is comfortable and dry and will be sleeping on the roof of the lean-to, and to meet him in the morning.' " Baldyga had stamped and carved out a place for himself in the 4 feet of snow that sat on the lean-to's roof. Before climbing up onto his perch, he even thought to grab all of their wallets and driver's licenses and credit cards, in addition to dry clothes and food and water.

Overnight, Sheridan returned several times to check on Baldyga. "The rest of us had a comfortable evening in the cabin, listening to the radio and worrying about him," McCaughey says. "And feeling really bad that we were warm and cozy and he was stranded out there. Though we couldn't have really done anything about it."

Early the next morning—around 4:30 or 5:00 a.m.—the water had receded slightly, and Sheridan was able to get close enough to throw a line and a life preserver to Baldyga, who donned the life vest and tied in to the rope. Then Sheridan nervously belayed him through a swift current of slush and snow underlain by 3 feet of water. By midmorning, Sheridan and Baldyga had arrived safely back at the cabin.

Soon after, "the cavalry—a bunch of rangers—arrived on snowmobiles to take us out from there," McCaughey says. Rangers also brought warm, dry clothes for the men to change into. With the men deposited at the Loj near Lake Placid, a ranger drove Baldyga and

McCaughey to their cars at Upper Works. Then the two men drove back around to the Loj, picked up their friends, and that night drove home, just missing the worst of the ice storm.

The ice storm ended up damaging 18 million acres of forest throughout New York, Vermont, New Hampshire, and Maine. In Essex, Franklin, and Clinton counties of New York—in the heart of the Adirondack Park—rangers reported extensive damage. The crippling weight of the ice ravaged trees and left a lingering threat to hikers from falling ice, trees, and branches. On the Black River in the western Adirondacks, the heavy rains and melting snow caused record flood levels. The river crested at 16 feet in Watertown on January 10, the highest recorded flood on the river since 1869, and significantly above the 100-year floodplain. On that same day, then President Clinton declared counties throughout the Adirondacks as major disaster areas. The storm caused an estimated half a billion dollars in damage, and more than 3 million people in four U.S. states and two Canadian provinces were without electricity. Some communities were without power for as many as twenty-three days. In Maine, 80 percent of the state's population lost electricity service, many for more than two weeks.

"It didn't occur to us that there would be a flood and an ice jam near the lean-to," McCaughey says in retrospect. "That cabin and caretaker being there saved our lives." Sheridan adds: "Had they fallen through [and not been able to get back out of] the river, it would have been a nasty, terrible death. It was a snowy year, and their saving grace was the outpost. If they [had] had to hike out six miles, who knows what would have happened? That outpost saves lives."

Ironically, in March of that same year, just two months after the young men's misadventure, the Interior Outpost burned down due to a chimney fire. A 1985 DEC mandate restricted man-made structures in wilderness areas, and a debate raged over whether or not to rebuild the outpost. Due in part to a letter from McCaughey—sent in February after his ordeal, but before the cabin burned down—DEC, in July 1998, amended its mandate to permit the rebuilding of the outpost, and that fall, the Lake Colden Interior Outpost stood once again.

"If the outpost were not there, I would certainly be writing a different story, or not writing at all," McCaughey wrote in his letter to the DEC's Region 5 regional director, Stuart Buchanan. "I have thought many times about the course of events if certain situations were different—and I think most about what would have happened if the outpost was not there or if it were not manned . . . . I can't imagine how we would have helped our friend on the roof . . . . The 5-mile hike to Upper Works would not have been good in the snow, in the dark, in underwear and socks. I honestly can't imagine making that . . . . As I look back on the event, I remember the water, the cold, and feeling scared and helpless in the middle of it all. I remember also the network of support that came as a direct result of the presence and operation of the Lake Colden Outpost. My life and well-being, and that of my friends, was protected by the continued operation of the Outpost. I cannot express enough my gratitude . . . ."

Looking back, McCaughey can't help but remark at the timing of events—of the weather shifting from wintry cold to unseasonably warm and rainy, to one of the worst ice storms in the region's history. The rain prompted them to change their plans. They'd had enough of it. "Why stay another night when we could hike out today?" they had thought. Their decision to leave the forest then became a matter of incredibly unfortunate timing. "If we had been at that lean-to twenty minutes earlier, we probably would have hiked out and never known about the ice jam and flooding that came," McCaughey says. "And if [the ice jam and flooding] had happened earlier, we wouldn't have come down as far as we did and would have stayed on higher ground [away from the flood]. It hit us at the worst possible time . . . . From now on we'll be very wary of streams and floodplains when we camp."

16

AVALANCHE!

The anecdotal evidence suggests that Adirondack avalanches represent
more of a threat than winter adventurers realize . . . .

—James Vermeulen, "Slide Rules," *Adirondack Life* (1997)

I never thought I'd see a death in the High Peaks from an avalanche.

—Peter Benoit, former president, Lower Adirondack Search and Rescue

On Saturday, February 19, 2000—a beautiful winter day with clear, blue
skies and temperatures in the 20s—six friends left the Adirondak Loj
parking lot bound for Wright Peak. Their plan was to ski to Marcy Dam
and then head off-trail toward the base of Wright. During the previous
summer, torrential rains from Hurricane Floyd had caused a number of
landslides throughout the Adirondacks, forming new slides in the High
Peaks. A side-by-side pair on Wright Peak—a taller, narrower slide on
skier's left, and a shorter, wider slide on skier's right—were among them,
and the sextet of backcountry skiers planned to ski them both.

At forty-five years old, Ron Konowitz was the eldest member of
the group, and the most experienced. A consummate outdoorsman, he
loved the woods, and he took great joy in hiking, paddling, and rock and

ice climbing. And he especially loved to ski. Konowitz even became the first person to ski all forty-six of the High Peaks, a feat he accomplished for no other reason than his own personal satisfaction. He had also logged a twenty-plus-year history of doing search and rescue volunteer work throughout the Adirondacks.

That February day, he was joined by his twenty-nine-year-old wife, Lauren, who worked as a physician's assistant in operating rooms at Lake Placid Hospital. Less than a year earlier, in August of 1999, the couple had been married on the summit of Algonquin Peak, which neighbors Wright as part of the MacIntyre Range. Their dog, Otis, acted as the best man.

At the Loj parking lot, the couple and their dog met up with friends Rohan Roy, who had worked at the Loj for years, and Christina Ford, a former assistant forest ranger. They suited up for the day, stepping into their bindings and fitting their backcountry skis with skins—synthetic material stretched over the base of the skis, allowing them to slide forward but not backward, and permitting the group to climb uphill in their skis. While they finalized preparations for the day, the four friends and Otis coincidentally bumped into twenty-six-year-old Russ Cook and twenty-seven-year-old Toma Vcarich. As the friends chatted with Cook and Vcarich, whom they had met only once before, they discovered the two men were also headed for the Wright Peak slides. The two separate groups opted to merge into one party, and prepared for a day of fresh-powder skiing.

It had been consistently cold over the preceding six weeks. That Monday, a storm had dumped 2 feet of fresh snow on the MacIntyre Range, and the night before—on Friday—an additional 6 inches had fallen.

Earlier in the day on Friday, a group of forest rangers from the

New York State Department of Environmental Conservation (DEC) had been over at Smuggler's Notch in Vermont taking a class in avalanche preparedness. It was part of New York State's increased efforts to address what it perceived to be a serious hazard and liability in the mountains. In Avalanche Pass, between Mount Colden and the MacIntyre Range, the DEC had already posted a warning sign, well before snow began to blanket the ground. The warning alerted hikers and snowshoers to the threat of an avalanche from above on the Avalanche Pass Slide, since the trail passed directly beneath it and efforts to reroute the trail through a safer section of the pass had proven unsuccessful. The state wanted its rangers trained in avalanche preparedness and appropriate rescue procedures, should unwary hikers get caught in the wrong place at the wrong time by an avalanche in the pass or elsewhere.

The snow at Smuggler's Notch that Friday had been unstable, with a threat of triggered avalanches. A reporter covering the training asked New York State forest ranger Jim Giglinto whether there was a potential for avalanches in the Adirondacks. "Possibly," he responded. "It could happen anywhere." They were five words casually uttered in the middle of an interview. But just a day later, they would prove tragically prophetic.

All six backcountry skiers had completed a run down the taller and narrower of the two new slides when they took a break to eat lunch. Lauren, in fact, had even taken two laps on the slide. She was a strong skier and highly motivated that day, Ron said, and she "took off" faster than the others as the group skinned up from Marcy Dam to the base of the slide.

Even before that Saturday, some members of the group had already visited the slide on skis. Lauren had skied it the day before, on

Friday, and Ron and Lauren had skied it together the Saturday before that. Toma Vcarich had also been up on the slide previously. The shorter, wider slide, which they planned to ski after lunch, was another story— Saturday, February 19, would be the first time anyone in the group had ever skied down it.

Roy was the first to go down the shorter slide, "hootin' and hollerin'" the whole way, while the others still sat at the base, finishing their lunches. Then they all climbed up to the top together to take their turn in the 2.5 feet of fresh powder that sat on the slide. In Ron Konowitz's words, they would be "farming" the slide—taking turns skiing the slide, starting from the right side and moving slightly to the left with each successive run to preserve the untracked powder. When everyone had had their turn, they'd skin back to the top and take a second run.

With the group together at the top, having eaten lunch and witnessed Roy's first run, Ron was the first to head down. He was soon followed by Lauren, who stopped alongside him about 100 vertical feet down the slide. Then came Cook, who made six or seven turns, and was about 50 vertical feet above Ron and Lauren, when his binding—a Voile releasable Telemark binding—broke. Ron reached into his daypack to pull out a screwdriver to help fix Cook's ski while Vcarich started coming down, with Roy watching from above. Ford, meanwhile, was out of sight above the top of the slide.

Being the fourth person to come down, Vcarich was toward the middle of the slide, where the snow ran over a slightly steeper section. He was about three turns into his run when he fell.

It isn't clear whether his fall caused an avalanche, or whether the slope avalanching caused him to fall. But when Ron and Lauren, standing side by side, looked up from their lower position on the slide, they saw a fracture line propagate out horizontally from Vcarich, 150 feet in both directions. Then they felt the snow slope settle, and heard an audible *whoompf.*

A slab avalanche was coming down on top of them. "I remember seeing chunks [of snow] floating in it like a river as it came towards us," Ron remembers. "I couldn't believe it was happening. Then my next thought was that we're all gonna die."

They never had a chance to get out of the way. Within three seconds of releasing, a slab avalanche can reach speeds of up to 20 miles per hour, and within another three seconds, it can hit 80 MPH—much faster than most people can ski, and certainly faster than Ron and Lauren could ski starting from a dead stop just 100 feet below the fracture line. The snow slope beneath their skis started to move—and then swallowed them into the bowels of the avalanche.

The subtler complexities aside, an avalanche requires three basic elements to occur: a steep slope, an unstable snowpack, and a trigger. Most avalanches (more than 90 percent of them) occur on slopes between 30 and 45 degrees. The Wright Peak slide measured about 36 degrees.

Although in retrospect the Wright Peak slide seems like a prime candidate for an avalanche, the idea was still far from most people's minds on that day. Avalanches have not historically been a part of the Adirondack experience, or at least were not a common part of the collective memory of the Adirondacks' outdoor community in early 2000. One article in the November/December 2003 issue of *Adirondack Explorer* cited fifteen major avalanches in recent Adirondack history, though most were on ice climbing routes such as Chapel Pond Slab and the immense North Face of Gothics, rather than on slides. Ten of the avalanches cited in the *Adirondack Explorer* article happened on ice routes—the domain of climbers—while three occurred on slides, the domain of skiers and snowshoers.

National statistics bear this ratio out. Since the winter of 1950–51, climbing has been the top-ranking cause of avalanche-related fatalities in the United States; backcountry skiing ranks second. For the most recent five-year period, however, snowmobiling has taken the top spot, pushing climbing and backcountry skiing to second and third, respectively.

Even with backcountry skiing ranking slightly lower for avalanche risk than other causes, the fifteen avalanches cited in the *Adirondack Explorer* article (of which just three were related to backcountry skiing) occurred over a time span of more than thirty years—working out to an average of one avalanche every two years, and just one every ten years for backcountry skiers alone. This is hardly a fearsome statistic for skiers. As the *Adirondack Explorer* article points out, though, the low avalanche number may be the result of a relatively low use of the slides by winter recreationists more than anything else. In more than 90 percent of avalanche-related fatalities, the avalanche was triggered by the victim or by someone in the victim's party. And as more people ventured onto Adirondack slides, avalanches and injuries caused by them were bound to occur more frequently.

Saturday, February 19, was part of the Presidents' Day weekend, and around midday, when the avalanche occurred, Marcy Dam was host to as many as forty people. From the Dam, the new slides on Wright Peak are plainly visible, and the mass of people casually watched as the six skiers started down the shorter, wider slide in turn. Then they saw the snow slide, and watched the whole slope come down.

One witness described it as being like a curtain coming down, "like pulling a shade." At first they could only see it happening. The sound of the avalanche arrived some thirty seconds later. With it, they saw the powder cloud grow, and watched the skiers disappear.

The avalanche, especially from the skiers' perspective on the slide, was enormous. "There was really no way to get away from it," Ron Konowitz remembers. The avalanche fractured 5 feet deep at the crown line—the point where the avalanche separates from the snowfield above. The mass of snow was 300 feet wide and ran for 1,200 vertical feet. As it fell, it "stepped down" into the deepest layers of the snowpack, stripping the slide of its snow cover down to virtually bare rock and ice.

For the skiers, the snow opened up like a trapdoor. Roy was just above the fracture line, and Ford was farther up and didn't see the avalanche release. Vcarich, Cook, and the Konowitzes, on the other hand, were sucked into the avalanche.

Ron was engulfed in snow for the entire duration of the avalanche. He remembers hitting things on the way down, tumbling like he was inside a washing machine. *Take your skis off. Ditch your poles. Get your pack off*, he thought to himself. He didn't have to. By the time he reached the bottom of the slide along with the avalanche, it had all been torn off his body. His jacket and pants were ripped, the ice ax torn from his backpack.

He was in total disbelief. "I realized we were going to die," he recalls. "There was no question in my mind that I wasn't going to be able to survive this." At first it was terrifying, but then he grew calm. "I was still trying to fight it, trying to swim," he says. "But at the same time, my body was really relaxed . . . almost like I was waiting to get hit in the head with something and knocked out."

When the avalanche had first started, he had reached out for Lauren, who had been standing next to him, but like the others, she too was sucked beneath the snow. In an interview with *Adirondack Explorer* years after the accident, she likened the experience to being crushed by a large, breaking ocean wave. Her ride in the avalanche lasted for what she estimated as only ten or fifteen seconds. Sometime during the tumble, her head struck a rock forcefully, but she remained conscious the entire time. Then she stopped moving. "I went under the snow, and I never resurfaced," she told the *Adirondack Explorer*.

Her body was frozen in place into the snow, packed in by the hard slab that set up like concrete. At that point she felt no pain, and strangely, her body felt warm. Snow filled her nose and mouth, though she could still breathe. With no other choice, she lay motionless, trapped beneath the snow.

When the avalanche came to rest at the base of the slide, the debris pile at the bottom was estimated to be the size of a football field. Avalanched snow and other debris had accumulated up to twenty-five feet deep. The avalanche had crested a debris pile that had been left at the base of the slide following Hurricane Floyd, and the force of the avalanche tearing into the forest at the base of the slide had snapped the tops off of trees, including birch trees with trunks 8 inches in diameter.

Roy, who had been standing just above the fracture line when the snow slope had released, watched the whole thing happen. He had seen the powder cloud, and had watched where each person had disappeared into the avalanche, and how far into the forest the snow had traveled at the base.

Like Lauren, Ron had also been completely buried beneath the snow. *Boy, I'm in trouble now*, he thought. Then the snow around him shifted—or a secondary slough came down from above—and pushed him over several big drops before shooting him 75 to 100 feet into the air.

It was the first time he'd seen daylight since getting sucked beneath the snow at the top of the slide. He catapulted straight forward, landing on his side with his head downhill. He looked back up and saw the remainder of the avalanche coming down. Fortunately, at the last moment, most of the avalanche doglegged to skier's left, and only reburied Ron up to his waist. He was able to dig himself out. Miraculously, he didn't have any broken bones, although one leg was injured, and one arm was useless, hanging limp at his side.

As he scanned the avalanche debris around him, his first thought was that everyone had died. "I dug my legs out, and I was looking around, and there was no one," he says. The forest was eerily quiet. Then he heard a sound. Roy came skiing down from above, quickly checked to see that Ron was all right, then moved on to start looking for the others. The two men felt helpless—no one wore avalanche beacons (transceivers that send out an electronic signal used to locate a person buried in an avalanche), and they didn't have probes they could plunge into the snow to try to locate their buried companions.

Then someone heard a sound from the trees. It was Cook. Like Ron, Cook had initially been buried and then brought to the surface when the second movement of snow hit. He wound up pinned against a tree, buried up to his waist in snow. He was more or less fine, save for a broken leg, and the upper half of his body hadn't sustained any injury. Seeing this, Roy and Ron left Cook to dig himself out and continued to look for the others. In a sense they were triaging members of their own group in a race against the clock. Lauren was nowhere to be found. The same was true of Vcarich.

The crowd at Marcy Dam had watched, dumbfounded, as the avalanche swept down the slide on Wright Peak. Jay Federman, a doctor from Saranac Lake who was at the Dam with his wife, called the rangers on his cell phone.

Forest rangers Jim Giglinto and Gary Hodgson had been patrolling the High Peaks on skis when a call came over their radio from DEC dispatch around noon: A group of backcountry skiers had been caught in an avalanche on one of the Wright Peak slides. Giglinto and Hodgson were at the height of Avalanche Pass, roughly 1.5 miles from the accident site. Giglinto, the faster skier, immediately struck out for Marcy Dam, with Hodgson following behind.

Meanwhile, Roy and Ron frantically looked for any sign of Lauren and Vcarich. "We couldn't find Toma. It was awful," Ron remembers. Then Roy spotted a small bit of red poking out of the snow beyond the trees and debris at the base of the slide. It was Lauren. In the course of the avalanche, Lauren's red anorak had been pulled up high over her head, and a small bit of its fabric had caught Roy's eye. He immediately started to pull the snow away from her face and head.

By the time they'd found her, precious minutes had elapsed, and she had already resigned herself to death. She had felt serene as she lay there, thinking about Ron, her sisters, parents, and friends. Then, as she began to fall asleep—a sleep from which she believed she might never awake—Roy's sudden appearance and his pulling the snow away from her head brought her back to reality. She started screaming, terrified that even though she had been found, they might not be able to pull her out in time to save her life. The snow around her was soaked with blood.

"Even when we found Lauren, I didn't think she was going to live," says Ron. "Just looking at her and seeing the extent of her injuries, and realizing how long it was going to take to get a helicopter in there. As a rescuer you have a game face. But this was the person I loved the most . . . my wife . . . and I didn't think she was going to live. But I had to make it sound like she was going to be fine."

Lauren had sustained a skull fracture and four major breaks to bones—two in her left leg and two in her right arm.

By then, Christina Ford had at last come down to rejoin the group. She and Roy left Ron to finish digging Lauren out with his one functional arm while they went off to find Vcarich.

The first outside person on scene at the accident site was Teresa Palen, whose husband, Ed, runs Adirondack Rock and River, a climbing and backcountry-skiing guide service whose offerings include skiing tours on Wright Peak. Palen happened to be cross-country skiing to Avalanche Lake that day and had arrived at Marcy Dam, en route, thirty seconds after the avalanche had happened.

To her surprise, most of the people crowded at Marcy Dam were reluctant to go and help. "We're going to go get the rangers," they told her. "No! You've gotta come up there now!" she exhorted them. Alone, Palen started in toward the slide and soon encountered the Konowitzes' dog, Otis. He was howling and moaning, and Palen—who knew the Konowitzes and their dog personally—immediately knew that Ron and Lauren were involved. Otis had also been involved in the avalanche, although no one knows exactly what happened to him when the snow slid.

Fifteen minutes behind Palen, Chris Heisen, a doctor, came up to the accident site as well. He had been skiing with his son, Peter, on Mount Marcy, and the pair was on their way down when they had arrived at Marcy Dam. Behind the elder Heisen, several of the original onlookers from the Dam had changed their minds and decided to come up to assist with the rescue.

By the time Palen, Heisen, and the others had arrived, Ron and the other survivors had almost gotten Lauren out of the snow, though Vcarich was still missing.

As soon as he had reached Marcy Dam, Ranger Giglinto had started in toward the slide while Hodgson stayed back to prepare a track through the snow that rescuers could use to bring in additional equipment and personnel. Within an hour after the accident, Giglinto arrived as the first forest ranger on the scene. His first priority was to get a helicopter in to the site. He moved higher onto the slide above the rescue efforts and started to stamp out a makeshift helicopter pad. Then he organized rescuers into a rudimentary and, at times, chaotic probe line—a group of searchers spread abreast in a line that would slowly move over the snow surface, probing down into the avalanche debris in the hopes of finding Vcarich—a task made all the more difficult since no one had an actual probe.

This rescue was different than most others. Many times, the major rescues involve local forest rangers and search and rescue personnel assisting people who come to the Adirondacks from out of the area. But this time, the rescuers and those needing rescue knew one another and were a part of the same community. They were working to save some of their own.

Around 2:30 p.m., roughly two hours after the avalanche, a helicopter finally arrived. Cook, Roy, and Ford were airlifted out in the first load, followed by Ron and Lauren. Ron didn't want to leave, and rescuers literally had to drag him uphill and into the helicopter. There, he finally let his guard down, and broke down crying. Vcarich was still somewhere under the snow, and he realized then that they wouldn't find Vcarich—at least not alive.

"It was difficult to be airlifted out without having found him,"

Ron says. "This was someone who, although I didn't know him well, was just with us, and I couldn't find him. After all my rescue work and all my training, I couldn't save him."

With the five survivors airlifted out and flying to the hospital, searchers continued to look for Vcarich. They formed a probe line low on the slide and worked their way up in a line strung out across the avalanche debris. One of the people probing got a strike; when they dug down into the snow, they discovered a pair of skis, which now focused the search around that area of the avalanche debris. Although it was the best lead searchers had to go on, they didn't realize then that the skis weren't Vcarich's—they belonged to Ron. Because he had already been airlifted out, however, Ron had no way of telling rescuers that they were following the wrong trail of clues.

Luckily, Robert Thomas and his dog—the same Bob Thomas who had spent years looking for his missing brother, Steven (detailed in chapter 8)—were on the scene as part of the search and rescue effort. Thomas's dog didn't need clues like skis and poles in the snow. He sensed something, and began digging in one spot, and started to whimper. The dog's insistence moved the probe line higher yet again, and there, under 3 feet of snow, rescuers discovered Vcarich's lifeless body.

His skis were still on his feet, possibly serving to anchor him deep under the snow as the avalanche roared down the slide. Every other person's skis had released—most of their cable binding systems were stretched more than 1.5 feet beyond their normal range by the force of the avalanche. However, while Vcarich's skis might have been a factor in his demise, the injuries he sustained during the avalanche were severe— possibly too severe to recover from, even if he had been found earlier.

The extent of his injuries aside, the depth and duration of his burial also didn't bode well. Avalanche victims buried within a foot of the surface have a survival rate of almost 90 percent. But by the time the burial depth reaches 3 feet—the depth at which Vcarich was found—the survival rate drops to just 30 percent. Similarly, buried victims found within the first fifteen minutes of an avalanche have a 90 percent survival rate. By the thirty-minute mark, the probability of being found alive drops to 50 percent. And at three hours and beyond—roughly how long it took to locate Vcarich—the survival rate is a dismal 5 percent.

In the wake of the tragedy, Adirondack Rock and River hosted a memorial service for Vcarich that was attended by more than a hundred people. Ron and Lauren Konowitz, who hadn't known Vcarich very well, met his family and friends at the service. They felt saddened by the loss of an individual many described as "a wonderful person." And Lauren, for her part, was wracked with survivor's guilt. "Why did he have to die and I survived?" she wondered. Others, such as Peter Benoit, the former president of Lower Adirondack Search and Rescue, were simply in shock. "I never thought I'd see a death in the High Peaks from an avalanche," he remembers.

During the days and weeks that followed, it seemed like every newspaper and morning show in the country wanted to talk to the survivors. On Internet discussion forums used by the outdoor community, everyone had an opinion about what went wrong and why. But those who actually lived through the avalanche remained resolutely silent, still absorbing the enormity of their experience and the depth of their loss.

The *Plattsburgh Press-Republican* quoted Ron: "We lost Toma, but we saved Lauren." For years those seven words stood as the only ones directly attributed to those who had actually lived through the ordeal of the avalanche. With every published report, the survivors grew increasingly angry over what they saw as an overwhelming number of inaccuracies that plagued accounts of what had happened. For example, one account said the skiers were on Mount Marcy, rather than Wright Peak. Other sources have led some people, to this day, to think the avalanche occurred on the slides on Mount Colden, rather than Wright.

"I was there, and I can tell you exactly what happened," says Ron. "It's unsettling to me. It was a bad enough experience to go through, and then to be chastised in the newspapers by people who had no idea what was going on.

"We didn't think there was an avalanche danger that day," he says, looking back. "If we thought there was, we wouldn't have been up there." He remembers no settling of the snow, no surface sloughing. In all his years of skiing Adirondack slides, including similar slides in similar snow conditions, he'd never seen anything remotely close to what happened on that fateful day. "We were so far away from thinking about avalanches," he continues. "We were experienced, but we weren't a ski-to-die group. We had skied together for years, and just didn't see the risk. It was just perfect snow and a perfect day." Almost.

Based upon the Adirondacks' history, his thinking wasn't far off the mark. Despite the findings of *Adirondack Explorer*, and despite the fact that statistically, February is the deadliest month for avalanches on a national scale, New York State ranks near the very bottom of the state-by-state list for avalanche fatalities among states for which avalanche statistics are recorded. In fact, Vcarich's death was the first, and still only, backcountry death due to an avalanche statewide. And there had only been one other avalanche-related death at all in the recorded history of the state: A motorist on the Taconic Parkway in the Hudson Valley was killed when his car was pushed off the road by an avalanche during the blizzard of 1993.

Recovery—both physical and psychological—took a long time for Ron and Lauren Konowitz, who have since divorced. At the time they lived in a house on 40 acres of land near Adirondack Rock and River, and that March, the Adirondacks received several big snowstorms. Just walking around in their yard with the snow falling triggered "weird vibes," Ron says.

Friends urged him to get back out and ski again, but a month after the accident, he discovered it was too soon. The smell of the snow and the movement of skiing triggered intense flashbacks. At the Whiteface Ski Center, he broke down crying partway down a run. The following ski season also proved difficult, with constant flashbacks, even at lift-serviced areas. Ron kept away from the slides, skiing trails, and taking runs through the trees.

It was years before he skied another slide. "Skiing has always been something that I love. It's always brought happy feelings," he explains. "Suddenly, skiing brought back these awful memories of not being able to find Toma, and being in this awful mess." In 2004 he finally got back into the Adirondack backcountry in earnest. "I'm able to go out and enjoy skiing again now. It's been a long time, though," he says.

Now, he carries a shovel, probe, and beacon every time he's in the woods. "I personally won't ski with someone anymore unless they're carrying [them]," he says. And perhaps just as important, Ron carries the equipment to help others if he's in the woods and another group gets caught in the way his did.

Looking back on the experience, he still tries to make sense of what happened. Why that slide? Why that day? Why, when other backcountry skiers had skied slides on Colden and Dix on that same day, without incident? He has one theory.

The summer leading up to Hurricane Floyd was extremely dry, spawning two months of forest fires, including the 90-acre Noonmark fire. Then, a week after Noonmark, Floyd dropped 12 inches of rain and created eighteen new slides. From then on, the weather pattern changed, raining for at least part of every day for a month and a half straight. Then it got cold. The slide on Wright that avalanched, unlike most Adirondack slides, wasn't completely clean. It was littered with mud, tree stumps, and other debris that had become saturated by the constant rain. That mud never fully dried out before winter set in, and the latent moisture may have been one of a deadly combination of factors contributing to avalanche-conducive conditions, such as the growth of hoarfrost, which would have provided a notoriously unstable sliding surface for an avalanche.

"I've gone through this scenario a hundred times in my head, trying to figure out what was so different about that day," he says. While we may never know, when asked if it could ever happen again, Ron answers, "Sure." While the "why" may forever linger in uncertainty, two things are certain: Konowitz and his group were involved in the worst avalanche in the history of New York State—the first, and still only, fatal backcountry avalanche statewide—and one of them didn't come back alive. The avalanche lasted just fifteen seconds from start to finish, from release to debris pile, but those fifteen seconds forever changed the lives of six skiers, along with the lives of their families, friends, rescuers, and the outdoor community. The face of Adirondack winters, and certainly slide skiing, will never be the same.

17

AN UNPLANNED EPIC: THE THIRD WORST SNOWSTORM IN ADK HISTORY SURPRISES TWO PAIRS OF HIKERS

Men's resources of energy in the face of death are inexhaustible. When the end seems imminent, there still remain reserves, though it needs tremendous willpower to call them up.

—Maurice Herzog, *The Quotable Climber* (2002)

During the wee hours of Sunday morning, March 4, 2001, a pair of Canadians—nineteen-year-old Phillip Mousseau from Hull, Quebec, and twenty-year-old Jean Richer from Chelsea, Quebec, near Ottawa, Ontario—set out from Adirondak Loj, destined for Lake Colden. They left the trailhead at 1:00 a.m. with plans to climb both Algonquin and Marcy, returning to the Loj by Monday afternoon. The men were experienced and relatively well prepared, with sleeping bags, a tent, and a stove, but with little food or fuel. They were planning to "go light" and make a continuous alpine-style traverse of the two peaks, pausing only long enough for a short catnap if necessary.

Sunday was a clear day, but a raging storm was closing in. It would come to be called the third worst snowstorm in the history of the Adirondacks—the Nor'easter of March 2001—and it would hit with an intensity many times greater than forecasted or expected.

Mousseau and Richer reached the top of Algonquin, the first of the two peaks on their itinerary, in time to watch the sun rise. From the summit they continued down to Lake Colden, arriving around 3:00 p.m. There they met Interior Outpost caretaker Margaret Hawthorne, and told her that they planned to nap for a few hours before continuing over Mount Marcy. But they slept through the night, not waking until nearly 8:00 a.m. on Monday, March 5.

While Mousseau and Richer slept in a lean-to near Colden's Interior Outpost that Sunday night, some 275 miles away, in Rochester, New York, young twenty-somethings Bryce Dalhaus and Ethan "E-Man" Marcello sat in the warmth and comfort of their respective homes, watching heavy snow fall in near whiteout conditions outside the windows. They were scheduled to embark that night on a weeklong winter camping trip in the High Peaks.

Marcello's mother pleaded with him not to go. Dalhaus, undeterred by the falling snow, convinced his friend that they would be okay. Besides, he pointed out, Lake Placid's forecast was only for 3 to 5 inches of snow, possibly 6 at the most; either way, nothing to worry about. But neither man had seen a recently revised weather forecast that told of a coming storm much worse than either of them was prepared for.

Marcello packed his gear, loaded his car, locked his house, and made the short drive to Dalhaus's house. There the two split the food they'd both shopped for in the preceding weeks, and sat their expedition packs in the rear seat of Marcello's car like two additional passengers.

By 11:00 p.m. they were on the road, en route to the Adirondacks. Already, the heavy snowfall was greatly impairing visibility and made for treacherous driving conditions. "On the road, I felt like this was a mistake," Marcello recalled. Any motorists brave enough to be on the road closely followed the plows of highway maintenance crews trying to keep up with the rate of snowfall.

More than six hours later, Dalhaus and Marcello pulled into a parking area on Route 3, which weaves east-west through the northwestern corner of the Adirondack Park from its border near Harrisville and past Cranberry and Tupper Lakes on the way to Saranac Lake and Lake Placid. Having driven through most of the night, they stopped for a much-needed two-hour nap. Dalhaus slept with his head against the door of the car, using his gloves as a pillow, until the bitter cold woke him from his slumber.

They resumed their journey, and an hour later, arrived at South Meadows, near the Adirondak Loj. They had full winter gear, heavy expedition packs, and snowshoes. They would need it all, and then some.

On Monday, March 5, Dalhaus and Marcello planned to hike from South Meadows to Marcy Dam, through Avalanche Pass, and across Lake Colden to the Beaver Point Lean-to on the lake's southwestern edge—about 6 miles. As they headed into the wintry wilderness, the temperature hovered in the 20s, and snow fell moderately. They carried five days' worth of food, plus extra clothing. At the High Peaks Wilderness Area boundary sign, they signed the trail register and took note of a DEC avalanche warning about the Avalanche Pass Slide (the same general warning errantly cited in newspapers in the wake of the Wright Peak avalanche, detailed in chapter 16).

Continuing their hike, the peaks were hidden from view, shrouded in thick clouds. Off-trail the snow was deep and unconsolidated, but on the trail, the snow was well packed, overlain by an inch or two of fresh powder (though soon, those inches would add up to feet). Dalhaus carried water bottles inside his jacket to prevent them from freezing, the bottles held up by the tension of his pack's waist belt cinched around his middle.

By and large, this was Marcello's first winter trip. All his gear was new. And already at this early stage in the trip, to Dalhaus, Marcello didn't seem to be enjoying any part of it. "I had no idea what I was getting into, nor was I prepared for it," Marcello later recalled. Even so, despite his demeanor on the trail, the trip was a liberating one for him: "I felt free for the first time in a long time. Free from the stresses of work."

Soon, the pair arrived at Marcy Dam. Marcello took the opportunity to rearrange his pack. While he shuffled and sorted his gear, a group of day hikers passed by. Everyone looked like they were having a good time, he noticed. Dalhaus, meanwhile, munched on a Clif Bar, but soon grew cold, so the two men reshouldered their packs and continued on the trail toward Avalanche Pass.

Shortly before noon, they reached the second of the Avalanche Pass lean-tos and dropped their packs to rest. Already, Marcello wanted to call it quits. Dalhaus felt differently. "I was determined to hike my own hike," he later recalled.

That afternoon, having resolved to continue their trip, the men met up with a cross-country skier. The skier had spoken with a forest ranger earlier in the day, and learned that strong winds and heavy snow would be moving in that night. But Dalhaus and Marcello didn't give the warning much attention. "All I could think about was climbing some mountain," Dalhaus recalled.

They pushed onward, passing beneath the base of the Avalanche Pass Slide—to which the DEC warning referred—and came to the cliffs that bound Avalanche Lake itself. Wispy trails of white powdery snow blew off the rocks high above, and the lake was frozen from end to end. The men chose to stick to the trail, hiking to the "Hitch-up Matildas" bolted to the cliffs along the edge of the lake. There they took another break, and Dalhaus ate another Clif Bar. "How far is it to the lean-to?" Marcello asked. "About a mile," Dalhaus answered, giving the same response each time the question was asked, no matter how far the actual distance.

With Avalanche Lake behind them, the men turned right at a trail junction to travel along Lake Colden's western shoreline and past the Interior Outpost toward the Beaver Point Lean-to. Dalhaus had considered taking a longer route to the lean-to around the lake's eastern shore, but "ignoring signs of the coming storm, I felt it would be better to rest up for our choice of mountains the next day," he recalled. As they hiked, the pair slowly separated, with Dalhaus ahead in the lead, and Marcello somewhere behind. At one point, Dalhaus's right leg plunged down into the snow up to his hip, possibly having fallen into a spruce trap. He decided then to wait for Marcello to catch up. As Marcello came into view, he had "a look of misery" on his face. Dalhaus, meanwhile, was "enjoying every minute of it."

Unsure of the exact location of the lean-to, Dalhaus hiked to the top of a small rise to scan the surrounding terrain. From his higher perch he spotted the lean-to not far ahead along the trail, and waved Marcello on ahead. When Dalhaus caught up five minutes later, Marcello was already sprawled out in the lean-to "as if he had died."

Across the lake from their lean-to, the men could see the Interior Outpost. Marcello was quick to get out his sleeping bag and pad to try and warm up in the fierce cold. Dalhaus, too, got out his sleeping bag, rated to minus-20 degrees. He had never used it before, although it was a few years old. Then Dalhaus hung his pant shell and jacket, plus his fleece vest, which was damp with sweat, from pegs on the wall of the lean-to and prepared to cook dinner.

Marcello, meanwhile, pulled his boots off and water literally poured out. Though his boots were waterproof, snow had been methodically sneaking its way in underneath his pants as he hiked and then melting, soaking his feet and socks. He quickly switched into a spare dry pair.

The storm the forest ranger had warned of was closing in, and would soon reach full force. Yet even so, Dalhaus asked Marcello which mountain he wanted to climb the next day: Algonquin, Colden, or Marcy. Then, around 3:30 p.m. that afternoon, both men took a nap.

Around that same time, Mousseau and Richer were high on Mount Marcy, fighting their way through the storm. After waking much later than they would have liked earlier that Monday morning, they had struck out from Lake Colden and were now near Marcy's summit. But the storm was too much, turning them back before they could reach the mountain's pinnacle. They took shelter on the northwest side of the peak, pitching their tent a few hundred yards below the summit. They would spend the night, they thought, and then continue over the summit and down the Van Hoevenberg trail to the Loj the next day.

Just before dark, Dalhaus woke from his nap to the sounds of a fierce storm blowing outside the lean-to. The winds blew stronger and stronger with each passing minute, and the snow fell hard and heavy, at times blowing horizontally. As he brought water to a boil to finish cooking dinner, darkness fell. He filled their water bottles with the boiling water, and then made hot soup. The men stuffed the hot bottles into their sleeping bags, but left everything else out in what they considered "the relative safety of the lean-to," including their camera, eyeglasses, and flashlight.

With dinner finished, they turned in for the evening around 7:00 p.m. Each man crawled deep into his sleeping bag, zipped it shut, and closed his eyes.

Around 11:50 p.m. that night—as Dalhaus and Marcello lay asleep ten minutes before midnight—Mousseau's mother called DEC dispatch and reported her son and Richer missing after they failed to return from their High Peaks overnight camping trip. Forest ranger Jim Giglinto received the call. Normally an in-the-field ranger, Giglinto was sitting in the regional headquarters office in Ray Brook fielding calls because the usual dispatcher couldn't make it in because of the raging storm. The DEC would have to wait until the storm abated, Giglinto told Mousseau's mother, before they could mount a serious search for the young men.

Back in the lean-to on Lake Colden's Beaver Point, Dalhaus used a fleece blanket as a pillow, and wore two hats and a pair of fleece gloves inside his subzero-degree sleeping bag. Around midnight, five hours after falling asleep—and just after Mousseau and Richer were reported missing—Dalhaus woke up. Not wearing his glasses, he couldn't see beyond the confines of the lean-to, but he could easily tell that the storm had intensified even further. He hoped that daylight would come soon, and that the weather would improve. In both cases, it wouldn't.

It was nearly one o'clock in the morning as Dalhaus lay there, trying to fall back asleep. He slowly realized that going up any mountain at daybreak was "out of the question due to the storm," but still, he hadn't given up all hope.

That night on Marcy, Mousseau and Richer hunkered down to ride out the brutal conditions high on the mountain, having dug in to take shelter on the northwest side of the peak before Dalhaus and Marcello ever reached the Beaver Point Lean-to.

In the early morning hours of Tuesday, March 6, Dalhaus woke and realized that his fleece blanket was no longer totally beneath his head. Pulling it back over, he dumped "a face full of snow" on himself. The howling winds had blown snow into the lean-to throughout the night, and Dalhaus lay covered beneath a foot of snow, "literally inside a snowdrift." His jacket, pants, and vest had fallen off their pegs and onto the floor. Anything left out on the floor of the lean-to was now buried beneath the snow, included Dalhaus's eyeglasses, which he couldn't find.

He woke up Marcello "to show him how bad it was." Marcello poked his head out of the top of his sleeping bag. "I looked in amazement as I saw nothing but the lean-to and white," he recalled. "The wind was screaming past the opening of the lean-to . . . . Then the thought came to me . . . the nor'easter was on top of us. Bryce was buried in the snow."

Needing to urinate, Dalhaus stepped out of the lean-to and immediately saw that their trail had vanished, and that a wall of snow crossed his path. He retreated to the lean-to, where he stood around, jumping up and down to keep warm.

As the sun slowly came up and the forest grew lighter, the pair began to unbury and pack their gear. Dalhaus's pants and jacket were full of snow. His fleece vest, which was damp when he hung it up the night before, had frozen solid in the bitter overnight temperatures. His sleeping bag was wet, and his sleeping pad was frozen to the floor of the lean-to.

Marcello opted to skip breakfast, and sat while Dalhaus downed four Nutri-Grain Bars. Their plan had originally been to eat hot oatmeal for breakfast, but with the stove buried beneath the snow, they opted not to try and light it. Then they pondered their options.

Around 7:00 a.m., with the storm still swirling around them, they strapped on their snowshoes, zipped their jackets tight, closed their hoods around their faces, and stepped out into the maelstrom. Dalhaus led, still with the intention of heading toward Mount Marcy. He pushed south head-on into the teeth of the storm. A cold, painful wind lashed at their faces, forcing them back. "It was just too much," Dalhaus at last admitted. The newly fallen snow was well over 3 or 4 feet deep. The pair turned back to head toward Marcy Dam. Even with their snowshoes, they plunged knee- and waist-deep with every step.

Snow continued to fall, and would for the entire day. Deep snowdrifts were everywhere. Each step was a fight. "I knew for certain we wouldn't make it to the car," Dalhaus later recalled. As they reached the northern end of Lake Colden, they struggled to locate the trail and pick the easiest route back through the snow. The pair alternately took turns falling—dozens of times—into deep snow.

They passed the Interior Outpost and then struck out for Avalanche Lake. The tall, steep cliffs on either side of the lake created a wind tunnel—often attributed to the Venturi effect and known as a gap or jet-effect wind—accelerating the wind to upward of 70 miles per hour. The wind chill plummeted to an estimated minus-40 degrees. Snow lashed at the exposed parts of their faces. On the lake itself, the constant wind had sculpted the snow, so that it was 2 inches deep in some places, and 6 feet deep in others. The men looked up only long enough to navigate, and then hunched over in the wind again. At this point, one man would lead the way until he fell. Then, the other would take over and do the same. Neither man quit as they slowly fought their way northward. Ice had by now built up thick on Dalhaus's beard, including a painful chunk the size of an egg that hung from his chin.

When they reached the "Hitch-up Matildas" they had passed the day before, they took a break. Marcello wondered whether or not they'd make it back to the car, or at all. He sunk into a state of utter despair. "I fell [again] and my soul left me. I gave up at that moment," he recalled. "My body was tired and cold and it decided to shut down for a period of time. The only thing that kept me going was Bryce, who kept going himself and urged me to get up."

At last, the men reached the northern end of Avalanche Lake. They saw a yellow trail marker on a tree and followed a trough into the woods, not realizing that it wasn't the trail. Half an hour later, they were lost. Marcello continued to try and forge a route ahead while Dalhaus backtracked to the lake to try and relocate the trail from the yellow marker they had seen. Eventually, he succeeded, and the pair regrouped and continued their march.

As they plodded through Avalanche Pass, two men "came out of nowhere" following Dalhaus and Marcello's tracks. The men had started out from another lean-to near Lake Colden and, having followed Dalhaus and Marcello's route up until that point, offered to take a turn breaking trail. The two pairs of men temporarily became a group of four. They passed beneath a giant icicle hanging from the cliffs. Each man continued to fall into the deep snow, fighting for every step back toward their cars and safety.

Two miles after starting out from the lean-tos on the south end of Lake Colden, the four men reached one of the Avalanche Pass lean-tos, where they took a break. Chatting with the two men, Dalhaus and Marcello learned that they were from the University of Buffalo, and had been out for five days. They planned to try and make it out to the Loj that day, or at least, hoped to make it to Marcy Dam, from which point someone else might have broken the trail back to the trailhead. Dalhaus and Marcello, though, were done for the day. They had decided to go no farther than the Avalanche Pass Lean-to that day, and the two pairs parted ways.

Earlier that day, Mousseau and Richer also awoke to several feet of snow; in their case, it was on their tent, rather than in front of a lean-to. The wind was still howling high on Marcy. It was the first time they realized that maybe they were in real danger. "We said, 'Now we're in trouble,'" they later told North Country Public Radio. "What do we do now?" They were only able to move downhill in the brutal conditions, forcing them to drop into the valley of the Opalescent River, which drains Marcy's northern and northwestern flanks, flowing generally westward before being joined by Feldspar Brook, and eventually reaching a spot between Lake Colden and Flowed Lands.

"We couldn't go forward . . . even with our 40-pound packs, the wind was pushing us back," they told reporters. The pair figured they could move their way around the peak, following the Opalescent drainage, until they reached a trail. But having been forced off-trail into the deepest snow, they only covered half a mile on March 6.

Having received the call from Mousseau's mother the night before, forest rangers Jim Giglinto and Charlie Platte skied in to Marcy Dam to check on conditions in the backcountry. The less-than-2-mile ski took them nearly three hours. The snow, which was still falling, was nearly waist-deep. When they skied downhill, the powder flowed chest-high. Giglinto and Platte realized then that Mousseau and Richer were probably in serious trouble. "The snowstorm was a big one," Giglinto recalls. "I don't think they were anticipating as much as we got."

While Dalhaus and Marcello sat in the lean-to late Tuesday afternoon, now on their own again, snow continued to fall. Marcello hadn't eaten all day, and the men were out of water. Sitting inactive, they soon became "chilled to the bone." Dalhaus's gloves were wet, and he didn't have a dry pair to change into. He operated their stove with his bare hands, frequently pausing to rewarm them from the painful cold. He boiled water and made a dinner of instant mashed potatoes for them to eat. He chose the garlic-flavored pouch, though he also carried plain, four-cheese, and sour cream and onion. Marcello managed to eat some potatoes, washing them down with some spare water from the stove. Dalhaus mixed part of a Jell-O packet into what little water remained from cooking dinner to make a flavored sugar drink. Then, Marcello fell asleep, and Dalhaus followed soon after.

Their plan for day three—Wednesday, March 7—was to travel from their Avalanche Pass lean-to Marcy Dam. There they planned to drop their packs, and then, improbably, Dalhaus still hoped to head up Phelps Mountain, or possibly toward Marcy, as far as Indian Falls. From either destination, they'd backtrack to their gear and hike out to the Loj and then to South Meadows where their car was parked.

Dalhaus opened his eyes that morning just before dawn and watched the sky fill with light. The storm had cleared, and the sky was a deep blue. The High Peaks gleamed a bright white with their bare, snow-covered summits. "When I woke up . . . I lay there in awe of Nature's beauty," Marcello recalled. The forest was silent, he noticed. The silence was so loud it made his ears hurt.

A final foot of snow had fallen since they had arrived at the lean-to the night before. High on Marcy, the two Canadians were still missing, up there somewhere. Later that Wednesday morning, Dalhaus and Marcello heard a helicopter overhead. The search for the missing Quebecois was finally under way.

At 7:00 a.m. that morning, the DEC sent a helicopter to comb

Mount Marcy from above while fifteen forest rangers, searching in three separate teams, converged on Marcy from below. One team started from Adirondack Loj, another from Johns Brook Valley, and a third from the Adirondack Mountain Reserve. They all fought with the deep snow, only able to cover half a mile an hour. They called the telephone numbers of any hikers who, according to trail registers, had been in the area recently (a column for telephone numbers had been added to trail register pages since the Carleton search). Another team led by Jim Giglinto was dropped off via helicopter in the wilderness with skis and snowshoes. Elsewhere, teams of rangers tried to make headway on snowmobiles. Progress was frustratingly slow. The snow was so deep and so unconsolidated that rangers were forced to get off their snowmobiles, walk with snowshoes for a quarter mile or so to pack down the trail, return to their sled, and then ride the snowmobiles. Then they'd have to repeat the process. It was the only way to get the machines into the backcountry.

The new day, and the beautiful weather, gave Dalhaus a renewed burst of energy. He hiked powerfully toward Marcy Dam, passing a large group of French-speaking students, and later, a DEC forest ranger. Dalhaus and Marcello finally learned of the plight of the two Canadians on Mount Marcy, who were fighting to survive at the same time that the two men from Rochester were struggling back from Lake Colden.

Marcello, meanwhile, felt dejected, and was singularly focused on getting out of the woods. To put it simply, he was miserable. "I had no intention of staying, even though it was something that I would have loved to do," he wrote in a personal account of the epic journey.

At Marcy Dam, Dalhaus found the nearest lean-to, dropped his pack, and went back to find his friend, who had again fallen behind. While at the lean-to, Dalhaus noticed that the trail toward Marcy and

Phelps was broken and, since Phelps was "only two miles from where we stood to the peak," wanted to know if climbing a mountain would snap Marcello out of his funk or not. The pair agreed to give it a try. They stashed their packs in the rear of the lean-to and set out with a little bit of food and water. Marcello's bottles were actually empty, and he resorted to eating snow as they hiked.

The men reached the summit of Phelps. Dalhaus's polypropylene top was drenched with sweat. He pulled his shirt off and stood barebacked on the summit of the mountain, soaking up the sun's rays. Then the men returned to the main trail and turned to head up toward Marcy. Just past Indian Falls, they caught up with a pair of forest rangers who were breaking trail up the mountain, looking for the missing Canadians.

By then, Richer's mother, Elaine, was giving up hope. "I thought he was not going to make it," she told reporters. "The first night I was positive . . . he's strong, has good judgment. But at the end I was no longer positive."

Out of fuel and eating snow for hydration, Mousseau and Richer ate orange peels out of their garbage bag as they continued their push down the Opalescent drainage on March 7. All day, a helicopter circled over the mountains, looking for tracks in the snow, signals, or even avalanches (since rangers expected any avalanches to be human-triggered, and possibly by the Canadians). Throughout the day, rangers didn't see any signs of the men. Then, just before dark, the same helicopter Dalhaus and Marcello had seen overhead earlier that morning spotted Mousseau and Richer's tracks near the Opalescent.

To what must have been Marcello's extreme pleasure, the pair finally headed out to the Loj. They reached the parking lot with 9 miles behind them that day. A reporter on skis who was covering the story of the missing Canadians approached the men, asking about conditions in the wilderness. Inside the Loj, Marcello breathed the heated air deep into his lungs.

Then they stepped out into the cold again, this time for the final walk to their car at South Meadows. There they were forced to sit and wait for a tow truck to come and extract their car from the deep snow, in which the tires had become irrevocably mired. They sat drinking hot coffee Dalhaus had gotten at the Loj and mixed with some remaining powdered hot chocolate. The pair pondered their experience, what they had endured, and the saga of the Canadians. "That we had fought our way through it is something of a legend for the two of us, but it is a fight that bows in comparison to the journey of the Quebecers," Dalhaus later wrote.

The Canadians, meanwhile, continued to forge through the unrelentingly difficult conditions, at last stumbling across a trail broken by rangers between the Uphill and Feldspar lean-tos. They followed that track to Colden's Interior Outpost, reaching the cabin around 7:30 p.m. on Wednesday night, and finally having some real food to eat. They were exhausted and a little cold and dehydrated, but otherwise okay.

Driving south from Quebec that night, Elaine Richer and her husband answered their cell phone and heard the good news, delivered directly from the forest rangers: Their son had been found.

Early Thursday morning, March 8, Mousseau and Richer were flown out of the wilderness. Forest rangers praised the pair's appropriate equipment, resourcefulness, and determination. All three were keys to "surviving the ordeal of being caught in the worst possible case, a storm that was many times more severe than originally predicted," wrote Tony Goodwin in his semiannual accident reports for *Adirondac*.

The Canadians had been out for four days, and missing in the nor'easter for three. And though there were times when they didn't think they would make it, in the end they successfully endured what they calculated was forty-five continuous hours of snowfall, dropped by a storm that shut down the Northway and came to be called the third worst snowstorm in the history of the Adirondacks. And despite the hardship, far from being turned off by the experience, they were exhilarated by the beauty of the High Peaks in winter, and plan to return again.

18

LIGHTNING STRIKE

Was that thunder? Very likely. But thundershowers are always brewing
in these mountain-fortresses, and it did not occur to me that there was
anything personal in it.

—Charles Dudley Warner, "Lost in the Woods,"
The Adirondack Reader (1964)*

Saturday, June 30, 2001, was a hot, muggy day. Forecasters were calling
for storms that afternoon, and "it started rumbling early," remembers
forest ranger Jim Giglinto. Thirteen hikers from several unaffiliated
groups lounged on the summit of 5,114-foot Algonquin Peak, including
Peter Church and his girlfriend, Cheryl Phoenix.

Two weeks earlier, Church had received a pair of trekking poles
for Father's Day. They had ergonomic handles, titanium shafts, and
integrated shock absorbers. This hike was one of their very first voyages
into the Adirondack backcountry.

Church and Phoenix reached the top of the peak around noon,
and sat admiring the views into the heart of the High Peaks, with the

* Excerpted from *The Adirondack Reader*, edited by Paul Jamieson and published (first
edition) by MacMillan in 1964. This copyrighted material is used with the permission of
Paul Jamieson. Subsequent editions of *The Adirondack Reader* published by Adirondack
Mountain Club Inc. (ADK), www.adk.org.

Great Range stretching across the horizon. Sometime close to 12:30 p.m., they ate lunch, but soon, a severe thunderstorm threatened as it approached the Adirondacks. "Then a few raindrops started falling," Church told the *Albany Times-Union*. He and Phoenix donned their rain gear and started down from the summit. So did the other eleven hikers who were also on top.

Within a few yards of leaving the summit, it started to pour. Church and Phoenix ducked under a rock overhang and waited for four or five minutes. The rain stopped, and the sky got lighter. "So we decided to bug out," he explained. A group of Canadians the couple had seen on the summit were also coming down roughly alongside them.

Then, when they were all 200 yards below the summit, a lightning bolt struck the mountain somewhere close behind them. "There was no warning. No hairs standing on the back of your neck. No smell of ozone. In fact, I had just heard a bird singing and told Cheryl that was a sign the storm was over," Church told reporters. He was wrong.

An intense bolt of lightning struck the bare summit cone of Algonquin. It didn't strike anyone directly, but the electricity traveled across the surface of the rain-soaked rock as a splash charge. In fact, although a bolt of lighting comes down as a 1- to 2-inch thick channel of electricity, it can spread out as much as 60 feet upon striking the earth's surface.

All thirteen hikers were affected by the jolt. Church and Phoenix were the worst hit; both were knocked unconscious, and Church was thrown to the ground, suffering a gash on his head that later required thirteen stitches to close. The others—mostly the larger group of Canadians—received smaller shocks and suffered minor burns, including a dog's paws and the soles of a twelve-year-old's hiking boots that melted.

Some minutes later, Church and Phoenix both regained consciousness, but with temporary paralysis in their legs. Other hikers helped them to their unsteady feet. "We couldn't feel anything from the knees down," Church said.

Matt Maloney, a Summit Steward, was also on the summit of Algonquin when the lightning hit. The Summit Steward program started in 1990 as a joint effort between the Adirondack Mountain Club, the New York State Department of Environmental Conservation, and the Nature Conservancy. It is a program designed to educate hikers about the fragile alpine vegetation on the summits of New York's highest peaks—all 85 acres of it. Maloney had been a Summit Steward for three or four years after first working at the ADK's Johns Brook Lodge.

He carried a cell phone, and after descending to just below treeline, used it to call for help. Then the whole group—thirteen hikers, one dog, and Maloney—started the long hike down the mountain. Shortly into the hike, they met up with an ADK volunteer who was coming up the mountain to provide preliminary first aid. Then, a mile later down the trail, they met the first forest ranger—Jim Giglinto (followed soon after by Jennifer Chapin)—coming to help. Back at the Loj parking lot, an ambulance waited to take everyone to a local hospital as a precaution.

Every year, according the National Lightning Safety Institute, an average 30 million ground points across the United States are struck by lightning. Some places are struck more than others, such as the Empire State Building, which is hit an average of twenty-one to twenty-five times per year. And some people, it seems, are struck more than others as well. Ray Sullivan, a United States Park Service ranger, was struck by lightning seven times between 1942 and 1976. He survived every strike.

(And never mind the fact that men are inexplicably struck five times more often than women.)

Sullivan for sure was the exception rather than the rule, but lightning is certainly more dangerous than most people realize. In a typical year, lightning causes more deaths than tornadoes, hurricanes, or any other weather event except for floods, killing on average sixty-seven people each year. For the thirty-six-year period spanning from 1959 until 1994, data compiled by the National Oceanic and Atmospheric Administration (NOAA), the National Weather Service (NWS), and the National Severe Storms Laboratory (NSSL) highlights more than 13,000 casualties (deaths and injuries combined) across the country, with nearly 25 percent of those being fatalities.

New England, thanks in part to its high population, has some of the highest casualty rates in the nation. Based on the raw data, New York, for example, ranks fourth for fatalities, and fifth for both injuries and casualties. Thankfully, when weighted for population, New York's fatality ranking drops to forty-third, with .20 deaths due to lightning per million people per year. It appears there's safety in numbers.

There's also safety, it would seem, in the mountainous North Country. The region stretching across northern New England from the Adirondacks through the Green Mountains and to the White Mountains is home to some of the lowest lightning flash densities in the country, and certainly of any region east of the Mississippi—less than one lightning flash per square kilometer per year (compared, for example, to Florida, the nation's most gluttonous state for lighting strikes, with more than sixteen per square kilometer per year). And when we look at a state like Vermont, whose whole geographic extent is confined to that lightning-starved North Country, the statistics seem to confirm the safety assumption.

Vermont, again based on raw data, ranks forty-third for fatalities due to lightning, and forty-seventh for injuries and casualties.

But when weighted for population, Vermont's fatality ranking suddenly jumps to fourteenth in the country. Perhaps the North Country is not as safe as we thought.

The problem is with lightning itself. Ancient Greeks believed that lightning was the weapon of Zeus, and that it was invented by Minerva, the Goddess of Wisdom. Scandinavian mythology holds that Thor, the Thunderer, hurled lightning bolts at his enemies. But thanks in part to Benjamin Franklin's now-famous kite-and-key experiments during 1752 and 1753, we today know that lightning is essentially a giant static electric spark that releases when the differential in charge between cloud and ground becomes great enough for a lightning bolt to "bridge the gap."

Lightning is a lazy beast, and seeks out the path of least resistance in its 90,000-mile-per-second journey from cloud to ground—which means that it looks for the easiest or shortest route (or both). When it comes to the North Country, the easiest and shortest route to the earth is through the summits of the highest peaks. And as the Adirondacks' second-highest mountain, Algonquin offers a shorter, easier route for Thor's lightning bolts than most.

Amazingly, on the same day—and almost at the same time—that thirteen unlucky hikers were struck by lightning on Algonquin Peak in the Adirondacks, a Roman Catholic priest had his own run-in with lightning on the 4,393-foot summit of Vermont's highest peak, Mount Mansfield. On that June Saturday in 2001, Rev. Philip Keane had just turned sixty years old. He taught medical ethics at the oldest Roman Catholic seminary in the United States—St. Mary's Seminary in Baltimore, Maryland—where he had been a member of the faculty for thirty-five years. About every other year for the twenty-five years leading up to 2001, Keane had spent his summers teaching at St. Michael's College, a small Catholic liberal arts college near Burlington, Vermont.

Keane was an avid outdoorsman who thoroughly enjoyed God's good creation. He started climbing in the Adirondacks as a teenager back in 1956. During his teen years and early twenties, Keane climbed roughly twenty of the Adirondack High Peaks. His Adirondack adventures went on temporary hiatus during stints in Honolulu, San Francisco, and Seattle. Then he returned to the East Coast, and his Adirondack climbs resumed not long thereafter. In 1989 he became an Adirondack Forty-Sixer for the first time, and then, just for good measure, finished the forty-six High Peaks a second time around a few years after that. Keane continues to hike in the Adirondacks "all the time," and has been up some peaks so many times—twenty times or more in some cases—that he's lost count: Giant, Marcy, Algonquin, Porter, Cascade, Whiteface, Big Slide, the Dixes. Now, Keane looks for new trails he hasn't yet been on.

And although he prefers the ruggedness of Adirondack peaks, Keane also hikes quite a bit in Vermont's Green Mountains, which are utterly convenient to access from the St. Michael's campus. So it was that on Saturday, June 30, Keane found himself at Underhill State Park at the trailhead for Mount Mansfield's Sunset Ridge Trail.

Keane wasn't teaching that day, and was looking to get away into the mountains. The weather forecast called for bad weather, but not until later in the day, he recalls. "I assumed I was going to have plenty of time to get up the mountain and down without any difficulty," he remembers. He left the college sometime between 7:30 and 8:00 a.m. that morning for the 15-mile drive to Underhill and the Sunset Ridge Trail. It was, and still is, Keane's favorite route up the mountain.

He set off alone up the trail, carrying a walking stick he's used since 1994 when he was involved in a serious bicycle accident, in which he was run over by an eighteen-wheeler. He didn't absolutely need the walking stick to hike, but it did make him more comfortable.

Hours later, Keane was coming up the Sunset Ridge Trail, some 500 vertical feet below Mansfield's summit, when he saw a severe thunderstorm blowing in, earlier than expected. He clambered under some rocks and huddled on the dirt for forty-five minutes to an hour, waiting for the storm to blow over. "I just sort of sat there and rested and thought about things," he recalls.

Then, even though it was still raining, it appeared to Keane that the storm had moved on. He resumed his hike to the summit, joining the Long Trail a quarter mile south of Mansfield's summit and continuing all the way to the top. Though he didn't know it, he wasn't out of danger yet. Lightning can strike more than 10 miles away from a storm in an area of clear sky, and, of greater concern to someone like Keane, who waited for a storm to pass over, lightning bolts can travel more than 60 miles from the front of a storm horizontally to the rear of a storm before touching down (the longest lightning bolt recorded to date reached 118 miles over the Dallas-Forth Worth area of Texas).

He reached the summit, spent a few minutes on the top, and started back down. Roughly 200 vertical feet below the summit—still on the Long Trail and not yet on the Sunset Ridge Trail—he placed his trekking pole on a rock as he walked, and suddenly saw an orange flash come from the bottom of his pole where it touched the rock. An "explosion" threw Keane to the ground. He had been knocked over by a blast of lightning. "I had no doubt what had happened to me," he says, though to this day he doesn't know if it was a direct strike or not.

Keane looked down at his watch—it was just before 1:00 p.m.

When the lightning bolt struck Keane, it superheated the air around it to a temperature greater than 50,000 degrees Fahrenheit, or three times hotter than the surface of the sun. Twenty thousand amps of electricity surged through his body—enough "juice" to light a 100-watt household lightbulb for three months straight. By comparison, an arc welder uses 250 to 400 amps to weld steel; an average single family home uses about 200 amps; and it takes just 20 milliamps (one fiftieth of an amp, or one millionth of the amperage contained in a lightning bolt) to cause a person's chest muscles to contract, stopping their breathing.

He made several attempts to stand up, but his legs were wobbly, and he fell over at least two or three times. The arm that held the walking stick was useless, hanging limp at his side, immobilized. Finally, fifteen minutes after being struck, Keane realized that he could stand and was able to walk. His first thought was that the best thing to do was continue down the trail and get off the mountain. From where he had been struck, it was 3 miles back to the car. The distance would normally take him two hours, or a little under; on that day, he would complete the hike in two and a half hours.

Partway down the mountain, Keane met up with three hikers from Philadelphia—a father (roughly sixty years old, like Keane), his daughter, and his prospective son-in-law. As Keane and the group greeted one another, they pointed out a bleeding cut on his chin. Keane hadn't even realized he had the injury. He explained what had just happened to him. The trio of hikers were concerned, and accompanied Keane down the trail for most of the distance back to the trailhead. Then, lower on the mountain, Keane and the group parted ways, convinced that the reverend would be okay to finish the hike on his own.

He continued down solo, finishing the rest of the hike back to his car. He even stopped to eat lunch on the way, which he had neglected to eat while back on the summit, as originally planned.

Keane drove back to St. Michael's College, took a shower, cleaned himself up, and then went to the hospital, not at all looking the part of a man who'd just been struck by lightning. He went to the Fanny Allen campus of what today is known as Fletcher Allen Hospital. The Allen campus was named after Ethan Allen's daughter, and was the closest medical facility to St. Michael's. He walked into the emergency room and told doctors, "I've been struck by lightning."

"You don't look like you've been struck by lightning," the ER doctors responded. But when they hooked Keane up to an electrocardiograph (EKG machine), all doubt was erased. Keane's irregular heartbeat hinted that something had happened. Doctors ushered him into an ambulance and drove him to the main hospital campus (Fletcher Hospital) at the University of Vermont. There an older Irish-American doctor taking over the ER for the night knew to look for the characteristic zigzag scarring indicative of a lightning strike. Sure enough, he found it on Keane, on the right side of the man's chest (the scarring eventually disappeared).

The doctor looked at his patient. "We all believed your story because you're a priest," he told Keane. "But now we know for sure that you've been struck by lightning." Doctors put Keane on an intravenous solution to help flush his kidneys in case there was any internally burned tissue that would get "hung up" in his filtering organs. His irregular heartbeat returned to normal within a few hours. ER staff sutured the cut on Keane's chin.

Doctors debated whether they should even keep Keane in the hospital or not. Ultimately, they decided to err on the side of caution and admitted him for two nights (a total of thirty-six hours). In the end, the doctors could basically find nothing wrong with Keane at all, and they released him early Monday morning, in time for him to teach his classes for the day. Within weeks, Keane was back in the mountains, including up on Algonquin where Church and Phoenix and the other Adirondack hikers had had their own run-in with lightning.

Keane suffered no permanent long-term effects from his lightning strike. He was one of the lucky ones. Of the 75 to 80 percent of lightning strike victims who survive, as many as one out of every four suffers serious long-term side effects, including heart and lung problems, nerve and brain damage, burns, skin scarring, hearing and vision impairments, memory loss, attention deficits, sleep disorders, numbness, dizziness, joint stiffness, irritability, fatigue, muscle spasms, restlessness, depression—and the list goes on.

On Monday, two days after being struck by lightning (and on the same day that Burlington doctors released Keane from the hospital), Church and Phoenix still had lingering pain in their legs, and sore muscles throughout their entire bodies. Even so, despite the experience, they hadn't sworn off hiking, although now with a few new prerequisites: "Oh, it'll be no humidity, not hazy, and blue skies," Church told reporters. "But we'll go again."

As for his modern trekking poles he received for Father's Day: "I told them [the Canadians who had picked up the poles] to throw them away. They're somewhere on that mountain," Church said. "When I go again, I'm pulling out my old hiking stick. It's wood."

Reverend Keane, for his part, plans to keep adventuring in the great outdoors as well. "I really haven't changed anything," he says. "Every summer since [the lightning strike] I've climbed a number of peaks in Vermont and the Adirondacks. I sail and ride my bicycle. I cross-country and downhill ski and snowshoe during the winter months. None of that has really changed at all. I love the hiking and all the other activities, and no, I would never stop.

"[People] wonder what I did with the staff," Keane concludes. "I still have that same walking stick . . . . I thought of changing to a wooden staff, but I haven't."

19

DEAD MAN WALKING: THE SEARCH FOR ARTHUR BIRCHMEYER

He may . . . escape the dangers without even knowing that they were there.
But if he affronts too often forces whose powers he had not attempted to
understand, he will in the long run succumb.

—Lord Schuster, *The Quotable Climber* (2002)

Fifty-eight-year-old Arthur Birchmeyer, a real estate agent and housing
inspector from the Syracuse, New York, suburb of Onondaga, was an
experienced hunter and outdoorsman. A member of a hunting and
fishing club, he often hunted alone, and was known to spend unplanned
nights in the woods.

In late November 2002 he spent a week at a friend's hunting camp
in Hamilton County in the Western Adirondacks, near Inlet among the
Fulton Chain of Lakes. Then, early Saturday morning, November 30,
he drove 9 miles to the southeast, parked his truck, and headed into the
Moose River Plains Wild Forest on his own. He was due home Sunday
night, and when he didn't return by Monday morning, his wife, Sheila,
contacted authorities—at 7:05 a.m.—and reported him missing.

Every year, it seems, hunters go missing in the Adirondacks. Most
often, they come out of the woods late, but otherwise none the worse
for wear. Hunters tend to be a hardy group, well versed in the ways of

the outdoors. But every now and then a hunter's trip into the woods becomes his last, such as it was for George Bombardier, who disappeared during the fall of 1971 while hunting in the Paul Smiths region of the Park. By the spring of 1972, searchers were still looking for him, but by then, only for his body. Everyone hoped Birchmeyer, a father of four and "good family man," as one forest ranger described him, wouldn't be a similar case.

More than thirty forest rangers went into the woods on Monday using snowmobiles to access the remote country of the Moose River Plains. Helicopters flew overhead, using night vision and heat-sensing technology to look for the missing man.

Sometime around midmorning, searchers found Birchmeyer's truck parked on a road just east of Squaw Lake. The road was remote, rugged, and not maintained in winter. Shortly beyond the point where Birchmeyer had parked his truck, the road closes to normal passenger vehicles and becomes a narrower snowmobile track that parallels Muskrat Creek, and then runs west-southwest just south of Little Indian Lake and 2,460-foot Indian Lake Mountain.

Birchmeyer's truck became the focal point of the search. It was, in search parlance, the Last Known Point (LKP) for the missing man. Searchers would have preferred a Point Last Seen (PLS)—the last confirmed sighting of a missing person in the woods—but they wouldn't get that lucky. Birchmeyer's truck, parked on a seldom-used road in one of the most remote corners of the Adirondack Park and more than 10 miles from the nearest civilization (the villages of Inlet and Raquette Lake), was all searchers had to go on. They knew for certain he had been at his vehicle. The only question now was, where did he go?

It wasn't an easy question to answer, especially considering the particularly deep and remote wilderness which faced searchers. In fact, at times, Adirondack wilderness like that of the Moose River Plains, in addition to hosting lost hikers or hunters, has also been used by fugitives and other criminals running, and hiding, from the law. Amidst the at-times impenetrable Adirondack wilds, criminals have remained undetected for days, weeks, and even months. One fugitive lived off the land for a hundred days, covering an estimated 300 miles during his clandestine travels within the Adirondack Park.

Searchers continued to look for Birchmeyer throughout the night on Monday and into Tuesday. The temperature was minus-18 degrees, and they could only stop for five minutes at a time because it was so cold.

Eighteen inches of fresh snow had fallen between the time when Birchmeyer had left his truck on Saturday morning and when forest rangers went in to search. Starting from the LKP—Birchmeyer's truck—rangers tracked the missing hunter by digging down to his frozen boot tracks in the older snow layers now hidden beneath the freshly fallen powder. Any suspicious depression in the snow attracted the attention of searchers, who then brought in specially trained rangers to painstakingly excavate each track to preserve its integrity.

As rangers found, then lost, then relocated Birchmeyer's track, a helicopter leapfrogged teams from one set of tracks to the next, hoping to link up the sections of track with Birchmeyer's LKP. Another storm was moving in, and they needed to find him quickly. But it wasn't easy. Animal tracks in the same vicinity as Birchmeyer's hampered efforts to follow the genuine track. Often, bear and moose tracks initially offered promise; the depressions they made in the snow above were only revealed to be false positives once rangers could dig down and discover their actual footprint shape.

By Tuesday night, December 3, there were thirty-five forest rangers in the field focusing their search on a 25-square-mile area of the Moose River Plains, which they closed to snowmobiles not directly a part of the search effort in order to facilitate the search and preserve any clues that might have still been out there. "We're keeping our hopes up that there's going to be a happy ending to this search," DEC spokesperson Dave Winchell told reporters.

There wouldn't be.

The search quickly grew to include not only DEC forest rangers, but also members of the Inlet police and fire departments, the Hamilton County Sheriff's Department, Lower Adirondack Search and Rescue (LASAR), and other volunteers. Because of the search's remote location, search and rescue volunteers were transported in to a spike camp—a remote camp prestocked with certain crucial supplies, such as snowmobiles, food, bunk beds, survival equipment—where searchers were served hot chili and offered the chance to warm up after being out in the extreme cold.

Dave Loomis from LASAR was one such searcher. He knew the Moose River Plains well. Loomis had a camp near Indian Lake, 5 miles into the woods off of Cedar River Road, and often snowmobiled over to Inlet through the same country he now searched. That Wednesday, as Loomis parked his car and walked past Birchmeyer's truck en route to his search assignment, he peered inside through the windows. The missing man looked well prepared, with extra boots, a sleeping bag, sandwiches, and other gear waiting in the truck.

Loomis's team searched the high ground on an unnamed mountain between Muskrat Creek and a beaver swamp on the north shore of the Indian River. The snow was up to their knees. Like the other teams, his found few clues, if any, to go on, and after finishing their assigned grid, Loomis's team hiked out to the road that Birchmeyer was never able to find in the midst of the snowstorm. Loomis didn't know it at the time, but the search was about to end.

At the same time that Loomis and company searched the high ridgeline, Ranger Steve Ovitt, LASAR members Tad Norton and Keith Fish, and a handful of local firemen were strung out in a line, searching another grid in the lowlands of the same forest. As they searched they could hear a helicopter flying search patterns overhead. Ovitt, the only one of his search crew to carry a radio, heard a report that a body had been located from the helicopter's aerial vantage point.

Suddenly, the other searchers in his team saw Ovitt take off running through the woods, aiming for a point below the hovering helicopter. Norton tied a piece of brightly colored flagging to a tree branch, marking the point where they left off searching their grid. Then, he and the others followed after Ovitt. Nearly half a mile later, they arrived on scene below the chopper. There, on the ground, was Birchmeyer— dead. It was 1:30 p.m. on Wednesday, December 4. Birchmeyer's body lay along the invisible borderline between the Moose River Plains Wild Forest and the West Canada Lake Wilderness. He was about 1 mile south of Little Indian Lake between the unnamed mountain that Loomis searched and the north shore of the Indian River. Birchmeyer was 3 miles, as the crow flies, from his truck, and less than a mile from the snowmobile track that could have led him back to the safety of his vehicle. He carried a map of the area, three separate compasses, and a Global Positioning System (GPS) unit.

Forest rangers and search teams thought it was an open-and-shut case. "99.9 percent he should have made it," recalls Loomis. Birchmeyer had simply screwed up, and he paid the ultimate price, finally succumbing to hypothermia, they thought. "The initial assumption was that he screwed up, didn't know where he was going, and didn't know how to use the technology [GPS]," adds forest ranger Will Giraud.

But that wasn't the whole story—a startling discovery turned everyone's thinking on its end. Birchmeyer's GPS unit was still operating and recording track points, leaving a detailed "account" of the hunter's desperate attempt to get out of the wilderness when he realized he was in trouble. Despite the harsh environment, extreme cold, and exposure to the elements, the unit never stopped functioning. Ranger Giraud worked on downloading the data. The rangers initially assumed the unit was broken because "it didn't seem to do anything," Giraud recalls. The LCD screen had frozen in the cold, giving the appearance that the unit was no longer working, but in fact, it was still communicating with satellites and recording data.

By coincidence, the Garmin-model GPS unit Birchmeyer carried was the same one used by the forest rangers. Giraud started working with Birchmeyer's unit and realized that it wasn't as nonfunctional as everyone had first thought. Partly on a whim, Giraud plugged it into his computer and was amazed when an avalanche of information downloaded. There, on the screen, GPS track point by GPS track point, was a detailed account of Birchmeyer's movements over the final days of his life.

Right away the rangers realized that many of their initial assumptions about Birchmeyer were wrong. He had known where he was going, and he knew how to use the technology. "He wasn't an idiot," says Giraud. While in the field, Birchmeyer had changed the timing interval of the GPS track points by extending the amount of time between each recorded data point. "That's not something you do by mistake," Giraud continues, speculating that Birchmeyer may have made such a change to preserve the unit's battery life in the cold temperatures, or to use fewer track points so that he wouldn't run out of memory space if he was in the woods for a long period of time.

Birchmeyer also had a waypoint—a preprogrammed coordinate position to which a user could navigate—loaded into his GPS, named "end of road." Its coordinates corresponded to the gate at the end of the road, marking where it changed to the snowmobile track.

As the rangers pored over the data and examined Birchmeyer's travels, they made a heartbreaking discovery: Birchmeyer had been making a beeline for the road—not quite for his waypoint, but definitely on course to intersect the snowmobile track not far beyond the gate. Then, just a half mile from his destination, he inexplicably turned around and backtracked to where he was later found dead. Rather than providing answers, the new data only raised more questions.

Piece by piece, rangers reconstructed Birchmeyer's last days, which, as best as can be surmised, were spent as follows:

On Saturday morning, November 30, Birchmeyer drove from his friend's hunting camp to the Squaw Lake trailhead in the Moose River Plains Wild Forest for a solo hunting excursion. In his truck, which had three-quarters of a tank's worth of gas, he left a portion of his gear: a sleeping bag, extra warm clothes, sandwiches, and possibly a tent. He hiked southwest toward Little Indian Lake, and then turned south toward the Indian River. The weather that day started in the 40s, or possibly even the 50s, as best as anyone can remember. Unexpectedly, a large weather front passed through, bringing with it a squall that dropped nearly 2 feet of heavy, wet, lake-effect snow. Then, an Alberta Clipper or equivalent cold-weather system moved in, and overnight, temperatures plummeted to more than 20 degrees below zero.

The rapid change in conditions prompted Birchmeyer to try and find a way back to his truck. Using his compass, GPS unit, and waypoints, he traveled north, looking to intersect the road, or at least the snowmobile track, and then follow it back to the safety of his vehicle. As he neared the vicinity of the snowmobile route, Birchmeyer temporarily abandoned his GPS and focused on finding the track in the nearby forest. "It makes sense . . . he wasn't screwing around," says Giraud. "He was trying to make his way back to the trail and get to his truck in the storm."

Although Birchmeyer's truck would have been snowed in, the vehicle would have at least offered shelter, food, clothing, the sleeping bag, and other supplies. Plus, it offered the opportunity to turn on the engine every few hours to warm up from the bitter cold. From there, Birchmeyer could have survived for days while waiting for help to come, or he could have resupplied and then hiked out along the road to get help.

But Birchmeyer never found the track. In fact, he blew right past it. It was 9:00 or 10:00 p.m. on Saturday night, long past dark. A whiteout blizzard raged all around. Heavy snow on the birches and balsams bent their limbs so that they hung down over the snowmobile track, disguising its look. Birchmeyer never saw what he was looking for. "It's easy to see how he could have gone past it," says Giraud. At some point during the night, Birchmeyer turned around and crossed back over the track—just 300 yards from the gate—heading south. He hiked over the small unnamed mountain searched by Loomis and then descended into a beaver swamp on the north side of the Indian River.

He fell into the swamp, soaking his legs. Then he reached the north shore of the Indian River, and probably had a demoralizing revelation. "He must have realized [at that point], 'I've really screwed up,' " Giraud thinks. Birchmeyer stopped for the night below the south slopes of the mountain and built a fire.

The next day—Sunday—again using his GPS, Birchmeyer headed north a second time in search of the snowmobile track. Half a mile away, he inexplicably turned around and headed back to his camp from the night before. Again he fell into the beaver swamp, soaking his legs another time. Although, according to forest rangers, there was plenty of fuel in the surrounding forest to build a fire, Birchmeyer instead tried to use gunpowder from one of his bullets to start a fire. He plugged the bullet into the front of the barrel of his rifle and wiggled it back and forth until he loosened the shell casing, allowing him to access the gunpowder contained within. Somehow during that process, he cut his hand, leaving spots of red blood in the snow.

He never left that spot again, succumbing to the elements sometime on Sunday night or shortly thereafter. Then, days later, rangers found his body.

Looking back, forest rangers are baffled as to why Birchmeyer turned around and headed back to his camp when he did, and why he didn't survive. Perhaps he had lost some of his mental faculties in the cold, or perhaps the disorientation and emotional and psychological trauma of realizing he was lost caused him to panic. Or maybe he had a heart condition or other medical condition that was exacerbated by the snow and cold.

It has taken much less, and circumstances far less severe, for people to irretrievably lose their way, or their senses, in the woods. Gary Hodgson, a retired DEC forest ranger who participated in 714 search and rescue missions, has seen it all. "Anyone who sits down and really tries to figure things out and do the best they can has a pretty good chance of coming out [of the woods]. It's almost impossible to travel in a straight line for any great distance and not come across some kind of logging road or foot trail," he notes. "In the Adirondacks, you're talking about a piece of country that's a pretty good size and it's pretty rugged, but there are a lot of hiking trails in it. Streams feed into bigger streams that will eventually come out someplace. You might go a long ways, but let's face it . . . if you walk steady for [a few days] . . . ."

But lose your cool head and panic, and all bets are off. In Hodgson's thirty-five years in the woods as a ranger, he's seen lost hunters and hikers unknowingly cross hiking trails, the Hudson River, and even the Northway—an interstate highway. Unbelievable, but true.

When it comes to Birchmeyer, however, "I'm not sure what the lesson is . . . he did a lot of things right, really. I don't know if we'll ever be able to answer," says Giraud. "He just got into a bad situation. It could happen to anybody. It was weird for us . . . the GPS data opened up a whole can of worms . . . we thought we had it figured out. Maybe he didn't mess up as much as we thought he did. A couple of bad decisions maybe left him out there longer than he needed to be."

And in this case, those bad decisions were enough to leave Birchmeyer a dead man walking.

20

BEACON OF CONTROVERSY: ONE CANOEIST, TWO RESCUES, AND THE PERSONAL LOCATOR BEACON THAT MADE HISTORY

One gets lost in the woods when he least expects it.

—J. T. Headley, *The Adirondack: Or, Life in the Woods* (1849)

Fifty-five-year-old Carl Skalak was a freelance photographer and community college administrator from Cleveland, Ohio, and a regular visitor to the Adirondacks. He was a man who always prepared for the worst . . . at least, almost always. Before each trip he would leave a detailed itinerary with the local forest ranger, including maps and copies of his driver's license and blood donor card. He brought only the best, most state-of-the-art gear, including extra changes of polypro, down, wool, and Gore-Tex. When he returned to civilization from the Adirondack wilderness, he would telephone the ranger to say he was out, and dropped a pre-addressed postcard in the mail indicating the same.

On November 10, 2003, Skalak set off for another Adirondack adventure. This time he brought his canoe, and put in from Long Pond Road in the Watson's East Triangle tract. From there he traveled solo 4 miles to the north, paddling for two hours until he reached the remote Alder Bed Flow on the Middle Branch of the Oswegatchie River in the far western Adirondacks. He planned to hunt, read a book, "sit on my butt," and perhaps take some photos, he later told *Adirondack Life* magazine.

Skalak paddled the deep stretches of river and pulled his canoe over sections that were too shallow. Soon after setting up his camp near Alder Bed Flow, the weather changed. At first, there were high winds and rain. Then it turned colder and the storm, according to Skalak, dropped several feet of snow—upward of 4 feet, he estimated—in the Five Ponds Wilderness (in reality, according to DEC documents, 12 to 18 inches of snow had fallen). Skalak was camping near the flats (floodplain), along a slack-water stretch of river. During the storm, the flats flooded, and then froze—at least partially—making the slushy, frozen river too thick to paddle and too thin to walk on.

The surrounding forest was still a tangle of blowdown from the 1995 microburst (chapter 13), Skalak knew, and he was reluctant to bushwhack through such country in deep snow. In short, he was stranded in the middle of the wilderness.

Trapped in his tent, and with many more hours of darkness than of daylight, he had plenty of time to ponder his fate. Worst-case scenarios came to his mind. He thought back to his native Midwest, where, in his experience, even a few inches of snow can cause a river to come up, "and people die," he later said. Then his thoughts shifted to what midwesterners refer to as the Blizzard of '78, which shut down the state of Ohio for a week.

Faced with the cruel reality of his predicament, and battling the thoughts swirling in his head, Skalak pulled out a Personal Locator Beacon (PLB)—purchased from ACR Electronics for $599—and flipped the switch. Miles overhead, and far out of sight, a satellite orbiting the earth received an electronic signal that initiated an elaborate search and rescue response that would save his life.

PLBs like the one Skalak carried actually belong to a larger grouping of emergency beacons that also include Emergency Position Indicating Radio Beacons (EPIRBs), used in maritime emergencies, and Emergency Locator Transmitters (ELTs), used in aviation emergencies, such as the one used to locate Bill and Mary Black after their plane crashed in the Adirondacks' Sawtooth Range (chapter 14).

It wasn't until July 1, 2003—less than five months before Skalak paddled into the Adirondack wilderness—that the Federal Communications Commission (FCC) authorized PLBs (portable units designed for individual people, and particularly, outdoor recreationists) for use throughout the continental United States. Prior to July 1, PLBs were only authorized for use by residents of Alaska, where officials were testing PLBs' capabilities and impact on search and rescue resources. The trial program was overwhelmingly successful, having been credited with helping to save nearly 400 lives, while generating only a small number of false alerts, prompting the FCC to roll out the technology nationally. In activating his PLB on November 14, 2003, Skalak became the first backcountry user in the country to rely on the technology.

PLBs, which operate on the accurate 406-megahertz frequency and also transmit a 121.5-megahertz homing beacon that rescuers can zero in on, once in the general area of a signal's location, utilize a complex network of search and rescue resources.

When a PLB is activated, its signal is initially picked up by satellites orbiting high above the earth. In the United States, that signal is first detected by the National Oceanic and Atmospheric Administration's Geostationary Operational Environmental Satellites

(GOES), which hover in fixed orbit over the earth. They receive the signal, which contains registration information about the beacon and its owner, including the person's name, address, telephone number, and a way to contact family members. The information is then relayed to Polar-Orbiting Operational Environmental Satellites (POES), which constantly circle the globe.

The U.S. system is part of a larger worldwide satellite search and rescue system known as COSPAS-SARSAT, the Search and Rescue Satellite-Aided Tracking System. Created in 1982, it is a network of American and Russian satellites that together can detect a PLB signal anywhere in the world.

The signal's information is relayed from the satellites to the Mission Control Center in Suitland, Maryland, and finally, on to the Air Force Rescue Coordination Center (AFRCC) in Langley, Virginia. The AFRCC acts as the single federal agency responsible for coordinating search and rescue in inland regions of the forty-eight contiguous states, and notifies the appropriate state emergency agency in the region where a signal originates.

According to official DEC documents, at 11:05 a.m. on November 14, 2003, the State Emergency Management Office received information about a signal from a PLB located 7.8 nautical miles north of the Stillwater Hotel in Herkimer County. That information was relayed to the Herkimer County sheriff's office. At 11:15 a.m., that office determined that it would be a wild lands search and rescue, and called the forest rangers to turn the search over to them. At 11:35 a.m., Herkimer County 911 also called the forest rangers, this time with exact satellite reception coordinates—44° 01.6 N, 75° 02.8 W—obtained from AFRCC. The coordinates placed the signal source along the

Middle Branch of the Oswegatchie River, near Alder Bed Flow.

Rangers also knew that they were probably looking for Carl Skalak, after tracing the PLB's registration information. At 11:50 a.m., the DEC's Herkimer office sent forest rangers Michael Lewis and Joel Nowalk to respond, along with six additional rangers. At 12:40 p.m., DEC interviewed ranger Howard Graham, the last person to see Skalak. The two had spoken on Sunday, November 9, when Skalak told Graham of his plans to canoe into Alder Bed Flow, saying that he'd be out by Sunday, November 16. Graham also knew that Skalak had been to that area before, but always as part of a group. Skalak left Graham with a map of his intended destination, which forest rangers immediately realized corresponded directly to the location of the distress signal. Then they found Skalak's truck parked at the end of Long Pond Road.

At 2:25 p.m., Fort Drum Aviation near Watertown called to offer the use of their Huey helicopter. Twenty minutes later, at 2:45 p.m., forest rangers requested the use of the State Police helicopter, but it was unable to respond. Finally, at 3:00 p.m., rangers accepted the offer of the Fort Drum chopper. While the helicopter was en route from Fort Drum, rangers received a slightly revised set of coordinates—44° 01.9 N, 75° 02.5 W. State police arrived on scene at Long Pond Road at 3:45 p.m., and five minutes later and 4 miles away, the helicopter arrived over the source of the beacon signal and began flying search sweeps over the immediate area. Meanwhile, in the event that the helicopter would be unable to assist from the air, rangers started hiking downriver from Long Pond Road, aiming to reach Skalak's planned camp location.

At 5:15 p.m., rangers in the field heard their radios crackle with communications between State Police and the helicopter: A person had been spotted where the locator beacon was plotted. The chopper was unable to land at the immediate location, but was able to confirm that the person on the ground was Carl Skalak. Then, at 5:28 p.m., they successfully picked up Skalak, who was reported to be in good condition, and flew him to the Fort Drum Military Base. Forest ranger Michael Lewis picked up Skalak at the base and drove him back to his vehicle on Long Pond Road. By 11:00 p.m. that night, DEC noted that "the mission was secured."

Safely back at home in Cleveland, Skalak was inundated with calls from reporters. Both NOAA and ACR Electronics had launched a publicity campaign touting the first successful use of a PLB by a recreationist in the lower forty-eight, and Skalak was their poster child.

"The system worked like a gem," said Lieutenant Daniel Karlson, SARSAT operations support officer for NOAA, in a press release dated November 17, 2003. "In a matter of a few hours, Mr. Skalak might have become acutely hypothermic, putting his life at risk. Since he had properly registered his PLB, we were able to immediately confirm his whereabouts and set the wheels in motion for his rescue."

Skalak told reporters that he was glad no one got hurt coming to help him—by his own admission, an out-of-shape, middle-aged guy. "What do you think the chances are I'd pull that switch again unless I was inches away from death?" he told the *Cleveland Plain Dealer*. "I don't mind being first, but I sure don't want to be doing this two times in a row." But less than a month later, that's exactly what he did.

Later that same November, Skalak returned to the Five Ponds Wilderness to recover his gear that had been left behind during the rescue. Before heading back into the wilderness, he again made attempts to be cautious. He tried getting a buddy and coworkers to come with him, but no one did. He asked a hunter who lives near Croghan to guide him, but the hunter had other plans. His calls to the local DEC office went unanswered, he says.

Skalak made a first attempt to reach his campsite. He walked—again solo and again carrying a PLB—on the riverbed, wearing waterproof fly-fishing waders. When the river deepened, he moved onto land, but "softballs" of snow formed under the felt soles of the waders, making it difficult to walk. He abandoned the attempt. On a topographic map Skalak found an old logging road, and the next day followed that, but missed a fork in the road, and bushwhacked through the forest for most of the day until he returned to his truck.

He drove out from Long Pond Road and telephoned a forest ranger to let him know he was back out of the woods. Skalak had given himself two days to recover his gear, and didn't want anyone to come looking for him, thinking he was overdue. The next day he went to a local Laundromat, dried his sleeping bag, and then ate Thanksgiving dinner with a ranger he had gotten to know through previous trips to that corner of the Adirondacks.

On Thursday, November 27—Thanksgiving Day—he also spoke with ranger Graham, the same ranger with whom he had spoken prior to his first trip earlier in the month. Skalak said he planned to go back in on Friday, November 28, to try and retrieve his gear.

Finally, the next day, Skalak headed into the woods yet again, this time in the rain. Five and a half hours later, and soaking wet, he reached the campsite from which he had been rescued. His canoe, a $1,600 Curtis, was missing. That simple fact threw an enormous monkey wrench into his plans. He had anticipated having the canoe. In fact, his whole plan was predicated on the availability of that crucial piece of equipment. But with the canoe gone, "I was in trouble," he told

Adirondack Life. "I didn't have a margin of error at this point. I knew I had better be careful."

Skalak hung up his wet clothes, changed into dry long underwear, and crawled into his down sleeping bag—a three-season model—inside his tent. He also had a stove, fuel, one sandwich, a Lipton rice dinner, three packets of hot chocolate mix, and an 8-ounce package of salmon. Expecting to paddle out that same day, Skalak was now delayed and worried about hypothermia. He spent the next three and half days trying to dry out his Cordura nylon-exterior boots for the walk out. It didn't work. They stayed wet despite numerous attempts to dry them out, including placing Nalgene bottles filled with hot water inside the boots, and then trying to dry the boots over his Coleman lantern. Then the rain turned to snow.

By Monday, Skalak started to anticipate needing rescue. He mistakenly thought that the DEC would send personnel to check on hikers known to be two days overdue. But no one was coming, and in truth, no such policy exists. Ignorant of that reality, Skalak sat in his camp on Monday fully expecting a search party to show up at any moment. He sat in his tent, continuing his attempts to dry out his boots. Occasionally, Skalak stuck his head out to look for people, but there was no one. He thought the first place searchers would come looking for him was at his camp, he reasoned, so he decided that the prudent thing to do was to sit tight.

Then, on Tuesday, December 2, scared and unable to keep warm, he flicked the switch on his PLB. "I said, 'Screw it; I'll just live with the notoriety of doing it twice,' " he told *Paddler Magazine*.

At 4:48 a.m. on December 2, AFRCC in Langley, Virginia, received the satellite signal indicating that Skalak had again activated his PLB. At 10:00 A.M., Major Bill Clark from Langley spoke with forest ranger Barstow, and gave him the coordinates of the signal. There was absolutely no way the device could be activated accidentally, Clark assured Barstow. The coordinates placed Skalak in the vicinity of his original rescue.

Given the remoteness of the area, and the difficulty in reaching Skalak's location from the ground during the previous rescue, DEC forest rangers immediately chose to initiate a helicopter rescue as the quickest and safest method for everyone involved—Skalak and rangers alike. Rangers called State Police Aviation in Lake Clear to request the helicopter, and rangers Burns and Fox drove to the hangar to wait for a hopeful break in snow squalls that blanketed the region, during which time the chopper could take off.

Flying conditions didn't improve, and so forest rangers sent two teams in on the ground to try and reach Skalak. One team started from the south and headed north, following Skalak's intended route to camp. The second team started from the north and headed south, toward the coordinates of the signal.

Although the weather near Skalak had cleared, snow squalls continued in Lake Clear, grounding the helicopter. At 3:00 p.m., DEC determined that not enough daylight remained for the chopper to fly even if the weather cleared sometime later that afternoon. Meanwhile, search teams on the ground were confident they'd reach Skalak with some daylight left, but were concerned about evacuating him in the dark if he was injured or otherwise incapacitated. DEC notified Major Clark at Langley, who then made the decision to launch a helicopter out of Fort Drum. The chopper took to the air at 3:30 p.m., and at 4:45 p.m., located Skalak near his campsite with a signal fire burning.

The Huey helicopter picked him up that afternoon. Forest rangers in the field were notified and turned back, while another ranger drove Skalak from Fort Drum to a hotel in Lowville, where he spent the night. The next day Skalak was taken to the local DEC office and questioned about the incident. He was then driven to State Police barracks and charged with two counts of falsely reporting an incident, a misdemeanor. He was handcuffed, fingerprinted, and taken to Webb Town Court for his arraignment. With his wallet back in his truck, Skalak didn't have access to the $10,000 bond, and spent the night in Herkimer County Jail.

Officials alleged that, in the case of both rescues, Skalak was found in healthy condition with no imminent emergency. They didn't charge him to make him pay for the rescue, but rather to turn him into a lesson for others—to demonstrate that cases like Skalak's amount to an unacceptable abuse of rescue capability. Regardless, he was still the only person to use the device in the continental U.S., giving him claim to the first and second instances of its use there.

Year by year, the number of PLBs purchased, registered, and used has gone up. From their authorization on July 1, 2003, until the end of 2004, PLBs were credited with saving thirty-eight lives, including Skalak's. In 2005 alone, PLBs saved thirty-four lives in twenty incidents. And as more and more users bring PLBs into the backcountry, such numbers are sure to rise.

But their use, and especially Skalak's two rescues and subsequent arrest, have sparked much debate. People question the impact of PLBs on backcountry recreationists' self-reliance, accountability, and personal responsibility. They create a false sense of security, some argue, and prompt people to call for help under circumstances when they might not normally have done so. They encourage a lack of preparedness, and cause people to take risks they normally wouldn't.

At what point and under what circumstances and conditions, then, do you call for a rescue? What constitutes appropriate use of a PLB? Skalak later admitted: "If you get into a situation where self-rescue is dangerous or impossible, what are the alternatives? Somebody has got to come for you. I didn't feel like I was in dire straits. I just knew I couldn't get out on my own, and didn't know if that situation would change for the positive anytime soon." He also rationalized that things might have gotten worse—the weather, for example, or he might have gotten injured—so he opted to call for help during a spell of good weather that posed the least risk to rescuers and the greatest chance for a successful rescue.

But will New York follow the lead of other states such as New Hampshire, where people can be fined for "unnecessarily endangering the lives of rescue personnel?" Probably not. The Adirondacks remain resolutely committed to independence and self-reliance first, and second, to a network of state search and rescue resources. Still, in the wake of Skalak's incidents, the regional outdoor community remained strongly opinionated.

"There are plenty of people who will use PLBs (or cell phones or satellite phones) as a crutch," wrote one poster—who admittedly had no personal experience with a PLB—on Trailspace, an Internet discussion forum, "and allow themselves to get into situations they otherwise might avoid, because they think that rescue is just a button push away." That same poster harshly criticized Skalak for "expecting to be rescued." Skalak's backup plan was to get rescued, the critic noted, even though he "was less than six hours from his truck, over familiar ground, and in fine condition physically.

"In some respects, a PLB is worse than a cell phone," he continued. "With a cell phone call, rescuers at least have a chance to assess the victim's situation and, if appropriate, talk them out without having to mount an expensive and potentially dangerous rescue mission. With a PLB, it's pretty much all or nothing."

But cell phones in the Adirondacks have never offered much assurance. Cell coverage is spotty at best, and nonexistent at worst, and PLBs offer the kind of signal reliability that cell phones never will. "A PLB or phone can be a legitimate piece of backcountry equipment, but only if it's an absolute last resort and it does not affect your planning or decision-making," concluded another opinionated poster from the same forum. "PLB or none, if you don't have the ability to self-rescue from reasonably foreseeable circumstances, then you probably shouldn't be going at all."

"Don't rely on stuff like this to save you," added another. "Just because someone knows where you are, doesn't mean they can get to you . . . . Common sense can be the best thing you take with you."

Others, like the editor of Backpackinglight.com—rather than question the circumstances under which a beacon could reasonably be activated—instead wonder whether PLBs have a use in the lower forty-eight at all. "After all, the most remote location in the continental U.S. (in the far SE corner of Yellowstone National Park) is only thirty miles as a crow flies from the nearest road."

Skalak, on the other hand, remains convinced that he was justified in activating the beacon in both cases. On November 20, 2003—in between his two rescues—he wrote an e-mail to the manager of the Web site, Equipped to Survive: "A month ago I didn't know what a PLB was. Your story about the recently approved [PLBs] . . . gave me the information I needed to make the decision to purchase one for my solo canoe trip into a remote section of the [Adirondack Park]. When I became stranded by the severe blizzard conditions and the suddenly frozen river, I used the PLB to call for assistance. I can't say enough about the SAR folks who came after me, but thanks in part to your efforts, too, my heirs will have to wait a bit longer for their inheritances."

Which is perhaps the point. On the one hand, distress is in the eye of the beholder, notes Lieutenant Karlson from NOAA. But in addition, the fact remains that PLBs are saving lives, including (possibly) Skalak's. "We couldn't think of not having 911 . . . . False alerts, and even rare cases like Mr. Skalak's, are the price of doing business," Karlson concludes. "The bottom line is, these beacons are out there saving lives and doing their job, and the system does work."

EPILOGUE: LESSONS FROM THE BACKCOUNTRY

In the course of researching this book, one survivor of a misadventure recounted in these pages who declined to be interviewed asked me, "Why do you want to write about misadventures? There are so many great people and positive adventures happening in the Adirondacks that you can share . . . I don't understand why you focus on the negative." Her question gave me pause, and made me go back and re-center myself to bring renewed focus to why I was writing this book in the first place.

I felt then, as I do now, that my motives for writing this book are pure. As I set forth in the preface, I hope not only to entertain with these stories of outdoor misadventure, but to honor the memory of those people who have lost their lives in the Adirondack wilds, and to recognize the rescuers who selflessly come to the aid of those in need. But above all else, I hope that these stories help to raise awareness and to inform and educate other outdoor adventurers—readers like you—to go into the Adirondacks, or any wilderness environment, better prepared to handle the adventure, and the risk that comes along with it. In the end, it comes down to surviving. And surviving is not just about the will to live, and the choices we make, but also about what goes wrong and why, and how people successfully survive in the face of adversity.

To that end, I've tried to distill some "nuggets of wisdom" gleaned from the misadventures in the previous pages, and offer them to you as my most important answer to "why I write about misadventures." Borrowing a phrase from the search and rescue community, this book exists simply, "so that others may live."

THE RISK EQUATION

Every outdoor adventurer faces risk, and it is how we manage that risk that most often determines whether or not we come out of the backcountry alive. Risk, or the danger that creates it, comes in three types: perceived, subjective, and objective.

Perceived risk relates to the amount of risk we believe we are being exposed to, whether that risk is real or not. For example, a person with an intense fear of heights may perceive a high level of risk while walking on a trail above treeline, when in fact the actual risk of falling and being injured is very low.

Subjective risk relates to risks that are real, but that we have a high degree of control over. A person's physical fitness level, the amount of pre-trip planning they put into an adventure, and their technical skill level and training are all examples of factors that greatly impact the amount of risk that person is likely to experience in the backcountry. Fortunately, that person can decide to decrease the amount of risk they'd face by managing those factors—by exercising to improve their cardiovascular health, researching their route and carrying the appropriate maps, and seeking out instruction from an experienced guide.

Then there's *objective risk*—those risks over which we have little or no control, such as rockfall dangers, avalanche hazards, and the threat of sudden storms. We don't get to decide when a rock might fall on us, or when a snow slope will avalanche, or when a sudden thunderstorm will chase us off the mountaintops. Or do we? Even though we have little control over the hazard itself, we can still make decisions that will minimize our exposure to the risk it poses. We can choose to climb a route with less loose rock on it or to not pass beneath the base of a cliff, to dig a test pit and assess the snow's stability or to travel on safer slopes, or to be off of summits and other high points before we might expect thunderstorms to light up the mountain summits.

Ultimately, it's the choices we make in and out of the wilderness that enable us to manage, minimize, or neglect the risks we face as outdoor adventure seekers. And it's the conversion of risk to reality that leads to misadventures.

As outdoor enthusiasts, we're each tasked with answering a series of basic questions: How much risk am I willing to accept? How do I minimize the risks inherent in my outdoor adventures? How do I make sure that I am not caught in my own misadventure? And if one happens to me, how do I navigate the misadventure to reduce its consequences, and most fundamentally, to simply survive?

Fortunately, outdoor adventurers today can benefit from the collective experience of the outdoor and search and rescue communities, and take away lessons from those experiences that can then be carried into the wilderness.

The most important thing to remember is that misadventures can, do, and will happen. In the Adirondacks, as elsewhere, misadventure has proven itself to be adventure's constant companion; a yin to the other's yang. Throughout the years, decades, and even centuries, and across all disciplines of outdoor sports, misadventure is a guaranteed part of the equation. Some of those misadventures will be more epic than others, with greater negative consequences should things not turn out as we might like. But they happen nonetheless.

Beyond the fact that misadventure is a known part of the experience, however, how do we go about answering the other basic questions posed above? When we look to the collective experience of the outdoor and search and rescue communities for answers, a number of consistent themes emerge for the Adirondacks, whether we look to guide John Cheney in the nineteenth century or to Carl Skalak's history-making PLB rescues in the twenty-first century.

THE PRE-ADVENTURE CONTEXT

What we do before we ever set foot in the backcountry is just as important as what we do once we finally get there.

Prepare for your trip by seeking proper instruction in your outdoor discipline, practicing those skills, maintaining an appropriate level of physical fitness, and planning and packing for the worst-case scenario.

Common sense dictates that we follow these guidelines. Many of the misadventures recounted in this book illustrate that, to an extent, we can contribute to the success of our adventures: the amount of training and instruction we seek in a discipline, our accumulated experience in that endeavor, our preparation (physical, mental, and gear), and the planning that we put into a backcountry trip—all of these factors can lay the foundation for safety and success.

The decision to sign up for a basic rock climbing or winter camping course, to regularly exercise and improve our cardiovascular fitness, or to pack the type of survival and backup equipment that would allow us to tackle a worst-case scenario (i.e., carrying a sleeping bag or bivy sack on a winter mountaineering day trip, just in case we get caught out overnight)—all serve to minimize the risks we face once we actually set foot in the wilderness.

Understand the influence of group size on risk, and be willing to accept that risk, or alter the size or composition of your group, or the choice of route, to adjust the risk accordingly.

Extremes of group size—both large and small—also contribute to the risks we face in the woods. On the one extreme, the soloist leaves him- or herself with no margin for error. Should something go wrong, that person is left with little recourse, and must be self-reliant; and if the person becomes seriously injured or incapacitated, the opportunity for self-rescue vanishes, and the prospect of never coming back out of the woods alive becomes a sobering reality. Even traveling in pairs is not a guarantee of safety. If, for example, one person becomes injured, the remaining partner is forced to choose between staying with the injured partner and providing first aid, or leaving the person while he or she goes for help.

Yet, on the other extreme, groups that are excessively large—numbering eight to ten people or larger—face their own risks, though they may be different in nature. Larger groups exhibit a tendency to get strung out along a trail, for instance. As they do so, trip leaders and less-experienced members of the group lose contact with one another, and many times, a hiker gets lost. In the Adirondacks, such a scenario has happened so many times and so often that Tony Goodwin, editor of *Adirondac*'s twice-yearly Accident Report, dubs such events with the moniker "SGS"—Separated Group Syndrome. Another danger of larger groups is the risks they are willing to take. The concerns of individual group members become diluted or suppressed under the influence of the larger group size, and as a result, the group exposes itself to higher-than-expected levels of risk. Such scenarios are evidenced in avalanche statistics, where researchers have found a "risky shift," the tendency of larger groups to take more risk and ignore a higher number of signs of risk.

All other things being equal—training, experience, physical fitness—moderate group sizes offer the greatest margin of safety.

THE UNFOLDING OF THE ADVENTURE

Naturally, the choices we make in the face of the events that unfold in the course of our outdoor adventures have just as great an impact on the risks we face, and whether or not we wind up in our own misadventure.

Make decisions based upon a constantly updated evaluation of conditions; do not fall into the habit of complacency or of making routine assumptions, and be willing to deviate from your initial plan if it is the prudent thing to do.

Oftentimes, our own psychology can be our worst enemy. And most devious of all our psychological faults are what researchers call *heuristic traps*. Heuristics are unconscious rules of thumb that guide our decisions in everyday life and in the backcountry. The problem with heuristics is that they sometimes work, but not always.

One heuristic trap is known as *familiarity*. With familiarity, we rely upon the outcome of our past actions to guide our behavior in similar settings. For example, skiers experienced with skiing a particular snow slope may continue to do so without routinely studying the snow's stability if they have never before observed signs of avalanche potential. But familiarity becomes a dangerous trap when our assumptions, based upon that familiarity, no longer hold true. Similarly, familiarity becomes a serious danger when coupled with *non-event feedback*. Non-event feedback describes scenarios where we do not experience the potential consequences of our actions, resulting in desensitization to the hazard. For example, a rock climber who poorly places protection, but never falls on that rope system, does not receive the experiential feedback that would let him or her realize that the protection is inadequate. Then, when that person *does* fall in a high-risk scenario, he or she suddenly realizes the inadequacy of the belay system, although at that point, it's too late—the consequence will likely be fatal.

Another heuristic trap is known as *consistency*. Consistency describes our tendency to make subsequent decisions based upon an overriding initial decision. For example, if a group of hikers decides that they are going to hike to the top of Mount Marcy, their subsequent decisions throughout the day will likely lead them to continue their ascent, even if other factors, such as weather or fatigue, indicate that turning around might be the more prudent thing to do. Mountaineers call such a heuristic trap *summit fever*—the overwhelming desire and motivation to reach the top of a mountain, even when rational analysis would suggest it would be wiser to descend. But all outdoor recreationists, not just mountaineers, face such pressures, and must be open to the idea that plans may need to change.

Finally, we should learn to expect the unexpected. If we are open to the idea that things might not go according to plan, we will be less likely to get caught off guard when an adventure goes awry, and we will be more willing to change course and switch to Plan B when conditions dictate.

THE RESPONSE WHEN THINGS GO WRONG

Lastly, when things go wrong, our decisions then become paramount to our survival.

Your brain is your biggest asset.

Critical thinking in the face of an adverse situation is perhaps most important. Those people that remain calm, don't panic, and then logically reason out their situation are the ones who most often survive. When faced with a misadventure, our task is to deal with the reality of our situation; to self-rescue, to sit and wait, or to call for rescue when appropriate; to determine our options; to understand the severity of our situation; to help ourselves; to use our tools and training and common sense to determine our own outcome.

Technology is just one tool available to us in the face of a misadventure. Use it with discretion as part of a larger toolkit of resources that include self-sufficiency and self-reliance.

Technology does not guarantee rescue, and under certain circumstances, no matter how determined, a rescue team may not reach you. Cell phones, satellite telephones, and PLBs each have their own strengths and weaknesses, but ultimately, you must be your own best strength.

CONCLUSION

This epilogue is not meant to be an all-encompassing guide to wilderness survival. Entire books have been written on the topic for specific outdoor sports and accidents—avalanches, rock climbing, winter camping. Rather, this is a summary of many of the insights offered by the misadventures contained within this book's pages. You can gather many more insights by reading the stories themselves, but do use this condensation of insight to inform your own adventures.

For sure, not every outdoor sport carries equal risk. And similarly, not every misadventure need be the epic of a lifetime, where we are fighting for our very survival. But we can be certain that both risk and misadventure are a part of the outdoor experience. With misadventure, it is not a matter of *if* it will happen to us, but when, and how serious. The circumstances are not always in our control, and we don't always get to decide the outcome. But to the degree that the misadventure is in our hands, it becomes our decisions—at home, in the wilderness, and in the face of adversity—that determine whether we live or die.

TIME LINE OF MISADVENTURES AND
SEARCH AND RESCUES COVERED IN THIS BOOK

1800–1887 Adirondack guide John Cheney lived and died

1850 Mount Colden's Trap Dike first climbed by Robert Clarke and Alexander Ralph

1927 February Winifred Hathaway saves six men stranded on an ice floe on Lake Champlain

1933 August Three Boy Scouts—Tyler Gray, Bob Glenn, and Bill Ladue—were rescued after being stranded on the Wallface Cliff

1934 December Ernest Dyer, Dale Dyer, J. H. Brown, and P. D. Hambrook are all rescued alive after surviving their plane's crash in the Adirondack wilderness during an ice storm

1935 Winter Jim Goodwin and Ed Stanley complete first winter ascent of Mount Colden's Trap Dike

1936 March Abel Duso froze to death while crossing Lake Champlain from New York to Vermont

1937 February	A father and his two sons died when they broke through the ice of Lake Champlain returning from a day of fishing
1938 July	Maria Gersen is rescued after becoming stranded on cliffs above Chapel Pond
1942 Summer	Young teen disappears in Adirondack wilds; discovered alive after five days of subsisting on berries
1942 December	Charles Donnelly sustains serious injuries after falling off a short cliff near the summit of Whiteface Mountain
1951 August	E. F. Crumley disappears while on a fishing and camping trip; his remains accidentally discovered more than six years later by members of original search party
1954 Fall	Hunter treks 20 miles through woods to get out of wilderness after becoming separated from his group and lost
1961 Summer	Eight-year-old Douglass Legg walks away from his family's estate and disappears in the Adirondack wilderness; he is never found
1970s	A tough decade for airplane crashes throughout the Adirondacks, including six major accidents
1971 Fall	George Bombardier disappears in Adirondacks while on a hunting trip

1972 June Patrick Griffin dies while attempting to scale the forty-six High Peaks in five days with partner Chris Beattie

1973 March George Atkinson Jr. disappears on Mount Marcy; his remains are found more than three years later during the search for Steven Thomas

1975 March Peter Gough, Anthony Patane, and Ken Martin survive being avalanched down the Chapel Pond Slab ice climbing route

1976 April Steven Thomas disappears near Mount Marcy after walking away from the lean-to where his friends were located

1977 August William Mollet died after taking a serious fall while climbing Wallface Cliff

1977 October Jim DeGaetano and Bob Henry survive an unsuccessful attempt to run the Hudson River Gorge in a canoe

1983 July Lee Fowler and Andrew Metz died after their belay system failed and they took a groundfall while climbing Wallface Cliff

1983 Fall St. Lawrence University begins Peak Weekend, in which students attempt to collectively summit all forty-six High Peaks on a single day

1987 March Paul Junique and Jean Grenon are avalanched down Mount Colden's Trap Dike and survive, with injuries

1988 January An ice climber from Long Island, New York, is paralyzed after taking a serious fall while climbing Multiplication Gully in Wilmington Notch

1989 March Linda Hepburn dies after slipping and falling on the slides above Mount Colden's Trap Dike

1990 June David Boomhower disappears near Cedar River Flow on Northville-Placid Trail; his body discovered in October by hunters

1991 June Robert Mahar fell to his death after slipping off a ledge on Rogers Rock above Lake George

1991 June Jason Chicoine died after falling while attempting to scramble to the top of Roaring Brook Falls

1993 October Thomas Carleton disappears in the High Peaks after parking his car at Adirondak Loj trailhead; some of his equipment found years later, but he remains missing

1995 July Microburst storm catches hundreds of hikers and campers by surprise; blows down hundreds of thousands of acres of forest

1996 February One ice climber is left stranded in Chouinard's Gully above Chapel Pond after his partner dies rappelling off the end of their ropes

1996 August Bill and Mary Black crash into the Sawtooth Mountain Range after experiencing difficulty with their airplane; both survive

1998 January   Four college friends are caught by rising waters due to an ice jam on the Opalescent River during a terrible ice storm

1999 October   Middlebury College attempts to have students, faculty, staff, and alumni summit the forty-six High Peaks in honor of bicentennial; plans thwarted by blowdown from Hurricane Floyd earlier in the year

2000 February   Six backcountry skiers involved in a rare avalanche on Wright Peak; one skier dies

2001 March   Two pair of winter campers caught in third worst snowstorm in Adirondack history; all survive

2001 June   Day hikers struck by lightning near summit of Algonquin Peak; almost simultaneously, Rev. Philip Keane also struck by lightning descending from summit of Vermont's Mount Mansfield

2002 February   A Canadian ice climber dies when a large section of ice pulls off the Poke-o-Moonshine ice climb, Positive Thinking

2002 June   Ted "Cave Dog" Kaizer sets new High Peaks speed record by climbing all forty-six mountains in less than four days

2002 November   Arthur Birchmeyer disappears in Moose River Plains Wild Forest while on solo hunting trip; discovered dead

2003 November   Canoeist Carl Skalak rescued twice after using Personal Locator Beacon while facing difficult conditions at Alder Bed Flow

2004 Summer   Two pairs of hikers get stranded on steep slabs above Mount Colden's Trap Dike and require rescue

2004 December   Fred Vishnevsky and Alan Glick self-rescue after Glick slips and falls on slide above Mount Colden's Trap Dike

BIBLIOGRAPHY

BOOKS

Abbey, Edward. *Desert Solitaire: A Season in the Wilderness*. New York: Ballantine Books, 1968.

Accidents in North American Mountaineering, "Avalanche—New York, Adirondack Mountains," (American Alpine Club, 1988), 45–46.

Accidents in North American Mountaineering, "Avalanche, Poor Position—New York, Adirondack High Peaks, Wright Peak," (American Alpine Club, 2001), 71–72.

Accidents in North American Mountaineering, "Fall on Ice, Inadequate Equipment, Unclear Leadership/Decision Making—New York, Adirondacks," (American Alpine Club, 1990), 51–52.

Accidents in North American Mountaineering, "Fall on Rock, Failure to Follow Route, Failure to Test Hold, Inadequate Protection—New York, Adirondacks, Wallface Mountain," (American Alpine Club, 1978), 25–28.

Accidents in North American Mountaineering, "Fall on Rock, Inadequate Protection—New York, Adirondacks," (American Alpine Club, 1984), 41.

The Adirondack Forty-Sixers. Albany, NY: Peters Print, 1958.

Brumley, Charles. *Guides of the Adirondacks: A History*. Utica, NY: North Country Books, 1994.

Burdick, Neal, ed. *A Century Wild, 1885–1985: Essays Commemorating the Centennial of the Adirondack Forest Preserve.* Saranac Lake, NY: Chauncy Press, 1985.

Carson, Russell M. L. *Peaks and People of the Adirondacks.* Garden City, NY: Doubleday, Page & Company, 1927.

De Sormo, Maitland C., ed. *Told Around the Campfire: Henry Van Hoevenberg of Adirondack Lodge.* Saranac Lake, NY: Adirondack Yesteryears, 1967.

The Encyclopedia of Canada, s.v. "Exploration."

Freeborn, Frank. *Some Adirondack Paths: Climbs about the Keene Valley.* Boston: Appalachian Mountain Club, 1889.

Goodwin, Tony, ed. *Guide to Adirondack Trails I: High Peaks Region.* Lake George, NY: Adirondack Mountain Club, 1992.

Haeusser, Dorothy O., et al. *The Adirondack Forty-Sixers.* Albany: Peters Print, 1958.

Headley, J. T. *The Adirondack; or, Life in the Woods.* New York: Baker and Scribner, 1849.

Heller, Murray. *Call Me Adirondack: Names and Their Stories.* Saranac Lake, NY: Chauncy Press, 1989.

Holt, Charles. *Adirondack Frontier: Stories of Keene Flats after 1776.* Elizabethtown, NY: Denton Publications, 1976.

Jamieson, Paul F., ed. *The Adirondack Reader: The Best Writings on the Adventurous and Contemplative Life in One of America's Most Loved Regions.* New York: Macmillan, 1964.

Longstreth, T. Morris. *The Adirondacks.* New York: The Century Company, 1917.

Mellor, Don. *Climbing in the Adirondacks: A Guide to Rock and Ice Routes in the Adirondack Park.* Lake George, NY: Adirondack Mountain Club, 1995.

Pilcher, Edith, ed. *Up the Lake Road: The First Hundred Years of the Adirondack Mountain Reserve.* Keene Valley, NY: Centennial Committee for the Trustees of the Adirondack Mountain Reserve, 1987.

Roach, Gerry. *Colorado's Fourteeners: From Hikes to Climbs*. Golden, CO: Fulcrum Publishing, 1999.

Stoddard, Seneca Ray. *Old Times in the Adirondacks: The Narrative of a Trip into the Wilderness in 1873*. Edited, and with biographical sketch, by Maitland C. De Sormo. Saranac Lake, NY: Adirondack Yesteryears, 1971.

Sylvester, Nathaniel Bartlett. *Historical Sketches of Northern New York and the Adirondack Wilderness: Including Traditions of the Indians, Early Explorers, Pioneer Settlers, Hermit Hunters, & c.* Troy, NY: W. H. Young, 1877.

Waterman, Jonathan, ed. *The Quotable Climber*. Guilford, CT: The Lyons Press, 2002.

Waterman, Laura and Guy. *Yankee Rock and Ice: A History of Climbing in the Northeastern United States*. Harrisburg, PA: Stackpole Books, 2002.

Weber, Sandra. *Mount Marcy: The High Peak of New York*. Fleischmanns, NY: Purple Mountain Press, 2001.

Weston, Harold. *Freedom in the Wilds: A Saga of the Adirondacks*. St. Huberts, NY: Adirondack Trail Improvement Society, 1971.

MAGAZINES AND NEWSPAPERS

"2 Lost Boys Found Dead," *Adirondack Daily Enterprise*, 18 July 1974.

"29 from Coast Join Hunt for Boy," *The New York Times*, 18 July 1971.

"50 People Comb Peaks for Hiker," *Albany Times Union*, 18 October 1993.

"Abandon Search for Plane Victims," *Adirondack Record-Elizabethtown Post*, 20 August 1936.

"Adirondacks Scoured for Pilot," *Adirondack Daily Enterprise*, 22 March 1974.

"Air Patrol Finds Missing Pilot Dead," *Adirondack Daily Enterprise*, 24 June 1974.

"Body Keesville Man Found by State Troopers," *Adirondack Record-Elizabethtown Post*, 5 March 1936.

"Body of Missing Hunter Is Found," *Albany Times Union*, 5 December 2002.

"Bones Found Near Raquette," *Adirondack Daily Enterprise*, 27 November 1957.

"Boy, Lost Five Days, Found on Sunday," *Adirondack Record-Elizabethtown Post*, 9 July 1942.

"Boy Rescues Lives of 6 Adrift on Ice," *Adirondack Record-Elizabethtown Post*, 17 February 1927.

Brickman, Leonard. "Letters: Those 46 Peaks, a Questionable Challenge," *The New York Times*, 18 March 1973.

Brown, Phil. "Avalanche! The risk is real," *Adirondack Explorer*, November/December 2003, 30–31, 40-42.

Brown, Phil. "The Wright Story," *Adirondack Explorer*, November/December 2003, 6–7, 43.

Carpenter, Chris. "Marcy in Winter," *Adirondack Life*, November/December 1977, 10–13, 34–37.

Carpenter, Chris. "Rescue in the Hudson River Gorge," *Adirondack Life*, March/April 1979, 12–15, 44–47.

"Chicago Woman Physician Alone All Night on Mt. Whiteface." *The Elizabethtown Post*, July 5, 1906.

Clarity, James F. "400 Searching for Boy Lost in Adirondacks," *The New York Times*, 22 July 1971.

" 'Copter rescues Giant Mt. Hiker," *Adirondack Daily Enterprise*, 31 July 1975.

Crowe II, Kenneth C. "Heat And Humidity Bubble Up to Explode in a Rare Meteorological Phenomenon," *Albany Times Union*, 16 July 1995.

"Crumley's Death Said Accidental; His Bones Found in Mt. Country," *Adirondack Record-Elizabethtown Post*, 23 January 1958.

"David Boomhower; Hiker, Postal Worker," *Albany Times Union*, 23 October 1990.

Decker, Charles. "Identification Made of Atkinson's Gear," *Adirondack Daily Enterprise*, 16 June 1976.

Decker, Charles. "Solution of Mystery Nears as Skeleton Is Discovered," *Adirondack Daily Enterprise*, 28 July 1976.

Demare, Carol. "Couple Recovering After Plane Crash," *Albany Times Union*, 9 August 1996.

DiMeo, Sam. "Hikers Found Unhurt in Adirondacks," *Plattsburgh Press-Republican*, 8 March 2001.

Doolittle, William; Riley, Howard; and Outcalt, Evelyn. "Jet Plane Crashes near Airport; Searchers Find Two Bodies, Hunt Continues for Third," *Adirondack Daily Enterprise*, 28 December 1972.

Doolittle, William. "Massive Search Organized for Missing Light Plane with Pilot and Passenger," *Adirondack Daily Enterprise*, 20 December 1972.

Doolittle, William. "Relatives Await Word of Plane," *Adirondack Daily Enterprise*, 27 December 1972.

Doolittle, William. "Snow and Clouds Hinder Search for Two Lost Men," *Adirondack Daily Enterprise*, 21 December 1972.

"E'town Man Walks 20 Miles to Get Out of Woods; Was Lost," *Adirondack Record-Elizabethtown Post*, 25 November 1954.

"Fall from Cliff Kills Hiker; Many Searches in Progress," *Adirondack Daily Enterprise*, 28 October 1976.

"Family Searches for Missing Hiker," *Albany Times Union*, 10 July 1990.

"Father and Two Sons Drowned in Lake Champlain," *Adirondack Record-Elizabethtown Post*, 25 February 1937.

"Find Bones of Lost Man in Woods; Ends Mystery of 6 Years," *Adirondack Record-Elizabethtown Post*, 5 December 1957.

Fish, Glenn. "Letters: Those 46 Peaks, a Questionable Challenge," *The New York Times*, 18 March 1973.

"Five Ponds Wilderness Area Inaccessible After Storm," *Adirondac*, November/December 1995.

Forrest, Lisa. "Quebec Ice Climber Falls to His Death," *Plattsburgh Press-Republican*, 28 February 1996.

"Fort Ann Mayor Died Accidentally," *Adirondack Daily Enterprise*, 15 January 1958.

"Foul Weather Hampers Party Searching Plane," *Adirondack Record-Elizabethtown Post*, 25 January 1962.

Frenette, Liza. "No Margin for Error: In an Unforgettable Way, Three Hikers Find Mount Marcy Never Forgives," *Adirondack Life*, January/February 1988, 50–53.

Gallos, Phil. "Avalanche on Round Mt. Injures 4 Ice Climbers," *Adirondack Daily Enterprise*, 10 March 1975.

Gardinier, Bob. "Avalanche Kills Skier; 5 Rescued," *Albany Times Union*, 20 February 2000.

"Girl Is Rescued from Adirondack Ledge; Ropes Used to Haul Nursemaid to Safety," *The New York Times*, 8 July 1938.

"Girl Rescued From Keene Valley Cliff," *Adirondack Record-Elizabethtown Post*, 14 July 1938.

Goodwin, Tony. "Accident Report," *Adirondac*, January/February 1997, 30–31.

Goodwin, Tony. "Accident Report—Avalanche!," *Adirondac*, July/August 2000, 28–30.

Goodwin, Tony. "Accident Report—Summer 1988–Winter 1989," *Adirondac*, June 1989, 10–11.

Goodwin, Tony. "Accident Report—Summer 1990," *Adirondac*, November/December 1990, 36–37, 41.

Goodwin, Tony. "Accident Report—Summer 1991," *Adirondac*, January/February 1992, 32–33.

Goodwin, Tony. "Accident Report—Summer 1993," *Adirondac*, January/February 1994, 34–36.

Goodwin, Tony. "Accident Report—Summer 1995," *Adirondac*, January/February 1996, 34–35.

Goodwin, Tony. "Accident Report—Summer, 1999," *Adirondac*, January/February 2000, 34–35.

Goodwin, Tony. "Accident Report—Summer 2001," *Adirondac*, January/February 2002, 8–9.

Goodwin, Tony. "Accident Report—Winter 1986–87," *Adirondac*, July 1987, 22–23.

Goodwin, Tony. "Accident Report—Winter 1987–88," *Adirondac*, July/August 1988, 10.

Goodwin, Tony. "Accident Report—Winter 1990–91," *Adirondac*, July/August 1991, 23–24.

Goodwin, Tony. "Accident Report—Winter 1992–93," *Adirondac*, July/August 1993, 30–31.

Goodwin, Tony. "Accident Report—Winter 1993–94," *Adirondac*, July/August 1994, 34–35.

Goodwin, Tony. "Accident Report—Winter 1995–96," *Adirondac*, July/August 1996, 32–34.

Goodwin, Tony. "Accident Report—Winter 1996–97," *Adirondac*, July/August 1997, 28–29.

Goodwin, Tony. "Accident Report—Winter 1997–98," *Adirondac*, July 1998, 32–33.

Goodwin, Tony. "Accident Report—Winter 1998–99," *Adirondac*, July/August 1999, 32–33.

Goodwin, Tony. "Accident Report—Winter 2001," *Adirondac*, July/August 2001, 16–17.

Goodwin, Tony. "Accident Report—Winter 2001–2002," *Adirondac*, July/August 2002, 10–11.

Goodwin, Tony. "Accident Report—Winter 2003–2004," *Adirondac*, July/August 2004, 10–11.

Goodwin, Tony. "Rangers in the Night: Ripping the Safety Net of Wilderness Rescues," *Adirondack Life*, January/February 1990, 66–71.

Hale, Ed. "The Search for Steven Thomas," *Adirondack Life*, March/April 1982, 14–18, 46–47.

"Helicopters Scanning Marcy for Hiker Missing 4 Days," *Adirondack Daily Enterprise*, 16 April 1976.

"Hikers Lost Two Nights Rescued from Mt. Marcy," *Adirondack Daily Enterprise*, 14 January 1976.

"Hunt for Airliner a Radio Triumph," *The New York Times*, 1 January 1935.

"Indian Pass Gorges Are Unsurpassed in Country," *Ticonderoga Sentinel*, 27 July 1933.

"Inquest Ordered in E. F. Crumley Death," *Adirondack Record-Elizabethtown Post*, 19 December 1957.

"Keene Valley Resident Wins Rescue Award," *Adirondack Record-Elizabethtown Post*, 24 November 1938.

Kurp, Patrick. " 'Very, Very Ill' Latham Hiker's Diary Details His Last Days in The Woods," *Albany Times Union*, 24 October 1990.

"Lads After 31 Hours on 2-Foot Adirondack Niche Are Hauled Up, Little the Worse for Ordeal," *The New York Times*, 31 August 1933.

"Lake Placid Man Badly Injured in Fall on Whiteface," *Adirondack Record-Elizabethtown Post*, 3 December 1942.

Lange, William. "A Death on Marcy," *Adirondack Life*, November/December 1981, 14–17.

"Lost in the Adirondacks—Warning to Visitors to the North Woods; What Not to Do When You Lose Your Way and How Not to Lose It," *The New York Times*, March 16, 1890.

McFadden, Robert D. "Rare Avalanche Kills One on an Adirondack Slope," *The New York Times*, 21 February 2000.

McLaughlin, Bill. "Father Still Hopeful Hiker Will Be Found," *Adirondack Daily Enterprise*, 19 April 1976.

McLaughlin, Bill. "Green Berets Join Search," *Adirondack Daily Enterprise*, 26 March 1974.

McLaughlin, Bill. "No New Clues in Search for Hunter," *Adirondack Daily Enterprise*, 22 May 1972.

McLaughlin, Bill. "Rangers Have Busy Summer," *Adirondack Daily Enterprise*, 1 October 1974.

McLaughlin, Bill. "Search for Downed Pilot," *Adirondack Daily Enterprise*, 20 March 1974.

McLaughlin, Bill. "Search for Hunter Will Be Resumed," *Adirondack Daily Enterprise*, 18 May 1972.

McLaughlin, Bill. "Thousands of Square Miles Combed for Missing Pilot," *Adirondack Daily Enterprise*, 21 March 1974.

McLaughlin, Bill. "Trail Ends at Mountain Scar," *Adirondack Daily Enterprise*, 25 June 1974.

McLaughlin, Bill. "Weekend Search Is Futile," *Adirondack Daily Enterprise*, 25 March 1974.

McMammon, Ian. "Evidence of Heuristic Traps in Recreational Avalanche Accidents," *Couloir*, October 2005, 76–80.

"Missing Boy Feared Drowning Victim in Au Sable River Pool," *Adirondack Record-Elizabethtown Post*, 19 July 1956.

"Missing Hikers Track to Safety," *Albany Times Union*, 8 March 2001.

"Missing Men Search Fruitless," *Adirondack Daily Enterprise*, 26 December 1972.

Moody, Emily. "A Day with a Ranger," *Plattsburgh Press-Republican*, 19 September 1994.

"No Verdict in Case of 4 Bones Found in the Adk. Mountains," *Adirondack Record-Elizabethtown Post*, 26 December 1957.

"No Verdict Yet on Adirondack Bones," *Adirondack Daily Enterprise*, 21 December 1957.

"Ohio Man Lost, Found, Lost, Found and Charged," *Albany Times Union*, 7 December 2003.

Pawlaczyk, George. "The Last Days of David Boomhower, According to His Journal," *Adirondac*, July/August 1993, 8–11.

Petryk, Diane; and Seguin, Susan. "High Peaks Horror," *Plattsburgh Press-Republican*, 20 February 2000.

"Plane Crash on De Bar," *Adirondack Daily Enterprise*, 7 June 1972.

"Plane Crash Victims Rescued Monday Night," *Fort Covington Sun*, 3 January 1935.

"Plane in Gale Hits Whiteface Peak," *The New York Times*, 9 February 1943.

"Plane, Missing 11 months, Is Found near Ragged Lake," *Adirondack Daily Enterprise*, 5 November 1973.

"Plane Survivor Praises the Pilot," *The New York Times*, 2 January 1935.

"Plane Survivors Rescued in Exhausted Condition; Three Taken to Hospital," *The New York Times*, 1 January 1935.

Post, Todd. "The Power of Positive Thinking," *Adirondack Life*, January/February 1997, 10–16.

Quindlen, Anna. "Determination Marks Air Search for 3." *The New York Times*, 6 January 1979.

"Rangers Press Search for Hiker," *Albany Times Union*, 18 October 1993.

"Rangers, Volunteers Join Search for Man Missing in Adirondacks," *Albany Times Union*, 16 October 1993.

"Ready to Sleep to Death in Cold," *The New York Times*, 1 January 1935.

"Remains of Hiker Missing Since June Found," *Adirondac*, January 1991, 6.

"Rescue 3 Youths from Ad'k Lodge," *Ticonderoga Sentinel*, 31 August 1933.

"Rescuers Near 4 Fliers on Adirondack Mountain; Food Dropped by Planes," *The New York Times*, 31 December 1934.

Rinaldi, Ray. "Body of Lost Hiker Found by Hunter," *Albany Times Union*, 22 October 1990.

Rockwell, Winthrop A. "The Challenging Mountains: Two Men Attempt 46 Peaks in 5 Days," *The New York Times*, 18 February 1973.

Saxon, Wolfgang. "A Plane Missing Since December Found by C.A.P." *The New York Times*, 30 April 1979.

Scruton, Bruce A. "For Hiker, Lightning Struck Without Warning," *Albany Times Union*, 3 July 2001.

Scruton, Bruce A. "Missing Hiker Said to Be a Careful Planner," *Albany Times Union*, 22 June 1990.

"Searchers Seek Hiker on Marcy," *Adirondack Daily Enterprise*, 14 April 1976.

"Search for Hiker in Eighth Day," *Adirondack Daily Enterprise*, 20 April 1976.

"Search for Missing Latham Hiker Called Off," *Albany Times Union*, 9 July 1990.

"Search Slows," *Adirondack Daily Enterprise*, 2 April 1973.

Smith, Mason. "Always on the Lookout: Wilderness Ranger Pete Fish Schools Hikers on Safety in the Adirondacks," *Adirondack Life*, May/June 1983, 14–16, 33–35.

"Spring May Solve Disappearance of Two in Mountains," *Adirondack Record-Elizabethtown Post*, 19 April 1951.

"The Storm and Its Impact: What's a Microburst?" *Adirondac*, November/December 1995, 12–15.

Sturgis, Chris. "Forest Rangers Search for Missing Hiker," *Albany Times Union*, 15 October 1993.

Thill, Mary. "Civilians and Satellite Devices: Offering Rescues and Records? Personal Locator Beacon (PLB) Activation Leads to a Recovery and an Arrest in the Adirondack Forest Preserve," *Adirondack Life*, February 2004.

"Three Boys Trapped on Mountain Return for Rope," *Ticonderoga Sentinel*, 7 September 1933.

"Three Boys Trapped on Mountainside," *Adirondack Record-Elizabethtown Post*, 31 August 1933.

Vermeulen, James. "Slide Rules: The Very Real Threat of Adirondack Avalanches," *Adirondack Life*, January/February 1997, 18–24.

Wardenburg, Martha. "Did Her Aunt, the Ghost, Have this Carnegie Medal in Mind?" *Adirondack Life*, Spring 1971.

"Why Can't I Outrun an Avalanche?" *Skiing*, October 2005, 76.

"Woman Sought for Clues on Hiker," *Albany Times Union*, 28 October 1993.

"Young Rock Climber Falls to Death as Brother Watches," *Lake Placid News*, 4 November 1976.

OTHER

Adirondack Regional Tourism Council, "Adirondack Waterways: A Guide to Paddling Routes in the Northeast's Last Great Wilderness."

Carnegie Hero Fund Commission, "Case Minute 4979."

Clinton County Historical Association, "Three Scouts *Finally* Tell True Tale of Wallface Ascent."

Jenkins, Jerry. Wildlife Conservation Society, "Notes on the Adirondack Blowdown of July 15, 1995: Scientific Background, Observations, and Policy Issues," Working Paper No. 5, December 1995.

National Transportation Safety Board, "Factual Report Aviation = NTSB ID: IAD96LA129."

New York State Department of Environmental Conservation, "Avalanche Preparedness in the Adirondacks," Brochure.

New York State Department of Environmental Conservation—Bureau of Recreation, "Special Incident Report—Baldyga Incident."

New York State Department of Environmental Conservation—Forest Protection and Fire Management, "Search and Rescue Report—Boomhower Incident."

New York State Department of Environmental Conservation—Forest Protection and Fire Management, "Search and Rescue Report—Microburst 95 Incident."

New York State Department of Environmental Conservation—Forest Protection and Fire Management, "Search and Rescue Report—Sawtooth Plane Crash Incident."

New York State Department of Environmental Conservation—Forest Rangers, "Search and Rescue Report—Birchmeyer Search Incident."

New York State Department of Environmental Conservation—Forest Rangers, "Search and Rescue Report—Church/Phoenix Incident."

New York State Department of Environmental Conservation—Forest Rangers, "Search and Rescue Report—Skalak Rescue Incident."

New York State Department of Environmental Conservation—Forest Rangers, "Search and Rescue Report—Skalak Rescue II Incident."

New York State Department of Environmental Conservation—Office of Natural Resources, Region 5. "Final Draft—High Peaks Wilderness Complex Unit Management Plan: Wilderness Management for the High Peaks of the Adirondack Park," March 1999.

BIBLIOGRAPHY

TELEVISION AND RADIO

"Avalanche Awareness." *Outdoor Recreation*. Host Brian Mann. North Country Public Radio. 15 January 2001. http://www.ncpr.org

"Canadian Dies While Ice Climbing in Adirondacks." *Outdoor Recreation*. Host Brian Mann. North Country Public Radio. 25 February 2002. http://www.ncpr.org

"Hunter's Body Found Near Inlet." *Outdoor Recreation*. Host Brian Mann. North Country Public Radio. 5 December 2002. http://www.ncpr.org

"Lost Hikers Describe Struggle to Survive Blizzard." *Outdoor Recreation*. Host Brian Mann. North Country Public Radio. 9 March 2001. http://www.ncpr.org

"Search Ends: Canadian Hikers Found." *Outdoor Recreation*. Host Brian Mann. North Country Public Radio. 8 March 2001. http://www.ncpr.org

"Search Under Way: Hunter Lost in Hamilton County." *Outdoor Recreation*. Host Brian Mann. North Country Public Radio. 4 December 2002. http://www.ncpr.org

WEB SITES

Adirondack Connections, "The Adirondack Park," http://adirondackconnections.com/adkpark.htm (2 October 2005)

Adirondack Park Agency, "Geology of the Adirondack Park," http://www.apa.state.ny.us/About_Park/geology.htm (2 October 2005)

Adirondack Park Agency, "History of the Adirondack Park," http://www.apa.state.ny.us/About_Park/history.htm (2 October 2005)

Adirondack Regional Tourism Council, "The Adirondack Park," http://adk.com/home/park.cfm (2 October 2005)

BIBLIOGRAPHY

Adirondack Regional Tourism Council, "Media Fast Facts," http://adk.com/media/facts.cfm (3 October 2005)

Adirondack Rock and River Guide Service, "Backcountry Skiing," http://www.rockandriver.com/backcountry-skiing.htm (8 December 2005)

American Airlines C. R. Smith Museum, "American Airlines through the Years," http://www.crsmithmuseum.org/AAhistory/AA_text.htm (30 October 2005)

America's Roof, "Rescue Teams Dropped by Helicopters on Marcy," http://www.network54.com/Forum/message?forumid=3897&messageid=984156890 (26 September 2005)

Backpacking Light, "Personal Locator Beacons as a Rescue Device for Backcountry Travelers," http://www.backpackinglight.com/cgi-bin/backpackinglight/00205.html (14 December 2005)

Carnegie Hero Fund Commission, "Andrew Carnegie's Life in Brief," http://www.carnegiehero.org/fund_bio.php (29 October 2005)

Carnegie Hero Fund Commission, "Carnegie Hero Fund Commission," http://www.carnegiehero.org/heroFund.php (29 October 2005)

Carnegie Hero Fund Commission, "Carnegie Medal," http://www.carnegiehero.org/fund_medal.php (29 October 2005)

Carnegie Hero Fund Commission, "The History of the Carnegie Hero Fund," http://www.carnegiehero.org/fund_history.php (29 October 2005)

Carnegie Hero Fund Commission, "Latest Carnegie Medal Awardees," http://www.carnegiehero.org/awardees_recent.php (29 October 2005)

Carnegie Hero Fund Commission, "Requirements for a Carnegie Medal," http://www.carnegiehero.org/nominate.php (29 October 2005)

Colorado Avalanche Information Center, "Burial Depth and Survival Probability," http://geosurvey.state.co.us/avalanche/Default.aspx?tabid=123 (19 December 2005)

Colorado Avalanche Information Center, "Percent Survival vs. Burial Time," http://geosurvey.state.co.us/avalanche/Default.aspx?tabid=129 (19 December 2005)

Colorado Avalanche Information Center, "U.S. Avalanche Fatalities by Activity," http://geosurvey.state.co.us/avalanche/Default.aspx?tabid=120 (19 December 2005)

Colorado Avalanche Information Center, "U.S. Avalanche Fatalities by Month," http://geosurvey.state.co.us/avalanche/Default.aspx?tabid=115 (19 December 2005)

Colorado Avalanche Information Center, "U.S. Avalanche Fatalities by State," http://geosurvey.state.co.us/avalanche/Default.aspx?tabid=117 (19 December 2005)

Colorado Avalanche Information Center, "U.S. Avalanche Fatalities by State, 1985/86–2004/05," http://geosurvey.state.co.us/avalanche/Default.aspx?tabid=49 (19 December 2005)

"Earthquake!" 20 April 2002, http://www.snowjournal.com/page.php?cid=topic787 (2 October 2005)

Epodunk, "Willsboro, NY," http://www.epodunk.com/cgi-bin/genInfo.php?locIndex=1963 (29 October 2005)

Equipped to Survive, "Ohio Man Saved in First Use of a Personal Locator Beacon in Contiguous U.S. Credits Equipped to Survive," http://www.equipped.com/plb_first_use.htm (22 August 2005)

Federal Emergency Management Agency, "FEMA: January 1998 New York Ice Storm—Ice Storm Overview," http://www.fema.gov/regions/ii/1998/nyice2.shtm (12 January 2006)

Galvin, Rachel. "A Peopled Wilderness: A New Exhibition Explores Adirondack History," *Humanities*, July/August 1999, http://www.neh.gov/news/humanities/1999-07/adirondacks.html (12 September 2005)

Lake Champlain Angler, "Lake Champlain Ice Fishing Locations," http://www.angelfire.com/home/lake/slide.html (29 October 2005)

Lake Champlain Basin Program, "Lake and Basin Facts," *Nature of the Basin: Lake Champlain Basin Atlas*, http://www.lcbp.org/Atlas/HTML/nat_lakefax.htm (29 October 2005)

Lake Champlain Visitors Center, "Living Here: Historic Towns—Willsboro," http://www.lakechamplainregion.com/content_pages/liveWillsboro.cfm (29 October 2005)

Linsley, John B. "Out There!" *St. Lawrence Magazine*, http://web.stlawu.edu/magazine/out_there.html (8 December 2005)

L.L. Bean, "Adirondack Park," http://www.llbean.com/parksearch/parks/html/8869gd.htm (2 October 2005)

Middlebury College, "September 20, 1999: Middlebury College Community Celebrates Bicentennial by Climbing Mountains on Oct. 9—Students Lead Faculty, Staff, Alumni, Parents, and Friends in Climb of 50 Peaks in the Adirondacks and Green Mountains," http://www.middlebury.edu/about/pubaff/news_releases/news_1999/summit.htm (8 December 2005)

"Mt. Colden (Adirondacks) Hiking Accident," 31 December 2004, http://neice.com/ubbthreads/showflat.php?Cat=0&Number=3058&page=2&fpart=all&vc=1 (13 September 2005)

National Aeronautics and Space Administration, "Human Voltage: What Happens When People and Lightning Converge," http://science.nasa.gov/newhome/headlines/essd18jun99_1.htm (13 December 2005)

"Nat. Geo Explorer—David Boomhower—RIP—1991," Views from the Top, 10 October 2005—22 April 2005, http://www.viewsfromthetop.com/forums/showthread.php?t=9589&highlight=boomhower (1 December 2005)

National Lightning Safety Institute, "Information for the Media," http://www.lightningsafety.com/nlsi_info/media.html (13 December 2005)

National Lightning Safety Institute, "Little Known Lightning Information," http://www.lightningsafey.com/nlsi_info/little_known_facts.html (13 December 2005)

National Lightning Safety Institute, "Mastery, Mystery and Myths about Lightning," http://www.lightningsafety.com/nlsi_info/myths.html (13 December 2005)

National Lightning Safety Institute, "Weather Factoids," http://www.lightningsafety.com/nlsi_info/weather_factoids.html (13 December 2005)

National Oceanic and Atmospheric Administration—National Severe Storms Laboratory, "NOAA Technical Memorandum NWS SR-193: Lightning Fatalities, Injuries, and Damage Reports in the United States From 1959–1994," http://www.nssl.noaa.gov/papers/techmemos/NWS-SR-193/techmemo-sr193.html (13 December 2005)

National Oceanic and Atmospheric Administration—National Severe Storms Laboratory, "Questions and Answers about Lightning," http://www.nssl.noaa.gov/edu/ltg (13 December 2005)

National Oceanic and Atmospheric Administration—NOAA News Online, "NOAA Satellites Play Key Role in 260 Rescues in 2004," http://www.noaanews.noaa.gov/stories2005/s2382.htm (14 December 2005)

National Oceanic and Atmospheric Administration—NOAA News Online, "Ohio Man Saved by Using Personal Locator Beacon," http://www.noaanews.noaa.gov/stories2003/s2124.htm (14 December 2005)

National Oceanic and Atmospheric Administration—NOAA Satellite and Information Service, "Emergency Beacons," http://www.sarsat.noaa.gov/emerbcns.html (14 December 2005)

National Transportation Safety Board, "Aviation Accident Database and Synopses—Identification # IAD96LA129," http://www.ntsb.gov/ntsb/brief2.asp?ev_id=2001208X06529&ntsbno=IAD96LA129&akey=1 (22 November 2005)

National Transportation Safety Board, "Aviation Accident Statistics—Table 10. Accidents, Fatalities, and Rates, 1985 through 2004, U.S. General Aviation," http://www.ntsb.gov/aviation/Table10.htm (30 September 2005)

National Weather Service Lightning Safety Program, "Lightning Kills, Play It Safe," http://www.lightningsafety.noaa.gov (13 December 2005)

BIBLIOGRAPHY

New York State Department of Environmental Conservation, "The Adirondack Forest Preserve," http://www.dec.state.ny.us/website/dlf/publands/adk (2 October 2005)

New York State Department of Environmental Conservation, "News— DEC Closes Avalanche Pass Slide in Adirondack High Peaks," http://www.dec .state.ny.us/website/press/pressrel/2001/2001x31.html (16 December 2005)

New York State Department of Environmental Conservation, "News— DEC Warns of Avalanche Danger in the Adirondacks: Backcountry Visitors Cautioned about Snow Conditions," http://www.dec.state.ny.us/website/press/pressrel/2005/200511.html (16 December 2005)

New York State Geological Survey, "The Geology of New York: A Simplified Account," http://gretchen.geo.rpi.edu/roecker/nys/adir_txt.html (2 October 2005)

Outside Online, " 'Cave Dog' Nails Adirondack Peaks Record," http://outside.away.com/news/headlines/20020701_1.html (12 September 2005)

Paddler Magazine Online, "Canoe Rescue: Stranded Canoeist Becomes First Person in Lower 48 to Be Rescued with Personal Locator Beacon," http://www.paddlermagazine.com/issues/2004_2/article_243.shtml (22 August 2005)

"Personal Locator Beacon," TrailSpace, 15 June 2005, http://www .trailspace.com/forums/backcountry/topics/31200.html (22 August 2005)

Saint Lawrence University, "NetNews," http://web.stlawu.edu/netnews/peak.html (8 December 2005)

Saint Lawrence University, "NetNews," http://web.stlawu.edu/netnews/peak2002.html (8 December 2005)

Saint Lawrence University, "NetNews," http://web.stlawu.edu/netnews/peakweekend05.html (8 December 2005)

Smith, Greg. "A Geological History of the Adirondacks," http://adirondack-park.net/history/geological.html (2 October 2005)

Team Lake, "The Lake Renegade, Universally at Home," http://www .teamlake.com/simon%20renegade.htm (13 January 2006)

Vermonter, "Ice Fishing in Vermont," http://www.vermonter.com/icefishing.asp (29 October 2005)

WeatherMatrix, "Remembering the Blizzard of '93," http://www.weathermatrix.net/education/blizzard93 (16 December 2005)

Westwide Accident Report Database, "Accident Report," http://www.avalanche.org/proc-show.php3?OID=17260 (8 December 2005)

Wikipedia, "Adirondack Mountains," http://en.wikipedia.org/wiki/Adirondack_Mountains (2 October 2005)

Wikipedia, "Columbia River," http://en.wikipedia.org/wiki/Columbia_River (3 October 2005)

Wikipedia, "History of the Nile," http://en.wikipedia.org/wiki/Nile (3 October 2005)

Wikipedia, "Lake Tear of the Clouds," http://en.wikipedia.org/wiki/Lake_Tear_of_the_Clouds (3 October 2005)

Wikipedia, "Lewis and Clark Expedition," http://en.wikipedia.org/wiki/Lewis_and_Clark_Expedition (3 October 2005)

ACKNOWLEDGMENTS

This project would not have been possible without the support, encouragement, and assistance of many people.

Thank you to my agent, Jim Cypher, and editor, Rob Kirkpatrick.

Invaluable research assistance was provided by: Phil Brown, Doug Chambers, the Clinton County Historical Association, David Glenn, Jim Goodwin, Tony Goodwin, the Keene Valley Library (especially Patricia Galeski and Nona LeClair), Emily Ladue, Mary Lou Record (and the Adirondack Forty-Sixers), the Saranac Lake Free Library (especially Susan Stiles in the William Chapman White Memorial Room Adirondack Research Center), Jim Schaad, John Streiff, and Dave Winchell.

I am deeply indebted to the survivors of the misadventures about which I write, who were so graciously willing to be interviewed and share their story for this book: Chris Beattie, Bill Black, Bryce Dalhaus, Jim DeGaetano, Peter Gough, Bob Henry, Rev. Philip Keane, Ron Konowitz, James McCaughey, William Moskal Sr., and Anthony Patane.

My sincerest thanks also go out to the rescuers who similarly shared their perspectives on the events within these pages: David Ames, Doug Bissonette, James Giglinto, Will Giraud, Gary Hodgson, Lower Adirondack Search and Rescue (especially Peter Benoit, Larry Gordon, Joe "Coach" Iuliano, Dave Loomis, Pat McGinn, and Tad Norton), Robert Marrone, Ed Palen, Vic Sasse, and Michael Sheridan.

ACKNOWLEDGMENTS

Long before this book was even an idea, and throughout the publishing process, my family and friends provided constant and unconditional support and encouragement, especially as difficult deadlines approached. Thank you, thank you, thank you! I especially want to thank my mother, Georgann, for believing in my passion for writing, for giving me strong roots in people, places, and values, and for giving me wings to follow my dreams.

Thank you, most of all, to my wife, Kelli. Your love and support, constructive criticism, endless patience, careful proofreading, thoughtful insight, and willingness to become a temporary "book widow" as I became hopelessly attached to my laptop computer during deadlines, all mean more than I can ever say. This is our book.

INDEX

INDEX

INDEX

INDEX

INDEX

INDEX

INDEX

INDEX

ABOUT THE AUTHOR

Peter Bronski (www.peterbronski.com) is an award-winning author, speaker, and adventurer. His articles regularly appear in magazines across the country, including *5280: Denver's Mile High Magazine*, *Adirondack Life*, *AMC Outdoors*, *Cornell Alumni Magazine*, *Men's Journal*, *Rocky Mountain Sports*, *Sea Kayaker*, *Vermont Life*, and *Westchester Magazine*. A former member of Lower Adirondack Search and Rescue, Mr. Bronski is New York State–certified in wild lands search and rescue, and has extensive outdoor experience in the Adirondacks, with rock and ice climbing, hiking, winter mountaineering, backcountry and lift-serviced skiing, snowshoeing, and canoeing. He is a First Prize winner in the 2005 North American Travel Journalists Association Awards Competition, and a recipient of the Summit Award from Lower Adirondack Search and Rescue. Mr. Bronski is an active member of the American Alpine Club. He lives in Boulder, Colorado, with his wife, Kelli, and their dog, Altai.